THEOLOGY, HISTORY, AND ARCHAEOLOGY IN THE CHRONICLER'S ACCOUNT OF HEZEKIAH

ARCHAEOLOGY AND BIBLICAL STUDIES

published jointly by

The Society of Biblical Literature
and
The American Schools of Oriental Research

Series Editor
Diana V. Edelman

Number 4
THEOLOGY, HISTORY, AND ARCHAEOLOGY
IN THE CHRONICLER'S
ACCOUNT OF HEZEKIAH

by
Andrew G. Vaughn

THEOLOGY, HISTORY, AND ARCHAEOLOGY IN THE CHRONICLER'S ACCOUNT OF HEZEKIAH

by
Andrew G. Vaughn

Scholars Press
Atlanta, Georgia

THEOLOGY, HISTORY, AND ARCHAEOLOGY IN THE CHRONICLER'S ACCOUNT OF HEZEKIAH

by
Andrew G. Vaughn

Copyright © 1999 by
The Society of Biblical Literature
The American Schools of Oriental Research

Library of Congress Cataloging-in-Publication Data

Vaughn, Andrew G.
  Theology, history, and archaeology in the Chronicler's account of Hezekiah / by Andrew G. Vaughn.
    p. cm. — (Archaeology and biblical studies ; no. 4)
  Includes bibliographical references.
  ISBN 0-7885-0594-7 (pbk. : alk. paper)
    1. Bible. O.T. Chronicles, 2nd, XXIX-XXXII—History of Biblical events. 2. Bible. O.T. Chronicles, 2nd, XXIX-XXXII—Antiquities. 3. Hezekiah, King of Judah I. Title. II. Series.

BS1345.2 . V38 1999
222'.64067—dc21
                                                          99-046954
                                                          CIP

08 07 06 05 04   5 4 3 2
Printed in the United States of America
on acid-free paper

To my parents

Silas M. and Catherine S. Vaughn

TABLE OF CONTENTS

LIST OF TABLES

ACKNOWLEDGMENTS

This monograph is a revision of the author's doctoral dissertation written under the supervision of Patrick D. Miller. The dissertation was completed in November, 1995, and the bibliography has been updated only sporadically since that time. Apart from revisions, the present volume differs from the dissertation in several ways. Chapters 1 and 2 of the dissertation have been combined into one introductory chapter with much of the material being published in a separate article (*BASOR* 313 [1999] 43-64). Appendix II (new readings and photographs of official seal impressions) of the dissertation has been removed and published as a separate article co-authored by Gabriel Barkay (*BASOR* 304 [1996] 29-54). The other two appendices have been abbreviated. Additional details from these appendices will be published in separate articles.

I am grateful to Princeton Theological Seminary for a postdoctoral grant for the 1996-1997 academic year and to Gustavus Adolphus College for a reduced load during the 1997-1998 academic year. The revisions of the present monograph were completed during those years.

As the research for this monograph was undertaken on three continents and the archaeological items studied are stored at fourteen public collections and numerous private collections around the world, many individuals and institutions assisted the author and made this research possible. The sheer number of people who assisted me allows only brief mention of each. Appreciation is expressed below in the following list arranged alphabetically according to institution followed by an alphabetical listing of private collections.

Badé Institute of Biblical Archaeology: K. Kaiser on behalf of the Institute granted permission for the examination and publication of *lmlk* and official seal impressions to G. Barkay. Barkay in turn shared his findings with me, and Kaiser provided me with photographs.

Bible Lands Museum, Jerusalem: J. Westenholtz on behalf of the BLMJ granted permission to examine, photograph, and publish the *lmlk* and official seal impressions in their collection.

British Museum: J. Tubb and J. E. Curtis on behalf of the British Museum granted permission to examine, photograph, and publish the *lmlk* and official seal impressions. The items themselves were made available for examination and photography by P. Magrill. Ms. Magrill was also very kind to share her own research about the locations of other official and *lmlk* impressions from Lachish that are kept in other collections.

British School of Archaeology in Jerusalem: K. Prag on behalf of the British School granted permission to publish the impressions. She also supplied several photographs and other documentation. G. Barkay made his lists of the material from the British School available to me.

Brooklyn Museum: J. F. Romano on behalf of The Museum granted permission for the examination of the *lmlk* impressions in their collection.

Cambridge University Museum of Archaeology and Anthropology: C. Chippindale on behalf of the Museum granted permission for the examination, photography, and publication of the seal impressions. R. E. Whitaker, Princeton Theological Seminary, assisted me in examining and photographing these handles.

Hecht Museum, University of Haifa: O. Rimon on behalf of the Hecht Museum granted permission for the examination of the *lmlk* impressions in this collection, and she assisted me in my visit to the Hecht Museum.

Israel Antiquities Authority: R. Peled on behalf of the I.A.A. granted permission for the examination and photography of *lmlk* and official seal impressions found at the Israel Museum, the Rockefeller Museum, and in storage. The items themselves were made available for examination and photography by curators B. Brandl, M. Dayagi-Mendels, G. Horwitz, D. Peretz, E. Peretz, and J. Zias.

Jewish Museum of New York: S. Braunstein granted permission for me to study the finds and shared detailed lists of the collection.

Tel Aviv University, Institute of Archaeology: D. Ussishkin, director of the renewed Lachish excavations, granted permission for the examination and photography of items from the renewed Lachish excavations. Their full publication will appear in the Lachish final reports in cases where they have not already been published by Ussishkin. The impressions themselves were made available for examination and photography by Y. Dagan and O. Zimhoni.

University Museum of Archaeology and Anthropology of the University of Pennsylvania: R. L. Zettler on behalf of The University Museum granted permission for the examination, photography, and publication of the impressions used in this study. I was assisted in my research by curators L. Bregstein and M. de Schauensee.

University of Southern California, Department of Ancient Near Eastern Studies Study Collection: B. Zuckerman provided me with the details of a *lmlk* impression from this collection.

The following individuals allowed me to study seal impressions in their collections: S. Adler, Barakat, J. Charlesworth, R. Deutsch, D. Friedenberg, H. Herbert, A. Spaer, W. Stern, M. Welch, and L. A. Wolfe.

I also benefited from specialized photographic training that enabled much of my epigraphic research to result in improved readings. I am indebted to a dissertation research grant from Princeton Theological Seminary that paid for my expenses to work with B. Zuckerman and K. Zuckerman, West Semitic Research. In addition, R. Heyman, Jerusalem, provided photographic training and support.

The majority of my research in Israel was conducted while at Tel Aviv University during the 1993-1994 academic year on a Fulbright Fellowship administered by the United States-Israel Education Foundation. I am also grateful to Princeton Theological Seminary for a grant to pay for photography expenses and travel during the 1993-1995 academic years. My examination of material in August 1995 was conducted while I was in Israel on an Endowment for Biblical Research/American Schools of Oriental Research Travel Grant.

Gratitude is also due to my many teachers and senior colleagues in Israel who gave me advice and in some cases suggested research topics. G. Barkay, Bar-Ilan University, collaborated with me in documenting thousands of *lmlk* and official seal impressions. Barkay and I spent literally hundreds of hours working on this project, and I am most grateful for his help, his expertise, and his interest. This project would not have been possible without his help. A. F. Rainey, Tel Aviv University, served as my adviser during my Fulbright Fellowship year at Tel Aviv University. In Israel, I also benefited from numerous consultations with the follow scholars: I. Finkelstein, Y. Garfinkel, S. Gitin, the late J. Greenfield, A. Killebrew, Z. Lederman, A. Mazar, Z. Meshel, D. Ussishkin, and the lateO. Zimhoni. I also benefited from the collegial exchange with scholars in residence at the Albright Institute, Jerusalem, where I was an honorary fellow for the 1993-1994 academic year.

I am also indebted to colleagues apart from my dissertation committee who have read parts or all of the manuscript of this monograph: D. Armstrong, G. Barkay, J. W. Hardin, G. Knoppers, S. McKenzie, A. F. Rainey, and J. Rosenbaum. I am also grateful to L. M. White, editor of the SBL/ASOR series in which this monograph is published.

I have saved the mention of my teachers at Princeton Theological Seminary for the end because they have trained and encouraged me throughout my twenties. I am particularly grateful to the members of my dissertation committee: P. D. Miller (chair), R. E. Whitaker, and C. L. Seow. My work on the *lmlk* jars began with a seminar paper for K. D. Sakenfeld. J. J. M. Roberts also made important contributions at various stages in my research for this monograph.

Finally, and most important, I thank my family. My parents, Si and Cathy Vaughn, have supported my academic and intellectual development all of my life. My wife, Amy, provided the most important support both in terms of morale and intellectual stimulus. Amy was also willing to modify her career plans to spend a year in Israel and limit her search for work as a pastor to New Jersey so that I could be near Princeton as I finished the dissertation. She has also been a constant help as I revised the present work into a monograph.

ABBREVIATIONS

AB	Anchor Bible
ABRL	Anchor Bible Reference Library
AION	*Annali dell'istituto orientali di Napoli*
ANEP	J. B. Pritchard (ed.), *Ancient Near East in Pictures*
ANET	J. B. Pritchard (ed.), *Ancient Near Eastern Texts*
AOS	American Oriental Series
AASOR	Annual of the American Schools of Oriental Research
ASOR	American Schools of Oriental Research
ASORMS	American Schools of Oriental Research Monograph Series
BA	*Biblical Archaeologist*
BASOR	*Bulletin of American Schools of Oriental Research*
BBET	Beiträge zur biblischen Exegese und Theologie
BDB	F. Brown, S. R. Driver, and C. A. Briggs, *Hebrew and English Lexicon of theOld Testament*
BFCT	Beiträge zur Förderung christlicher Theologie
BH	Biblical Hebrew
BHS	*Biblia Hebraica Stuttgartensia*
BJRL	*Bulletin of the John Rylands University Library of Manchester*
BLMJ	Bible Lands Museum, Jerusalem
BM	British Museum
BWANT	Beiträge zur Wissenschaft vom Alten und Neuen Testament
cc	concentric circles
CTM	*Concordia Theological Monthly*
Dtr.	Deuteronomistic History
EI	*Eretz Israel*
ESI	*Excavations and Surveys in Israel*
GN(N)	geographic name(s)
HALAT	W. Baumgartner, et al., *Hebräisches und aramäisches Lexikon zum Alten Testament*
HSM	Harvard Semitic Monographs
HTR	*Harvard Theological Review*
I.A.A.	Israel Antiquities Authority
IEJ	*Israel Exploration Society*
JAOS	*Journal of the American Oriental Society*
JBL	*Journal of Biblical Literature*
JSOT	*Journal for the Study of the Old Testament*
JSOTSup	Journal for the Study of the Old Testament Supplement Series
JSS	*Journal of Semitic Studies*

KAI	H. Donner and R. Röllig, *Kanaanäische und aramäische Inschriften*
LXX	Septuagint
MT	Masoretic Text
n(n).	note(s)
NEAEHL	E. Stern (ed.), *New Encyclopedia of Archaeological Excavations In the Holy Land*
OBO	Orbis Biblicus et Orientalis
OTL	Old Testament Library
pl(s)	plate(s)
p(p).	page(s)
PEQ	*Palestine Exploration Quarterly*
PEFQS	*Palestine Exploration Fund Quarterly Statement*
PJb	*Palästinajahrbuch des Deutschen evangelischen Instituts für Altertums Wissenschaft des Heiligen Landes zu Jerusalem*
PN(N)	personal name(s)
Qad	*Qadmoniot*
ResQ	*Restoration Quarterly*
RSO	*Rivista degli studi orientali*
SBLDS	Society of Biblical Literature Dissertation Series
SJOT	*Scandinavian Journal of the Old Testament*
SWBA	Social World of Biblical Antiquity
SWJA	*Southwestern Journal of Anthropology*
Tel Aviv	*Journal of the Institute of Archaeology of Tel Aviv University*
TSSI	J. C. L. Gibson, *Textbook of Syrian Semitic Inscriptions*
TynBul	*Tyndale Bulletin*
UMI	University Microfilms International
VT	*Vetus Testamentum*
VTSup	Vetus Testamentum, Supplements
WMANT	Wissenschaftliche Monographien Zum Alten und Neuen Testament
WSS	N. Avigad, *Corpus of West Semitic Stamp Seals*
WVDOG	Wissenschafliche Veröffentlichung der deutschen Orientgesellschaft
ZAW	*Zeitschrift für die alttestamentliche Wissenschaft*
ZDMG	*Zeitschrift der deutschen morgenländischen Gesellschaft*
ZDPV	*Zeitschrift des deutschen Palästina-Vereins*

INTRODUCTION
BACKGROUND AND STATEMENT OF THESIS

A. Background

The monograph addresses the relationship of historical data to an interpretation of the Chronicler's[1] treatment of Hezekiah in 2 Chronicles 29-32. This topic has its roots in the 18th and 19th century debate that questioned the feasibility of using Chronicles to reconstruct Israelite history. The negative assessment of Chronicles as a historical source is seen clearly as early as 1806 with the work of W. M. L. de Wette, who concluded that Chronicles could not be used to reconstruct Israelite history.[2] J. Wellhausen developed this position during the last quarter of the 19th century by arguing that while Chronicles might be helpful for understanding post-exilic Israelite history, the books were not reliable for examining the pre-exilic period. Representing the other side of the debate, Rawlinson and Sayce used archaeological data as a means of vindicating Chronicles as a historical source.[3]

M. P. Graham shows in his dissertation that although such polar opinions may be avoided in more recent twentieth-century scholarship on Chronicles, the issue of the usefulness of Chronicles in reconstructing Israelite history continues to be debated.[4] Rosenbaum, Halpern, Friedman, Japhet, and Rainey each argue that Chronicles contains at least some historically reliable sources apart from the Deuteronomistic History.[5] The

---

[1]The use of the term "Chronicler" is meant to refer to the author of the book of Chronicles by itself and not to a single author of Chronicles, Ezra, and Nehemiah. For arguments refuting the single author theory, compare S. Japhet, "The Supposed Common Authorship of Chronicles and Ezra-Nehemiah Investigated Anew," *VT* 18 (1968) 330-71; and H. G. M. Williamson, *Israel in the Book of Chronicles* (Cambridge: Cambridge University Press, 1977) 5-70.

[2]W. M. L. de Wette, *Kritischer Versuch über die* Glaubwürdigkeit der Bücher der Chronik *mit Hinsicht auf die Geschichte der Mosaischen Bücher und Gesetzgebung* (*Halle, 1806*).

[3]Cf. discussion in M. P. Graham, *The Utilization of 1 and 2 Chronicles in the Reconstruction of Israelite History in the Nineteenth Century* (SBLDS 116; Atlanta: Scholars Press, 1990) 141-151, 200-205, 208-18, 244-46.

[4]Graham, *Utilization of 1 and 2 Chronicles*, 243-49.

[5]J. Rosenbaum, "Hezekiah's Reform and the Deuteronomistic Tradition," *HTR* 72 (1979) 24-43. Baruch Halpern, "Sacred History and Ideology: Chronicles' Thematic Structure— Indications of an Earlier Source," *The Creation of Sacred Literature: Composition and Redaction of the Biblical Text* (ed. R. E. Friedman; Berkeley: University of California Press, 1981) 35-54. R. E. Friedman, "The Tabernacle in the Temple," *BA* 43 (1980) 241-48. S. Japhet, "The Historical Reliability of Chronicles:

common denominator in all of their arguments is that a historically reliable source often lies behind the passages in Chronicles that have no parallel text in Kings. In other words, not all of the passages unique to Chronicles are the theological invention of the Chronicler. The logical conclusion from their studies is that at least some of these unique passages arise from another source, and that if the verses stemming from this original source can be distinguished, they can be helpful in reconstructing Israelite history. On the other hand, Klein, Welten, and Ackroyd have suggested that in at least some (all?) cases the Chronicler's own theology, rather than another historical source, may be responsible for the additional material.[6]

In light of these two opposing approaches, commentators tend to ask whether or not selected passages unique to Chronicles reflect an accurate historical source. For scholars who maintain that the Chronicler utilized reliable sources other than the Deuteronomistic History, issues of historical reliability are important and are used to help isolate these theorized sources. On the other hand, for those scholars who have determined that the Chronicler's sources are more theological than historical, historical categories and questions have been relegated to a position of minimal importance. The monograph demonstrates that even if an interpreter brackets the minute identification of theoretical sources, historical categories and historical questions are still important for a theological interpretation. This point can be seen through a statement of methodology by Peter R. Ackroyd, a scholar who tends to emphasize the theological decisions of the Chronicler as opposed to historical sources the Chronicler may have used. He says, "However good his [the Chronicler's] sources, it is the way he uses them which ultimately counts."[7] Ackroyd is correct; yet, to begin to understand how the Chronicler used his sources or remembrances of past events, one must give historical questions an important and integral position in any theological investigation.

The History of the Problem and Its Place in Biblical Research," *JSOT* 33 (1985) 83-107, esp. 99. S. Japhet, *I & II Chronicles: A Commentary* (OTL; Louisville: Westminster/John Knox Press, 1993) esp. 18-23. A. F. Rainey, "The Chronicles of the Kings of Judah: A Source Used by the Chronicler," *The Chronicler as Historian;* ed. M. P. Graham; (Sheffield: Sheffield Academic Press, 1997, 30-72).

[6]R. W. Klein, "Abijah's Campaign Against the North (II Chr 13)— What Were the Chronicler's Sources?" *ZAW* 95 (1983) 210-17. P. Welten, *Geschichte und Gesichdarstellung und der Chronikbüchern* (WMANT 42; Tübingen: Neukirchener Verlag, 1973) 191-94. P. R. Ackroyd, "History and Theology in the Writings of the Chronicler," *CTM* 38 (1967) 501-15.

[7]Ackroyd, "History and Theology," 506.

B. Statement of Thesis

The Chronicler's treatment of Hezekiah in 2 Chronicles 29-32 is an excellent place to test the relationship of extra-biblical historical data to an interpretation of Chronicles. About seventy percent of this section has no parallel in Kings.[8] Many commentators question the reliability of the detailed account of Hezekiah's economic buildup and civil strength found in 2 Chronicles 29-32 because the Chronicler tends to glorify kings who are held to be pious. However, study shows that the Chronicler's detailed account of Hezekiah's economic buildup and civil power is consistent with the known extrabiblical historical data. The monograph argues that this historical consistency must be addressed, even if the identification of particular verses that may belong to a historically reliable source in Chronicles is bracketed. The investigation of this historical consistency shows that at least in the case of the Chronicler's account of Hezekiah, traditions or remembrances that were historically accurate were utilized in constructing the Chronicler's ideological message. Thus, the conclusion is drawn that even while presenting an ideologically laden message to the post-exilic community, the Chronicler was still concerned with historiography, or the writing of history. This conclusion is important for the study of Chronicles because Welten has recently suggested that the Chronicler's work should not be considered historiography.[9]

C. Method

Before a demonstration of the Chronicler's use of historically reliable traditions or remembrances is undertaken, several presuppositions are examined briefly in the first chapter. Chapter 1 outlines some presuppositional issues. The first section briefly discusses the chronology of Hezekiah's reign and explains the ramifications of the various theories

---

[8]S. L. McKenzie (*The Chronicler's Use of the Deuteronomistic History* [Atlanta: Scholars Press, 1985] esp. pp. 72, 170) and W. E. Lemke ("The Synoptic Problem in the Chronicler's History," *HTR* 58 [1965] esp. pp. 362-363) have used the appearance of the Qumran fragments to show that the Chronicler only very rarely makes a significant change to a parallel passage found in both Samuel-Kings and Chronicles. McKenzie (p. 72) states that "to a much greater extent the Chronicler's interests are apparent in his omissions and his independent material."

[9]Welten, *Geschichte*, 205-6. Japhet ("Historical Reliability," 107, n. 84) also explains that Welten's concept of *"Freie parabolische Geschichtsdarstellung"* is borrowed by H. Junker.

for the arguments presented in the monograph. The second section briefly summarizes arguments for the dating of the book of Chronicles and impact those theories have on the present work. Finally, there is a discussion on the use of the Siloam Tunnel and Siloam Tunnel Inscription in analyzing the relationship of extra-biblical sources in Chronicles. Previous works, including Welten's, have paleographically dated this inscription to the time period of Hezekiah and used it as a starting point in discussing the historicity of the Chronicler's account of Hezekiah. Even though the common paleographic dating of the Siloam Tunnel Inscription to Hezekiah's reign would support the thesis of this monograph by providing a convenient starting point for a discussion of historically reliable elements in Chronicles, the paleographic study presented in a separate report (see below, Chapter 1, n. 32) calls the certainty of the paleographic dating of the Siloam Tunnel Inscription into question. Thus, in an effort to base the discussion of historically reliable references on solid ground, this common assumption about the Siloam Tunnel Inscription is considered uncertain and does not form the basis for the assertion that Chronicles contains historically reliable elements. In the conclusion to the monograph, it is suggested that the Siloam Tunnel Inscription most likely dates from Hezekiah's reign, but this conclusion is drawn from an analysis of a reference found in 2 Chr 32:30, not from extra-biblical historical data.

The second chapter evaluates the archaeological material that relates to the period of Hezekiah. These data substantiate the positive details of Hezekiah's economic buildup found in 2 Chr 32:27-30 and show that the Chronicler's use of these verses was meant to provide historical legitimacy to his ideological message. A secondary goal of Chapter 2 is to support Rosenbaum's explanation of why these specific details were omitted by Dtr.[10] Rosenbaum assumes at least a major redaction of Dtr during the reign of Josiah, and presents a coherent argument for Hezekiah as a rival to Josiah. Thus, he theorizes that the Josianic redactor of Dtr omits details of Hezekiah's prosperity in an effort to highlight the importance of Josiah. The archaeological data presented in Chapter 2 show that economic buildup and prosperity in the time of Hezekiah were greater than in the time of Josiah.[11]

Chapter 3 reexamines the *lmlk* jar phenomenon in light of new data that are presented in the appendices to the monograph. The monograph advances the state of research with regard to the *lmlk* jar

---

[10]Rosenbaum, "Hezekiah's Reform," 29-33.

[11]Even if one were to conclude that the Deuteronomistic History was written/ redacted only in the post-exilic period, the conclusion presented in this monograph with respect to Chronicles remain valid if the post-exilic writer has a bias for Josiah as the reformer *par excellence*.

phenomenon by more than doubling the number of official seal impressions known and by increasing the number of *lmlk* impressions reported by more than 500. Appendix I presents a list of all the known *lmlk* impressions,[12] and Appendix II lists all of the known official seal impressions.[13] Chapter 3 shows how these new data affect the interpretation of Hezekiah's reign and specifically illumine the Chronicler's historically reliable traditions or remembrances in 2 Chr 32:27-30.

---

[12]This section includes only a preliminary listing of the excavated impressions from several sites that have not been previously published. The full publication of these impressions will be found in the respective reports by the excavators.

[13]The corpus of the official seal impressions is only a preliminary listing of the impressions with collection numbers. Their complete publication will appear in a forthcoming monograph by G. Barkay and me.

ONE
PRESUPPOSITIONAL ISSUES

A. Presuppositions About Chronology

1. Background

A focused analysis of the exact chronology of Hezekiah's reign and of the validity of the so-called "two-campaign" theory of Sennacherib is beyond the scope of this monograph. This question has already received much scholarly treatment, and with the currently available data, no conclusive resolution is possible. At the same time, it must be recognized that these issues are central to understanding Hezekiah's kingdom. It is prudent to review the history of research surrounding these issues and to present a limited number of conclusions that can be drawn without resolving the chronological problem completely.

2. The Chronology Problem

The chronology of Hezekiah's reign is difficult to determine because two different and irreconcilable synchronisms are found in 2 Kings 18. 2 Kgs 18:10 states that the Assyrians destroyed Samaria during the sixth year of Hezekiah. Since Samaria was destroyed about 722 BCE, this verse would place Hezekiah's ascension to the throne in 727/726 BCE. If this observation is combined with the statement in 2 Kgs 18:2 that Hezekiah reigned for 29 years, one arrives at the date of 698 BCE for the end of his rule.

The problem with this chronology arises in 2 Kgs 18:13, which states that "in the 14th year of King Hezekiah, King Sennacherib of Assyria went up against all the fortified towns of Judah and seized them." As Sennacherib's campaign is well dated to 701 BCE, the reference to Hezekiah's 14th year in 2 Kgs 18:13 would place his ascension to the throne in 715/714 BCE. Since one synchronism places Hezekiah's ascension in 727/726 BCE and the other puts it in 715/714 BCE, a problem is posed that is difficult to resolve.

3. Approaches to the Chronology Problem

The various approaches to the problem posed by the irreconcilable synchronisms in 2 Kgs 18:10 and 2 Kgs 18:13 have sparked scholarly debate. It is not necessary to repeat every view. In general, the approach taken in this chapter follows that found in P. K. Hooker's dissertation.[1] Hooker organizes the scholarly debate into four types of approaches to the problem. Although his conclusions and resolution are not as conclusive as he suggests, his outline of the broad categories is a helpful means of discovering what minimal conclusions can safely be made and what must be left unresolved with the present data.

a. Preference for 2 Kgs 18:13 and 2 Kgs 19:9

One approach to the chronology problem gives precedence to the datum in 2 Kgs 18:13 that Sennacherib's campaign of 701 BCE took place in Hezekiah's 14th year. W. F. Albright[2] and J. Bright,[3] among others, made this view well known. Albright says, "There is no rational escape from this date [of 715] for Hezekiah's ascension, since the campaign of Sennacherib in the summer of 701 is dated in the fourteenth year of Hezekiah."[4]

α. The Ethiopian Tirhaka

The date of 715/714 for Hezekiah's ascension is also connected to a theory that Sennacherib conducted two campaigns against Judah.[5] Proponents of this theory hold that the two accounts of Sennacherib's aggressions in 2 Kgs 18:17-19:37 (// Isa 36) actually point to two campaigns instead of just the one in 701 BCE. Central to that argument is the fact that 2 Kgs 19:9 mentions that an Ethiopian, Tirhaka, attacked Sennacherib at Eltekah. Since Tirhaka did not ascend to the throne until 690 BCE, it is argued that 2 Kgs 19:9 provides evidence that the second account of Sennacherib's campaign was actually a description of a later campaign.[6]

---

[1]P. K. Hooker, *The Kingdom of Hezekiah: Judah in the Geo-Political Context of the Late Eighth Century* (Ph.D. Dissertation, Emory University; Ann Arbor: UMI, 1993) 139-51.

[2]W. F. Albright, "The Chronology of the Divided Monarchy of Israel," *BASOR* 100 (1945) 22.

[3]J. Bright, *A History of Israel* (3rd ed.; Philadelphia: Westminster Press, 1981) 276, n. 21.

[4]Albright, "Chronology," 22, n. 28.

[5]Albright, "Chronology," 22, n. 28. Bright, *History of Israel*, 298-309.

[6]Cf. Albright, "Chronology," 22, n. 28; Bright, *History of Israel*, 298-309.

The situation involving Tirhaka is not as clearcut as Albright argued. According to Albright's chronology Tirhaka would have only been a child in 701 BCE; but K. A. Kitchen has since shown that Tirhaka was at least a young man in that year, and he could have been involved in the battle as a high ranking officer.[7] Moreover, Tirhaka was a famous Ethiopian ruler, so it would not be surprising for an anachronistic reference to link Tirhaka to a battle that included Ethiopian and Egyptian forces.[8] In light of both these considerations, the reference to Tirhakah in 2 Kgs 19:9 is not compelling as the sole support of a two-campaign theory or of a theory giving preference to the synchronism in 2 Kgs 18:13.

β. The Two-Campaign Theory

Although the entire case for the two-campaign theory did not rest on the Tirhaka reference in 2 Kgs 19:9, the recent correction of the date of Lachish Level III to 701 BCE has undermined the arguments favoring such a scenario.[9] Albright, Bright, and others argued that the campaign of 701 did not destroy Judah completely. However, evidence presented in Chapter 2 of this monograph shows that Judah was devastated by Sennacherib's campaign during 701 BCE, so there would have been no need for Sennacherib to return just ten years later to squelch another rebellion.[10] Moreover, the supposition that a second rebellion took place soon after Babylon had finally been wiped out in 689 BCE is also hard to support.[11]

---

[7]K. A. Kitchen, *Third Intermediate Period in Egypt (1100-650 B.C.)* (Warminster: Aris and Phillips, 1973) 383-87. Kitchen's argument was strengthened by Anson Rainey's subsequent syntactical study of the relevant Egyptian texts (A. F. Rainey, "Taharqa and Syntax," *Tel Aviv* 3 [1976] 38-41). Rainey shows that an important sentence that supports Kitchen's interpretation but taken as "ambiguous" by Kitchen is, in fact, clear. The result is "that Taharqa (= Tirharka) was definitely older than 20 years in 701 B.C.E." (Rainey, "Taharqa," 40).

[8]M. Cogan and H. Tadmor, *II Kings: A New Translation with Introduction and Commentary* (AB 11; Garden City, NY: Doubleday, 1988) 234.

[9]See Chapter 3 for a detailed justification of this dating.

[10]W. H. Shea's argument for a second campaign rests on dating various Assyrian texts later than 701 BCE ("Sennacherib's Second Palestinian Campaign," *JBL* 104 [1985] 410-18). Shea's arguments for dating these Assyrian texts have been called into question by F. J. Yurco ("The Shabaka-Shebitku Coregency and the Supposed Second Campaign of Sennacherib Against Judah: A Critical Assessment," *JBL* 110 [1991] 35-45, esp. 39-45). Yurco's challenge of Shea's data is valid, and the redating of Lachish Level III and the archaeological data presented in Chapter II provide a second means of refuting Shea's position.

[11]Cogan and Tadmor, *II Kings,* 249-50.

In light of these considerations, a theory for two campaigns by Sennacherib seems unlikely; rather, the reference to Tirhaka in 2 Kgs 19:9 seems to be an anachronistic reference to the well-known Ethiopian monarch. Thus, the argument for accepting the ascension of Hezekiah during 715/714 BCE without positing co-regencies to account for the synchronisms in 2 Kgs 18:1-2, 10 loses much of its strength. It must be concluded that in the absence of other support, the approach favoring the synchronism of 2 Kgs 18:13 over the reference in 2 Kgs 18:10 is not convincing, so this first of four approaches is ruled out for the purposes of the present study.

b. The Emendation Approach

The second approach is an attempt to reconcile the various synchronisms in 2 Kgs 18:1-2, 2 Kgs 18:10, and 2 Kgs 18:13 by emending the text of 2 Kgs 18:13. All of these emendations are analyzed in Hooker's dissertation.[12] It is not necessary to go into detail here, because each proposal rejects the more difficult reading in the MT of 2 Kgs 18:13 in favor of an emendation that would have been more likely to arise secondarily than the reading of the 14th year. It is difficult to understand why an editor would have modified a synchronism that was clear to one that was unclear. Therefore, this approach has also been rejected for the purposes of this study.

c. The Co-Regency Approach

A third approach posits several co-regencies to resolve the difficulties with the synchronisms in 2 Kgs 18:10 and 2 Kgs 18:13. This approach is primarily identified with its chief proponent, E. R. Thiele.[13] Thiele's work is not limited to the problems surrounding Hezekiah's chronology; he considers the overall system of chronology and synchronisms for both Israel and Judah. Through the positing of different forms of regnal dating in Judah and Israel and the existence of co-regencies at various times, Thiele develops a rationale that makes all of the synchronisms and chronologies agree. The problem with his system though, is that time after time, suppositions of changes in regnal dating and co-regencies must be accepted to make all of the numbers agree. Thiele's theory of chronology for all of the Judean and Israelite monarchs may be correct, but with the current data it is impossible to prove.

---

[12]Hooker, *Kingdom of Hezekiah*, 143-44.

[13]E. R. Thiele, *The Mysterious Numbers of the Hebrew Kings* (New Revised Edition; Grand Rapids, MI: Zondervan, 1983).

The situation with Hezekiah is a little different from other parts of Thiele's work, because there are several unquestionable dates provided by Assyrian texts. The fall of Samaria is fixed at 722 BCE, and the dating of Sennacherib's campaign to the summer of 701 BCE is also established. Further, by dating the first attack on Jerusalem by Nebuchadnezzar to 597 BCE, one is able to work backwards with the chronological record of the Judean kings and establish that Manasseh, Hezekiah's son, ended his reign in 642 BCE. Taking the datum that Manasseh ruled for fifty-five years, one can place his ascension to 698/697 BCE. Next, the reference that Hezekiah reigned twenty-nine years (2 Kgs 18:2) places the ascension for Hezekiah at 727/726 BCE, just as suggested by the approach that gives preference to the synchronism in 2 Kgs 18:10. A problem with this system of reckoning, however, arises with 2 Kgs 18:13. The datum contained in this verse must be regarded as secondary and incorrect if Hezekiah ascended to the throne in 727/726 BCE.

Albright is correct in his assessment that 2 Kgs 18:13 shows that "there is no rational escape from this date for Hezekiah's ascension [during ca. 715], since the campaign of Sennacherib in the summer of 701 is dated to the fourteenth year of Hezekiah."[14] It is difficult to imagine that a later redactor would have created such an inconsistency in the text of Kings by confusing a reference to Hezekiah's illness occurring during the fourteenth year of his reign with a reference to the campaign of Sennacherib. It seems most reasonable to follow Thiele in assuming that the redactor of Kings did not understand the dualdating for Pekah's reign as overlapping with the reigns of Menahem and Pekahiah. This error results in a discrepancy of twelve years between the synchronisms in 2 Kings 17-18 and the actual course of events. This twelve-year discrepancy also explains the synchronism in 2 Kgs 18:10 which would place Hoshea's death in 710 if the dualdating of Pekah's reign is not accepted.[15] Likewise, Thiele posits that Hezekiah's son, Manasseh, ruled as a co-regent for 10 years following the stunning defeat of Judah at the hands of Sennacherib. The supposition of that co-regency permits the placement of Manasseh's ascension to the throne in 698/697 BCE, as the reverse computation of the synchronisms from the first attack of Jerusalem in 596 suggests. This co-regency also accounts for Hezekiah's twenty-nine-year reign that began in 715 BCE.[16]

---

[14]Albright, "Chronology," 22, n. 28.

[15]Thiele, *Mysterious Numbers*, 122-38.

[16]Thiele, *Mysterious Numbers*, 174-78.

d. Preference for 2 Kgs 18:10

Even though the third approach is a reasonable way to make sense of all of the data, the co-regency approach does not rule out the possibility of a fourth way to look at the situation. The fourth approach accepts the synchronism in 2 Kgs 18:10 at face value and places the ascension of Hezekiah to the throne in 727/726 BCE. The strength of this theory is that it is in accord with the chronological information given in 2 Kgs 18:1-2, 9. 2 Kgs 18:1-2 states that Hezekiah began to reign in the third year of King Hoshea of Israel, and he reigned twenty-nine years. 2 Kgs 18:9 states that the siege of Samaria began during Hezekiah's fourth year and during the seventh year of King Hoshea of Israel. Even though the Judean chronographer of Kings was not aware that Hoshea was captured during the ninth and final year of his reign in 724 BCE (two years before Samaria itself fell), all of the synchronisms in Kings (2 Kgs 17:1, 4, 6; 18:1, 9) are consistent with this omission and assume that Hoshea remained on the throne until the fall of Samaria during his ninth year.[17] In the absence of the problem presented by the synchronism given in 2 Kgs 18:13, all of the other synchronisms in Kings make sense if Hezekiah ascended to the throne in 727/726 and ruled until 698 BCE.[18]

The preference for 2 Kgs 18:10 is also consistent with the common interpretation of Isa 14:28-29a as suggesting that both Ahaz and Tiglath Pileser III died in 727/726 BCE. Isa 14:28-29a reads:

בשנת־מות המלך אחז היה המשא הזה:
אל־תשמחי פלשת כלך כי נשבר שבט מכך

In the year that King Ahaz died came this oracle:
Do not rejoice all of you, Philistia, that the rod which smote
you has been broken.

Commentators note that Tiglath Pileser III was responsible for several campaigns against the coastal plain cities, and that this reference to the rod that smote Philistia being broken must refer to his death in 727 BCE. If this interpretation is correct, Ahaz's death would necessarily be placed in 727/726 as well, so Hezekiah must have ascended to the throne in this same year.[19]

---

[17]Cogan and Tadmor, *II Kings*, 195-96, 216.

[18]For bibliography see H. Tadmor, "The Chronology of the First Temple Period—A Presentation and Evaluation of the Sources," *A History of Ancient Israel from the Beginnings to the Bar Kochba Revolt, A.D. 135* (ed. J. A. Soggin; Philadelphia: Westminster Press, 1984) 380-81; Hooker, *Kingdom of Hezekiah*, 139-41.

[19]cf. Tadmor, "Chronology," 381; Cogan and Tadmor, *II Kings*, 216.

Proponents of giving precedence to the synchronism in 2 Kgs 18:10 further posit that the reference to Hezekiah's fourteenth year found in 2 Kgs 18:13 was originally attached to the account of Hezekiah's illness in 2 Kgs 20:1-11 and that a later redactor of Kings separated the datum from its original context. These scholars point out that the account of Hezekiah's miraculous recovery states that Hezekiah is granted an additional fifteen years of life (2 Kgs 20:6). Taking the total number of twenty-nine years on the throne as ascribed to Hezekiah in 2 Kgs 18:2, his sickness must have taken place during the fourteenth year of his reign. Because Sennacherib's campaign might have been seen by a later redactor as the cause for Hezekiah's sickness, these interpreters argue that this depiction accounts for the specification of the fourteenth year of Hezekiah's reign now found as a synchronism of Sennacherib's campaign in 2 Kgs 18:13.[20]

The strength of this approach lies in the fact that it takes into account the synchronisms found in 2 Kgs 18:1-2, 9-10. It also takes into account the synchronism found in Isa 14:28-29a, if that verse actually refers to the death of Tiglath Pileser III. On the other hand, Isa 14:28-29a could refer to the death of Ahaz in 714 BCE and be a warning about the general attitude of rebellion that developed in Philistia during the first few years of Sargon II's reign when the Assyrian ruler was too occupied in the East to be a threat in Palestine. In this case, the historical reference of the oracle in Isa 14:28ff could have been the eve of Sargon's campaign against Ashdod in 714 BCE, and the prophet would have been warning the Judeans not to follow in the disastrous steps of the Philistines.

The major drawback to a preference for the synchronisms of 2 Kgs 18:1-2, 9-10 over the reference in 2 Kgs 18:13 is that no compelling explanation exists for the datum that Sennacherib's campaign took place in the fourteenth year of Hezekiah. The supposition that a later redactor misplaced a reference to Hezekiah's sickness as occurring during the fourteenth year of his reign is possible, but it is not possible to prove this supposition beyond a reasonable doubt or even to offer evidence that indicates that this is the most probable possibility. However, the co-regency explanation that reconciles the synchronisms in 2 Kgs 18:10 and 2 Kgs 18:13 is also not foolproof, so the theory that posits Hezekiah's ascension to the throne in 727/726 must be accepted as one of two possible approaches.

---

[20]Cf. Cogan and Tadmor, *II Kings*, 228 with bibliography.

4. Summary: Relevance of the Chronology Problem

In the survey of the viable resolutions to the chronological problems of Hezekiah's reign presented by the irreconcilable synchronisms in 2 Kgs 18:10 and 2 Kgs 18:13, only two approaches are possible. A preference is expressed for the positing of co-regencies, because the synchronism of the fourteenth year of Hezekiah's reign to 701 is strong and impossible to reconcile with the other compelling synchronism in 2 Kgs 18:10 without a co-regency. Even though this approach seems to be the more probable, for the purposes of this study the co-regency approach is not accepted without reservation.

The purpose of this study is to evaluate the relationship of historical data to an interpretation of 2 Chronicles 29-32. To accomplish the task, it focuses on the economic buildup and civil power of Hezekiah and determines if the detailed accounts of these aspects of Hezekiah's reign found in Chronicles can be substantiated in the extrabiblical material. In the final analysis, the conclusions presented here are valid whether Hezekiah began to reign in 727/726 or in 715/14. In either case, he would have been on the throne following Sargon's last campaign against Palestine around 714. The loosening of Assyrian domination following that campaign until Sennacherib's reestablishment of Assyrian control in 701 would have given Hezekiah an opportunity to undertake significant economic development of his kingdom and to build a strong coalition regardless of whether he ascended the throne in 727/726 or in 715/714. Thus, the position taken in this study is that the redactor of Kings did not understand the dual dating for Pekah's reign. The mistake explains the synchronism in 2 Kgs 18:10 which incorrectly places Hoshea's death in 710 BCE and Hezekiah's accension in 727/726 BCE. Hezekiah most likely began his twenty-nine-year reign in 715/714, and he ruled with his son as co-regent during the final ten years. Even if the converse position— that Hezekiah became king in 727/726— is found to be true, the conclusions presented in this study concerning the economic development and civil power of Hezekiah's reign are still valid.

B. Presuppositions about Dating of the Book of Chronicles

Modern scholars have proposed a range of almost 400 years for the dating of Chronicles.[21] Some scholars argue for a major redaction of Chronicles during the time of Zerubbabel and thus posit a date in the late 6th century.[22] On the other hand, scholars such as Martin Noth link the work with the Samaritan schism and propose a date during the 3rd century.[23] The common ground among the above-mentioned efforts to date Chronicles is that each attempts to tie the book of Chronicles to particular historical events. However, as Sarah Japhet aptly points out:

> The actualities of the period, whether under Babylonian, Persian or Hellenistic rule, are not expressed in Chronicles in concrete references to events. . . The date and provenance of Chronicles must thus be determined mostly on the basis of general considerations, with no support from reference to precise historical events.[24]

Building on Japhet's comments, one may turn to several general indicators that suggest a date well after Zerubbabel. First, the language of Chronicles is "Late Biblical Hebrew" and has affinities with post-exilic books such as Ezra-Nehemiah, Esther, Daniel, etc. Japhet rightly concludes that this fact alone fixes "the upper limit of the composition of the book no earlier than the post-exilic period, and probably well into it."[25]

As a second means of pointing toward a date well into the post-exilic period, multiple scholars highlight specific references throughout the text of Chronicles that require a date well in the Persian period. In 1 Chr 29:7, there is a reference to 10,000 "darics" of silver. Williamson correctly concludes that "this coin was not minted before 515 BC at the earliest, and sufficient time must be allowed for the anachronism to have

---

[21]A convenient table that summarizes the various dates is found in M. A. Thronveit, *When Kings Speak: Royal Speech and Royal Prayer in Chronicles*, SBLDS, vol. 93 (Atlanta: Scholars Press, 1987) 97.

[22]For example see, among others, D. N. Freedman, "The Chronicler's Purpose," *CBQ* 23 (1961) 436-42; F. M. Cross, "A Reconstruction of the Judean Restoration," *JBL* 94 (1975) 4-18; also published in *Interpretation* 29 (1975) 187-201; recently Thronveit, *When Kings Speak*, 97-107.

[23]See M. Noth, *The Chronicler's History* (Sheffield: JSOT Press, 1987) 100-106.

[24]Japhet, *I and II Chronicles*, 25.

[25]Japhet, *I and II Chronicles*, 25.

been tolerated."[26] Further, 2 Chr 8:3-4 speaks of the association of Tadmor and Hamat-Zobah, and this association most likely "reflects the Assyrian-Babylonian-Persian system of administration."[27] Next, one notices that in 2 Chr 16:9, the Chronicler quotes Zech 4:10. Williamson correctly observes that this reference is made in conjunction with the quotation of "canonical writings," so a number of years mus be allowed for Zechariah to become authoritative. Similarly, the genealogy found in 1 Chr 3 lists six generations after Zerubbabel. Finally, the absence of material suggesting a Hellenistic influence argues for fixing the lower date at the end of the Persian period.[28]

These indicators point to a date well within the Persian period, somewhere in the 4th century BCE. It is difficult to arrive at a more specific date, but even this conclusion is important. If a 4th century date is accepted, one recognizes that the Chronicler writes at least 150 years after the completion of Dtr. Further, the Chronicler composes almost 400 years after Hezekiah's time. Therefore, whatever conclusions are drawn concerning the Chronicler's use of historical sources or remembrances, one must keep in mind that the Chronicler is concerned with revising or reinterpreting Israel's history for a community long after the exile.[29]

---

[26]H. G. M. Williamson, *1 and 2 Chronicles*, New Century Bible Commentary (Grand Rapids: W. B. Eerdmans Publ. Co., 1982) 15. This type of coin was first minted by Darius I. See also Williamson, *Israel in the Book of Chronicles*, 84.

[27]Williamson, *Israel in the Book of Chronicles*, 84. See also Welten, *Geschichte*, 35-36; and M. Noth, "Das Reich von Hamath als Grenznachbar des Reiches Israel," *PJb* 33 (1937) 36-51.

[28]Cf., among others, Williamson, *1 and 2 Chronicles*, 16; Japhet, *I and II Chronicles*, 25.

[29]A date in the 4th century is common among commentaries of Chronicles across the theological spectrum. For commentators who argue for a 4th century date, see among many, Japhet, *I and II Chronicles*, 23-28; M. J. Selman, *1 Chronicles: An Introduction and Commentary*, The Tyndale Old Testament Commentaries (Leicester, England; Downers Grove, Illinois: Inter-varsity Press, 1994) 71; Williamson, *1 and 2 Chronicles*, 15-17; and S. De Vries, *1 and 2 Chronicles*, The Forms of the Old Testament Literature, vol. XI (Grand Rapids: William B. Eerdmans Publishing Company, 1989) 16-17.

C. Presuppositions About the Paleographic Dating of the Siloam Tunnel Inscription

Almost all commentators assume that the Siloam Tunnel Inscription comes from the time of Hezekiah.[30] Even those who hold that Chronicles is almost completely devoid of historical value, concede that the Chronicler's account of the channel of water in 2 Chr 32:30a is an authentic remembrance of Hezekiah's water tunnel. Welten's work is a good example. He finds that when Chronicles contains material of a political nature or material detailing a Judean king's preparations for war, these additions are nonhistorical with the possible exception of four short passages. One of those passages is the brief reference in 2 Chr 32:30a to the Siloam Tunnel.[31]

It is important to determine if the Siloam Tunnel and the Siloam Tunnel Inscription can be assumed reliably as a starting point for discussion about the political work of Hezekiah. If so, this verse could provide a springboard from which to discuss other possibly reliable political references by the Chronicler. Although this consensus position of dating the Siloam Tunnel Inscription to Hezekiah by extrabiblical historical data would support the thesis of this monograph, the presupposition concerning that dating must be reexamined to insure that the argument contained in the monograph rests on solid ground.

When analyzing the historical reliability of 2 Chr 32:30a, one must take into account the arguments for the paleographic dating of the Siloam Tunnel Inscription, because paleography is one of the primary reasons that commentators who are skeptical of the general historical reliability of the Chronicler accept the validity of the reference to Hezekiah's tunnel in 2 Chr 32:30a. Most scholars use the paleography of the Siloam Tunnel Inscription to date the inscription to the late 8th century BCE. Even though the common paleographic dating to Hezekiah's reign would

---

[30]For the opposite view, cf. the discussion in R. North, "Does Archaeology Prove Chronicles Sources?" *A Light Unto My Path: Old Testament Studies in Honor of Jacob M. Myers* (eds. H. M. Bream, R. D. Heim, and C. A. Moore; Gettysburg Theological Studies; Philadelphia: Temple University Press, 1974) 375-81. See also the recent article by John Rogerson and Philip Davies that presents an argument for a Hasmonean date (J. Rogerson and P. R. Davies, "Was the Siloam Tunnel Built by Hezekiah?" *BA* 59 [1996] 138-49) and the paleographic response by Hendel (R. S. Hendel, "The Date of the Siloam Inscription: A Rejoinder to Rogerson and Davies," *BA* 59 [1996] 233-37).

[31]The other references with historical reliability are 2 Chr 11:5b; 2 Chr 11:6-10a; and 2 Chr 26:6a, 10. Welten, *Geschichte*, 195-96; cf. the analysis of Japhet, "Historical Reliability," 98.

support the argument presented in this monograph, paleographic data presented in a separate article[32] show that this common assumption about the Siloam Tunnel Inscription is still uncertain from a strictly paleographic viewpoint and should not form the basis for the assertion that Chronicles contains historically reliable elements. In other words, when the argument is made that there are elements of historical consistency in the Chronicler's account of Hezekiah, these elements can be supported even if the common paleographic dating of the Siloam Tunnel to Hezekiah's reign is rejected. In the conclusion to the monograph, it is suggested that the Siloam Tunnel Inscription most likely dates from Hezekiah's reign, but this conclusion is drawn from analysis of a reference found in 2 Chr 32:30, not from extrabiblical historical data.

---

[32]A. G. Vaughn, "Palaeographic Dating of Judaean Seals and Its Signigificance for Biblical Research," *BASOR* 313 (1999) 43-64; see esp. pp. 58-59. It should be emphasized at this point of the argument that paleographically the Siloam Tunnel inscription is definitely pre-exilic, and it would be a mistake to misuse the paleographic analysis presented here to suggest that the Siloam Tunnel dates to the Persian period.

TWO

AN ARCHAEOLOGICAL ASSESSMENT OF THE ECONOMIC BUILDUP OF HEZEKIAH AND JOSIAH

A. Introduction

Four major sections in 2 Chronicles 29-32 have no parallels in Kings: a) 29:3-36, which details the purification and restoration of the temple; b) 30:1-27, which describes the reestablishment of the Passover; c) 31:2-19, which specifies how the clergy will maintain the temple; and d) 32:27-30, which lists in some detail Hezekiah's economic buildup and his mighty acts. Archaeological data may be used to corroborate or to disprove only one of these sections. It is not possible with the present data to find material remains that have bearing on the rearrangement of the political structure of either the temple or Hezekiah's kingdom;. Nevertheless, archaeological data can be of assistance in evaluating the statements concerning Hezekiah's economic buildup and his great civil and administrative power that are detailed in 2 Chr 32:27-30. Thus, the primary goal of this chapter is to substantiate Hezekiah's great economic buildup and civil power.

The discrepancy created by the Chronicler's account of Hezekiah's economic buildup in 2 Chr 32:27-30 and the absence of such an account in Kings points to one of the central issues regarding the reliability of the Chronicler's account. Welten challenges in general the value of Chronicles to illucidate pre-exilic Israel, and he specifically challenges the value of any added material of a political nature (war reports, descriptions of military techniques, and reports about buildings and fortifications) except for four very brief passages.[1] On the other hand, Rosenbaum presents a logical explanation for the omission by Dtr. of political material supportive of Hezekiah. Rosenbaum accepts the view that at least a major redaction of the Deuteronomistic History took place during the reign of Josiah and postulates the desire to emphasize the material gains and prosperity of Josiah over Hezekiah—another monarch who was known for cultic reforms just a century earlier.[2] The present chapter builds on Rosenbaum's arguments. The chapter not only presents archaeological evidence to corroborate the account of great economic buildup by Hezekiah as described in 2 Chr 32:27-30, but also evaluates the archaeological evidence for the relative economic status of the other great Judean reformer, Josiah.

---

[1]Welten, *Geschichte*, esp. 195-96.

[2]Rosenbaum, "Hezekiah's Reform," 29-33.

One way of measuring Hezekiah's economic buildup relative to that of Josiah is to examine the settlement and population of Judah during both kingdoms. However, this is not a simple task. There are no accurate census records to compare. Even though one kingdom may have had a larger population, it does not necessarily follow that this particular kingdom would have had a greater economic buildup or civil strength than the other. Since there are no written sources, the investigator must rely on archaeological surveys and excavations for estimations of settlement patterns in the various areas of Judah during Hezekiah's and Josiah's reigns.

In preindustrial, agrarian societies, population had a more direct impact on economic buildup via the agricultural productivity of the area than it does in industrial societies today. However, one must ask if an increased population allowed for an increase in agricultural productivity, or if an increase in agricultural techniques, a more favorable climate, or more available land caused the increase in population and settlement.[3] Some historical considerations during the period of Hezekiah point toward at least some increase in the population and settlement of Judah caused by the immigration of northern Israelites after 722 BCE; however, it is not critical to an evaluation of Hezekiah's economic buildup and civil strength to know whether this population and settlement increase was the cause or the result of economic advances.

An increase in population as the cause for increased agricultural buildup is supported by anthropological models. D. E. Dumond explains that "population growth is not a simple effect of cultural change but is both a cause and effect of that change."[4] C. Clark goes further and claims,

> "The time comes, of course, when population growth does
> threaten to overtake the 'means of subsistence,' as they are
> understood in that time and place; and then the consequence is
> that population growth itself provides the necessary stimulus,
> inducing the community to change its existing methods of
> producing or obtaining food for more productive methods,
> which will enable it to support a larger population."[5]

---

[3]D. C. Hopkins, *The Highlands of Canaan: Agricultural Life in the Early Iron Age* (SWBA 3; Sheffield/ Decatur: Almond, 1985) 42-46.

[4]D. E. Dumond, "Population Growth and Cultural Change." *SWJA* 21 (1965) 302.

[5]C. Clark, *Population Growth and Land Use* (New York: Macmillan, 1967) 60.

It can thus be argued that an increase in population (in the case of Hezekiah, perhaps caused by immigration from northern tribes) caused increased agricultural buildup. Leaving aside the cause-and-effect question, sociological models of social stratification show that a higher rate of settlement and population lead to increased power and economic capacity. In his work on social stratification, G. Lenski states that "one measure of the power of any state is *the size of the territory it controls*."[6] Moreover, with respect to population, Lenski states that "*population size* is another measure of the power of [agrarian] states and also of the capacity of their economic systems."[7] Therefore, for the purposes of this study, an increase in population and settlement will be considered one component of an increase in the economic capacity and political power in an agrarian society, and little effort will be spent in determining if the increase in population is the cause or effect of this prosperity.

A secondary goal in this chapter is to use archaeological data to compare the economic buildup by Hezekiah with that of Josiah in order to support Rosenbaum's position that Hezekiah's status rivaled that of Josiah. In light of this second goal, every area of Judah is analyzed, whether or not it plays a major role in corroborating Hezekiah's economic buildup as described in 2 Chr 32:27-30. For instance, the Judean Desert does not play a major role in Hezekiah's economic development, but an analysis of the Judean Desert in the period of both monarchs is necessary for a comprehensive evaluation of the relative economic and political status of each king.

---

[6]G. E. Lenski, *Power and Privilege: A Theory of Social Stratification* (New York: Magraw-Hill Book Company, 1966) 194 (emphasis his). I thank John Brueggemann for calling my attention to Lenski's work and for discussing social stratification in agrarian societies with me.

[7]Lenski, *Power and Priviledge*, 195 (emphasis his).

B. Settlement and Economic Buildup During the Reigns of Hezekiah and Josiah

1. The Judean Shephelah

a. General Discussion

The Shephelah is the clearest area in Judah in which archaeological surveys indicate greater settlement and development during the period of Hezekiah than in the period of Josiah. These results are firm both due to the comprehensive survey work of Yehuda Dagan[8] and due to extensive excavations at Tel Batash (Timnah), Tell Beit-Mirsim, Tel Lachish, Tel Miqne (Ekron), and Beth Shemesh. Building on the results of the Lachish excavations, Dagan conducted an extensive survey of the Shephelah and recorded which sites contained pottery corresponding to Lachish Levels II and III. Due to the clear stratigraphy, it is commonly accepted that Lachish III corresponds to the late 8th century, whereas Lachish II corresponds to the early 6th century.[9] There was an occupation gap after the destruction of Lachish Level III in 701 BCE, so the pottery from the two levels is distinct. By recording which sites contained pottery corresponding to Level II or III, Dagan was able to estimate the density of settlement in the Shephelah from the late 8th through the early 6th century.

Dagan found that settlement reached a peak in the late 8th century. He says, "Archaeological survey shows that in most of the settlements that were surveyed, it was possible to find much pottery similar to the finds from Lachish Level III".[10] Moreover, this high settlement ratio is not found in either the periods preceding or those following, indicating an explosion in the population during the late 8th century. It is instructive to examine in more depth Dagan's findings from the various periods.

The majority of settlements were established during the Iron II (10th to early 6th century BCE). This increase is seen in all types of communities—tels, settlements, farming villages, and fortresses. Specifically, 15 of 40 tels, 130 of 132 sites with remains of residential dwellings,[11] 38 of 45 farming villages, and 8 of 8 fortresses that exhibited

---

[8]Y. Dagan, "The Shephelah During the Period of the Monarchy in Light of Archaeological Excavations and Surveys" (M.A. thesis, Tel Aviv University, 1992) (Hebrew).

[9]Cf. Ussishkin, "Destruction," 50-54. Cf. also Chapter 3 below

[10]Dagan, "Shephelah," 255.

[11]Dagan uses phrase "שריד יישוב." This term is translated as "sites with remains of residential dwellings" to convey the sense of Dagan's terminology.

signs of occupation during the Iron II were also founded during the Iron II. Moreover, most of this increased and new settlement took place in the latter part of the Iron II rather than at the beginning.[12]

Looking at the beginning of the Iron II, 17 tels and 4 sites with remains of residential dwellings contained pottery corresponding to Lachish Level V (roughly the 10th century BCE or the beginning of Iron II). Most of the settlements with pottery corresponding to Lachish Level V were principal tels that had a fairly continuous history of occupation throughout the time periods under discussion (e.g. Tel Batash, Tel Beth Shemesh, Tel Lachish, Tell Beit Mirsim). Only three settlements were found in the western part of the Shephelah (Hurbet Um el-baqar, Tel Kellek, and Tel Malḥah), and most of those were found at the eastern edge of the West Shephelah. Finally, even in sites with parallels to Lachish V, the proportion of that pottery to pottery from other periods was small.[13]

Turning next to the later Iron II period, Dagan found that 276 sites with a total built-up area of 4651 dunams[14] had pottery that corresponded to Lachish Level III.[15] Assuming that Lachish III was destroyed in 701 BCE, these data indicate settlement at these sites during the 9th and 8th centuries BCE. Table 1 details Dagan's conclusions:[16]

---

[12]Dagan, "Shephelah," 251-53, graph 1.

[13]Dagan, "Shephelah," 253-55.

[14]1 dunam = 0.247 acres.

[15]Dagan does not detail statistics for sites with pottery corresponding to Lachish IV. This is probably because there is no clear gap between Levels V and IV. Although Level IV can be clearly separated from Level III, there are no signs of destruction by fire. Further, many buildings of Level III are rebuilt upon the foundations from Level IV. Whatever the cause, the occupation is continuous between Levels IV and III so it is difficult to make clear distinctions in the pottery (cf. Ussishkin, "Destruction," 52). Nevertheless, there are small differences in the development of lug handles and bar handles on bowls and in the burnishing techniques (cf. discussion below on the pottery from the Western Hill of Jerusalem).

[16]Dagan, "Shephelah," 250.

TABLE 1: SITES WITH POTTERY PARALLELS TO LACHISH LEVEL III

Type of Settlement	Number of Sites	Area in dunams
Tel	40	1,809
sites with remains of residential settlements	132	2,393
farming settlement	45	198
fortress	8	32
single structure[17]	13	32
"isolated find"[18]	38	187
TOTAL:	276[19]	4,651

Although it is difficult to convert these data into a precise settlement estimate, it is clear that the Shephelah experienced an explosion of settlement during the 9th and 8th centuries. Since Dagan's survey only included about 51.3% of the Shephelah, he concluded that the actual settlement should be twice the size of the figures given.[20] This might·be questioned because one would assume that his survey included all settlements visible from the air. Assuming that those sites contain the largest built-up area, one might conclude that the additional sites that would be discovered through further survey would increase but not double the estimates presented here. On the other hand, Dagan also points out that surveys in the areas of Beth Shemesh and Kefar Menachem conducted since the end of his survey have accounted for an additional sixty-three sites with Lachish Level III pottery, so it is clear that a substantial number of smaller sites are not included in his calculations.[21]

---

[17]Dagan's term שריד בודד is translated as "single structure" to convey the sense of his usage. Dagan says that "this definition consists of 13 different sites where Iron Age II pottery was found, but it is not really possible to view them as one of the [four different] types of settlements defined above." He continues, "There is no doubt that isolated residents, who were separated from the larger concentrations of settlements, built in these sites isolated buildings for dwelling, and it is possible that these dwellings were seasonal" (Dagan, "Shephelah," 249).

[18]Dagan ("Shephelah," 250) defines an "isolated find" (נקודת ממצא) as a site where the archaeological finds consist primarily of concentrations of pottery found on the surface, but without any corresponding architectural ruins. This is to be contrasted with the term שרידי יישוב, translated here as "sites with remains of residential settlements." The salient difference between this term and the previous term שריד בודד is that the term "single structure" (שריד בודד) implies that it contains at least some architectural remains.

[19]Dagan reports that after the end of his survey in November 1991, new data surfaced in surveys near Beth Shemesh and Kefar Menachem. These additional data bring the total of sites with Lachish Level III pottery to 339.

[20]Dagan, "Shephelah," 256.

[21]Dagan, "Shephelah," 309.

Turning next to the very end of the Iron II (the late 7th to early 6th century BCE = Lachish Level II), Dagan found a dramatic drop in settlement of the Judean Shephelah. Pottery corresponding to Lachish Level II was found in only 38 sites. Table 2 details Dagan's conclusions:[22]

TABLE 2: SITES WITH POTTERY PARALLELS TO LACHISH LEVEL II

Type of Settlement	Number of Sites	Area in dunams
Tel	18	747
Site with remains of residential settlements	15	368
Farming Settlement	1	2
Fortress	0	0
Single Structure	1	2
"Isolated Find"	3	5
TOTAL:	38	1,124

Not only do these data point to a decrease in the built-up area of the Shephelah to less than one-fourth its size during the 8th century, they also point to the virtual extinction of the farming settlements and fortresses (one in the late 7th century compared to fifty-three in the 8th century). Moreover, there is also a dramatic drop in the number of sites with remains of residential settlements to one-tenth the number of the late 8th century (from 132 in the 8th century to only 15 in the late 7th century). There is also a drop of approximately one-half in the settlements at the major tels (40 in the 8th century compared to 18 in the late 7th). Finally, there is a virtual absence of Judean settlements in the western part of the Shephelah by the late 7th century.[23]

Inherent weaknesses of surveys must be examined. By nature, surveys do not present all the data; thus, the findings of any survey must be considered tentative and in need of confirmation by more extensive archaeological fieldwork. This issue has been addressed by I. Finkelstein in an article that incorporates population estimates made by surveys. Finkelstein points out that the most important feature of Dagan's survey is that it was conducted in conjunction with the large-scale excavations of Lachish, so it took into account the extensive excavations that have taken place in the Shephelah region since the beginning of the 20th century. In addition, Dagan's survey represents more than a small sampling of the area. More than fifty percent of the Shephelah was thoroughly covered.[24]

---

[22]Dagan, "Shephelah," 259-60.

[23]Dagan, "Shephelah," map 7.

[24]I. Finkelstein, "The Archaeology of the Days of Manasseh." *Scripture and Other Artifacts: Essays on the Bible and Archaeology in Honor of Philip J. King* (eds. M. D. Coogan, J. C. Exum, and L. E. Stager; Louisville: Westminster/John

Although archaeological surveys are prone to some degree of error, when the findings are as dramatic as in Dagan's surveys, the chance of error diminishes. It is possible that a limited number of sites might have contained pottery of Lachish Level II but were not identified, yet when hundreds of sites lack this type of pottery, the results cannot be ignored.[25]

As a result of Dagan's findings, several conclusions may be drawn that have ramifications for understanding Hezekiah's economic buildup and civil strength as measured against those of Josiah. The region of the Judean Shephelah experienced tremendous growth during the 9th and 8th centuries, in terms of both number of sites settled and population. Further, the growth seems to be "new growth;" that is, the majority of the settlements in the Shephelah were established at some point during those centuries. This observation is important for evaluating the status of Hezekiah. It shows that the extensive settlement of the Shephelah region should not be attributed to the period of the united monarchy. These data do not suggest that Hezekiah established all of these settlements, of course, but they do suggest that the settlements were still functioning during Hezekiah's reign and not long beyond. Thus, one may conclude that Hezekiah had a greater amount of economic buildup and civil strength in the Shephelah than did Josiah.

A further observation is that during Hezekiah's reign there were many Judean settlements without extensive fortification systems. As noted, Dagan found 132 sites with remains of residential settlements from the late 8th century as compared to only 15 during the period corresponding to Josiah. Although at least some of the sites may have had some type of fortification system, these fortifications systems, if they did exist, were not nearly as developed as the fortifications at the major tels. In addition, there were 45 farming settlements during Hezekiah's reign but only one during the reign of Josiah. Both factors indicate that not only were settlement and production of goods higher during Hezekiah's reign, but also that the area was more stable.

The large number of settlements without fortifications may be explained by the fact that there were eight fortresses documented in the Shephelah during the late 8th century,[26] but none were found from the

---

Knox Press, 1994) 172-74.

[25]I. Finkelstein, personal communication.

[26]As most of these fortresses do not have modern GNN, the following lists the GNN only when they exist. In all cases the sites are identified by Dagan's running numbering system with the map coordinates in parenthesis: a) Dagan no. 33 (14-12/64/1); b) Dagan no. 97 (15-12/12/2); c) Esh Sh es-Salihu: Dagan no. 102 (14-12/61/1; d) Kh. Rasm Ed dab^c: Dagan no. 131 (14-11/36/1); e) Dagan no. 195 (13-10/83/1); f) Rujm el Qas^ca: Dagan no. 232 (14-10/61/2); g)

reign of Josiah (late 7th century). These late 8th-century forts suggest a greater amount of Judean civil and military control in the Shephelah during Hezekiah's reign than during the reign of Josiah. In addition, there was little or no Judean settlement in the western part of the Shephelah during Josiah's reign, although this area was extensively developed during the reign of Hezekiah. It is possible, therefore, to draw the further conclusion that Judah had greater civil and military power over the areas closest to the inhabitants of the Coastal Plain during Hezekiah's reign than during Josiah's reign.

Finally, the fact that there were many more small settlements and farming communities under Hezekiah's reign than under Josiah's suggests that the land in the Shephelah was utilized to a higher degree in the late 8th century than in the late 7th. This greater utilization of land would mean that more goods would have been available to Hezekiah than to Josiah. Once again, evidence shows that Hezekiah had a greater economic buildup of resources in this area than Josiah.

b. Mareshah

The evidence from Dagan's surveys is confirmed by controlled excavations of major sites in the Shephelah such as Mareshah, Tell Beit Mirsim, Beth Shemesh, and Lachish. At the beginning of the 20th century, Bliss and Maclister conducted extensive excavations at Mareshah. Although the reports are not synchronized with the data obtained from the later excavations at Lachish, it is possible to compare the pottery discovered at Mareshah with that from Lachish. Such a comparison shows that pottery comparable finds at to Lachish Levels IV and III was found at Mareshah.[27] Dagan noted that there was also an absence of pottery corresponding to Lachish Level II.[28]

c. Tell Beit Mirsim

Tell Beit Mirsim was excavated in the early part of the 20th century by W. F. Albright, and he published ten levels dating from the third millennium until 589-587 BCE.[29] The last stratum at Tell Beit Mirsim (A)

Dagan no. 260 (14-10/50/2); h) Dagan no. 267 (14-10/70/2).

[27]F. J. Bliss, "Report on the Excavations at Tell Es-Sandahannah." *PEFQS* (1900):319-38; F. J. Bliss and R. A. S. Macalister, *Excavations in Palestine During the Years 1898-1900* (London: Committee of the Palestine Exploration Fund, 1902) 52-61, pl. 16-19.

[28]Dagan, "Shephelah," 47.

[29]W. F. Albright, *The Excavation of Tell Beit Mirsim in Palestine, Vol. I: The Pottery of the First Three Campaigns* (AASOR 12; New Haven: Yale University Press, 1932) xxi.

showed signs of extensive occupation, and Albright assigned it a destruction date of between 589 and 587 BCE.[30] If Albright's dates are correct, this site would seem to detract from the conclusion presented above. However, his dates have been challenged, so it is important to reevaluate his findings for the Iron Age II levels.

Levels A and B from Tell Beit Mirsim are the only levels containing Iron II pottery. Level A, the stratum found on top of the tell, contained two sublayers (A2 and A1). Level B, found beneath it, was published with three sublayers (B3, B2, and B1). Albright dated B1 to the pre-Philistine period (1230-1150), B2 to the Philistine period (1150-1000), and B3 to the united monarchy (1000-920).[31] Based largely on parallels with Lachish Level VI, R. Greenberg redated Tell Beit Mirsim Level B2 to the late 12th century or early 11th century, almost 100 years earlier than Albright's dating.[32] This modification in the earlier part of Albright's chronology suggests that modifications of later dates may be needed as well.

Albright's argument that Level A was destroyed by the Babylonians between 589 and 587 BCE was determined largely due to his misdating of Lachish Level III to 596 BCE. In addition, his attribution of the official seal impression of לאליקם / נער יוכן to the reign of Jehoiakin added another seemingly compelling reason to date the destruction of Level A to 587 BCE.[33] However, this seal impression and all the *lmlk* and official seal impressions in general have been reevaluated; and it is now clear that all of these impressions come from the late 8th century.[34] Noting these errors made by Albright, Yohanan Aharoni suggested redating the destruction of the majority of Level A2 to the campaign of Sennacherib in 701 BCE. Aharoni also postulated that the Western Tower and a limited portion of the tell were rebuilt during the 7th century. The destruction of the last layer of occupation of Level A (Y. Aharoni's Level A3) was dated to 586 BCE.[35] However, even this conclusion must be called into question because Y. Aharoni based his finding on the false assumption that the

---

[30]W. F. Albright, *The Excavation of Tell Beit Mirsim : The Iron Age* (AASOR 21-22; New Haven: ASOR, 1943) 39, 66-68.

[31]Albright, *Tell Beit Mirsim I*, xxi.

[32]R. Greenberg, "New Light on the Early Iron Age at Tell Beit Mirsim," *BASOR* 265 (1987) 55-80.

[33]Albright, *Tell Beit Mirsim III*, 39, 66-68.

[34]Cf. discussion below in Chapter 3.

[35]M. Aharoni and Y. Aharoni, "The Stratification of Judahite Sites in the 8th and 7th Centuries B.C.E.." *BASOR* 224 (1976) 73; Yohanan Aharoni, *The Archaeology of the Land of Israel: From the Prehistoric Beginnings to the End of the First Temple Period* (Philadelphia: Westminster Press, 1982) 261-62, 266.

נער יוכן / לאליקם seal should still be dated to the reign of Jehoiachin even though he dated the *lmlk* jars to the late 8th century.

O. Zimhoni has reexamined all of the pottery from Tell Beit Mirsim and compared it to assemblages from Tell ʿEton and Lachish. She builds on Aharoni's findings that the pottery from Tell Beit Mirsim is contemporary with that of Lachish Level III and furthers his work by showing that there is no pottery from Tell Beit Mirsim that corresponds to Lachish Level II. She says, "It is reasonable to assume that if there had existed at Tell Beit Mirsim, as Aharoni suggested, any settlement at all that could be dated a century or so later, some evidence, even the slightest, would have survived."[36] Noting that Aharoni's only justification for the 586 BCE destruction date of Level A3 is the misdated seal impression, Zimhoni correctly concludes that Tell Beit Mirsim was destroyed in 701 BCE and not reoccupied afterwards.[37] Thus, Tell Beit Mirsim is an example of a large, fortified settlement in the southern Shephelah that was inhabited during the reign of Hezekiah, but not during the reign of Josiah.[38]

d. Beth Shemesh

Beth Shemesh presents a confusing picture from the excavations undertaken in the early part of the 20th century. Unlike Tell Beit Mirsim where the findings were clearly published and recorded according to layers, the finds from Beth Shemesh are mixed, and it is difficult to separate pottery from the various strata and sublevels. The situation makes it impossible to redate precisely the various strata from the previous publications with the same precision possible with the reports of Tell Beit Mirsim; however, it is still possible to compare the pottery from Beth Shemesh with that from other stratified sites and to draw general conclusions.

The final publication of the most extensive excavations at Beth Shemesh was undertaken by G.E. Wright and E. Grant. A little background on that report is helpful. It is generally accepted that Grant's excavations at Beth Shemesh did not keep careful records, which was one of the primary reasons that Wright was recruited to help publish the material. Although Wright had never dug at Beth Shemesh, he was recommended to Grant by Albright as a promising young scholar who could make

---

[36]O. Zimhoni, "The Iron Age Pottery of Tel ʿEton and Its Relation to the Lachish, Tell Beit Mirsim and Arad Assemblages," *Tel Aviv* 12 (1985) 83.

[37]Zimhoni, "Pottery of Tel ʿEton," 82-84.

[38]Zimhoni ("Pottery of Tel ʿEton," 87-88) notes that Tell ʿEton is another site with systematic excavations that was destroyed in 701 BCE and not reinhabited.

sense out of the excavation records.[39] The directors of the renewed excavations of Beth Shemesh, Z. Lederman and S. Bunimovitz, assert that Wright "emphasized the inherent difficulties of his tentative analysis."[40]

Accordingly, Wright drew on historical texts to make sense of the data. As a result of study relevant to this period, Wright found that there was one basic stratum (Level II) with three sublayers, a, b, and c. He grouped the various finds into these substrata and concluded that Level IIc contained Iron II pottery. He dated its beginning to sometime during the late 9th century (ca. 825 BCE). Because when Wright published his report it was customary to date the *lmlk* jars to the early 6th century, he concluded that Level IIc was destroyed in 586 BCE.[41] If Grant and Wright were correct in this analysis, Beth Shemesh would not support the survey findings of Dagan. However, as was the case with Tell Beit Mirsim, there are indications that Grant and Wright were incorrect in their analysis and that Beth Shemesh was destroyed in 701 BCE and not resettled during the 7th century.

Such a conclusion about the redating of Level IIc was first reached by M. Aharoni and Y. Aharoni, who reexamined the pottery from Beth Shemesh and found that it was contemporary with the pottery from Lachish Level III. Aharoni and Aharoni found that 12 of 17 pottery types selected as representative of Lachish III were also attested at Beth Shemesh. This figure is conservative; it does not even include the multiple *lmlk* impressions found in Level IIc, because as Aharoni and Aharoni only considered restorable vessels.[42] In addition, Aharoni and Aharoni noted the absence of any pottery contemporary to Lachish Level II.[43] They thus concluded that Beth Shemesh Level IIc was destroyed in 701 BCE, and the site was not resettled during the 7th century.[44]

Aharoni and Aharoni's conclusion has been confirmed by the renewed excavations at Beth Shemesh. Two overview reports state that no pottery corresponding to Lachish Level II was found during the first

---

[39]Cf. S. Bunimovitz and Z. Lederman, "Beth Shemesh," *NEAEHL* (ed. Ephraim Stern; New York: Macmillan; Jerusalem: Israel Exploration Society, 1993) 249; Zvi Lederman, personal communication.)

[40]Bunimovitz and Lederman, "Beth Shemesh," 249.

[41]E. Grant and G. E. Wright, *Ain Shems Excavations (Palestine): Part V (Text)* (Biblical and Kindred Studies 8; Haverford, PA: Haverford College, 1939) 67-75.

[42]Aharoni and Aharoni, "Stratification of Judahite Sites," 76-85.

[43]Aharoni and Aharoni, "Stratification of Judahite Sites," 86-89.

[44]Aharoni and Aharoni, "Stratification of Judahite Sites," 73, 87.

several seasons of the renewed excavations.[45] The complete report has not been published, but Lederman and Bunimovitz shared their findings with the author on numerous visits to Beth Shemesh.[46] The directors reported that during the first five seasons of excavations, no pottery from Beth Shemesh that was contemporary to Lachish Level II was found.[47] Further, sherds and *lmlk* impressions were found that were contemporary to Lachish III. The problem, at this point, with drawing firm conclusions from the renewed excavations is that there is a dearth of reconstructable pottery from the late 8th century. Most of the finds similar to those from Lachish Level III come from fills. To date five reconstructable holemouth jars (first appearing in the very late 10th to early 9th century) and many sherds corresponding to Lachish Levels IV and III have been found.[48] Thus, while it is possible to conclude that there was no habitation at Beth Shemesh during the late 7th century, the lack of restorable pottery from the renewed excavations does not provide conclusive evidence for occupation at the end of the late 8th century. The issue of occupation at Beth Shemesh is discussed in depth below in the section on the *lmlk* jars. For the present, it is sufficient to note that the pottery published by Grant and Wright, when taken alongside the appearance of *lmlk* impressions, supports the interpretation that Beth Shemesh was inhabited until the end of the 8th century but not after.

e. Lachish

It is also important in this study to include an evaluation of a major Judean site that was resettled during the 7th century BCE. Lachish is probably the ideal site to study, because it was second only to Jerusalem in importance to the Judean kingdom.[49] One would not expect such an important city to be deserted entirely, even if the Shephelah experienced a major decline. Evidence of shrinkage in its size and importance from

---

[45]S. Bunimovitz, Z. Lederman, and R. Kletter, "Tel Bet Shemesh—1990," *ESI* 10 (1991) 143; Bunimovitz and Lederman, "Beth Shemesh," 252.

[46]The author also served as Field Director of an excavation area at Beth Shemesh during the summer of 1997.

[47]The renewed excavations at Beth Shemesh discovered some 7th-century pottery in a water cistern during the 1996 season. In addition, some 7th century pottery has been discovered in nearby tombs. However, to date there is no evidence of a 7th century settlement on the tel itself. The above-mentioned 7th-century pottery probably suggests a limited settlement around the water system at Beth Shemesh following its destruction in 701 BCE.

[48]Lederman, personal communication.

[49]D. Ussishkin, "Lachish," *NEAEHL*, (ed. E. Stern; New York: Macmillan; Jerusalem: Israel Exploration Society, 1993) 905.

the late 8th to the late 7th century may be seen as further confirmation of the survey findings presented by Dagan.

This scenario of the city shrinking in size and importance is exactly what is found at Lachish between Level III (destroyed in the late 8th century) and Level II (destroyed in the early 6th century). Ussishkin summarizes the situation as follows: "The stratum II city was poorer [than the Level III city], less densely inhabited, and had smaller fortifications than its predecessor."[50] It was noticed in the first excavations that although both cities were fortified, the fortification system of Level III was much more extensive and contained a more elaborate gate system than that of Level II. The large palace-fort area of Level III was left in ruins during Level II, and the houses that were found in abundance in Level III were much more sporadic in Level II.[51] The renewed excavations not only confirmed these conclusions but also showed that many houses and buildings that Tufnell was unable to classify to either Level III or Level II actually belonged to Level III.[52]

2. The Judean Hills and Towns Surrounding Jerusalem

a. General Discussion

Although the Shephelah is a central portion of the kingdom of Judah, it is obviously not the only area that is important to a discussion of the economic buildup and civil strength of Hezekiah and Josiah. Another important area is the Judean Hill Country and cities surrounding Jerusalem.

Survey work in the Judean Hills that is relevant to this discussion has been conducted by A. Ofer. The results of this survey were reported in detail in Ofer's dissertation and an article summarizing his dissertation.[53] He found that in the Judean Hill Country there was a steady increase in settlement from the early 9th through the late 8th century. He found that during the 9th century, "there were eighty-six sites, more than half of

---

[50]Ussishkin, "Lachish," 909.

[51]O. Tufnell, *Lachish III: The Iron Age* (Wellcome-Marston Archaeological Research Expedition to the Near East Publications; London: Oxford University Press, 1953) 48, 56-57; Ussishkin, "Destruction," 51.

[52]Ussishkin, "Destruction," 45-49.

[53]A. Ofer, "'All the Country of Judah': From a Settlment Fringe to a Prosperous Monarchy," *From Nomadism to Monarchy: Archaeological and Historical Aspects of Early Israel* (I. Finkelstein and N. Na'aman; Washington: Biblical Archaeology Society; Jerusalem: Israel Exploration Society, 1994) 92-121. Ofer's dissertation was unavailable to me. His results are known only from this 1994 article that summarizes his dissertation.

them small or very small" with an average built-up area of 554 dunams.[54] During the late 8th century, the number of settlements increased to 122 sites with a built-up area of 926 dunams, a peak that was not surpassed until the Byzantine period.[55]

Ofer's study indicated that this growth ended during the late 8th century, and he documented a decrease in settlement during the 7th. Ofer found that during the late 7th century, there were 113 sites with a total built-up area of 715 dunams. Further, the southern area of the Judean Hills experienced a greater loss of settlement than the area near Jerusalem. These findings caused Ofer to conclude that Judah suffered under the attack of Sennacherib in 701 BCE, and consequently the rate of settlement in the Judean Hill Country decreased.[56]

These conclusions are attractive to the thesis in this chapter. They appear to show that just as settlement and economic buildup decreased in the Shephelah region because of the campaign of Sennacherib, settlement, economic buildup, and civil strength likewise decreased in the area of the Judean hills. One could further postulate, as does Ofer, that it was only the negative influence of Sennacherib's campaign that reversed a 300-year growth trend. However, such a conclusion, albeit supportive of the thesis that Hezekiah rivaled Josiah, is not as easy to adopt without reservations as it is for the Shephelah region.

Perhaps the biggest difference between Ofer's and Dagan's surveys is their extent, in terms both of the actual area surveyed and of the conclusions. Due to the *intifada*, Ofer was unable to survey the Judean Hills as thoroughly as Dagan was able to survey the Shephelah. Moreover, Ofer's surveys point to a drop in settlement, but the decrease is not nearly as dramatic as in Dagan's surveys. Ofer finds a decrease from a builtup area of 926 dunams during the late 8th century to 715 dunams in the late 7th, whereas Dagan documented a drop from 4,651 to 1,124 dunams. Obviously the room for error with a 23% decrease is much higher than when a 76% decrease is indicated.

Room for error has caused I. Finkelstein to question the precision of Ofer's findings. Finkelstein rightly calls attention to the fact that only a limited number of pottery types allow for the distinction between Lachish Level III pottery and Lachish Level II pottery—in most cases only three clear types. Finkelstein warns that when a site is dated solely on the

---

[54]Ofer, "Country of Judah," 105. Ofer lists 55.4 hectares. Throughout the dissertation, all measurements are converted into dunams for the sake of consistency. 1 dunam = 1000 m²; 1 dunam = 0.247 acres; 1 hectare = 2.471 acres; 1 hectare = 10 dunams.

[55]Ofer, "Country of Judah," 105.

[56]Ofer, "Country of Judah," 106, 121.

basis that none of these types of pottery are found, there is a chance for error. He states that the possibility is compounded by the fact that many sites in the Judean Hill Country experienced heavy erosion which might have wiped away signs of late 7th-century occupation while leaving earlier pottery from the late 8th century.[57] The same possibility for error existed with Dagan's surveys, but the problems are mitigated both by the extensive nature of the survey and by the dramatic results. In other words, there is a chance of error, but this error could not result in a 76% decrease in settlement.[58]

Another difference between Dagan's surveys and Ofer's is that the decrease in settlement from Dagan's surveys is well supported by systematic excavations. This support is extremely important, because it is only with systematic excavation that the problems of erosion and the limited number of pottery types that allow for the identification of period may be overcome. The extensive excavation results supported and confirmed the decrease in settlement in the Shephelah suggested by Dagan's surveys; however, in the Judean Hills and Jerusalem, the systematic excavations point to a continuance of settlement at most sites during the 7th century with only a small decrease in settlement. This possible lack of conformity with the findings from the more developed excavations necessitates that Ofer's findings be viewed as suggestive but also interpreted with caution.[59]

b. Mizpah (Tell en-Naṣbeh)

Tell en-Naṣbeh (probably biblical Mizpah) is one site with extensive excavations that may challenge Ofer's findings. It is just north of Jerusalem in the Benjamin Hill Country instead of the area south of Jerusalem that Ofer surveyed. However, Finkelstein argues that one would expect that if a decline in settlement had taken place in the area south of Jerusalem, the same phenomenon would be seen just to the north.[60] Five extensive excavations at Tell en-Naṣbeh were carried out intermittently by W. F. Badè from 1926 to 1935, and about two-thirds of the tell was uncovered. Badè died unexpectedly during the last season of excavations,

---

[57]Finkelstein, "Days of Manasseh," 175. However, one should object to at least this portion of Finkelstein's reasoning because the erosion would not wipe out the 7th century pottery, only move it to another part of the tel. In any case, a survey would document both the earlier and later pottery.

[58]Finkelstein, personal communication.

[59]Finkelstein, "Days of Manasseh," 174-75.

[60]Yet, if Hezekiah turned Sennacherib back before the Assyrian king reach the area north of Jerusalem, then this would account for sites north of Jerusalem experiencing continuous occupation without destructions.

so the final report was published by two of his assistants, J. C. Wampler and C. C. McCown.[61] The material has been completely reinvestigated by J. Zorn.[62]

The stratigraphy of the site is somewhat confusing, primarily due to methodological errors on the part of Badè but also partly due to Badè's death before the final publication. It is almost impossible to determine precisely whether Tell en-Naṣbeh was more developed during Hezekiah's or Josiah's reign. Zorn states that "the major methodological problem is that the tell was not excavated according to debris layers,...[but rather] from the surface down to the point where three or more walls enclosed a space objects were only given a general designation."[63] Thus, Badè only excavated immense loci, and many loci were not recognized if at least three walls corresponding to a floor were not located.

Despite this confusing picture, B. Halpern argues on historical grounds that the itinerary of a foreign invader found in Isa 10:27b-32 must be the itinerary of Sennacherib in 701 BCE. He posits that Tell en-Naṣbeh was depopulated, if not partially destroyed, during Sennacherib's campaign. Halpern acknowledges that the excavators did not notice any signs of the destruction,[64] but he claims that "any Assyrian levee striking south from the province of Samerina passed this site, and will have reduced it to secure logistical links with the north".[65]

Halpern's historical arguments make sense if Isa 10:27b-32 does in fact refer to the Assyrians;[66] however, those arguments are not supported by archaeological data. While admitting that a precise dating of the sublayers of each room at Tell en-Naṣbeh is not possible, Zorn argues convincingly that Tell en-Naṣbeh was not destroyed in 701 BCE during

---

[61]C. C. McCown, *Tell En-Naṣbeh I: Archaeological and Historical Results*, (Berkeley: Palestine Institute of Pacific School of Religion; New Haven: ASOR, 1947); J. C. Wampler and C. C. McCown, *Tell En-Naṣbeh II: The Pottery* (Berkeley: Palestine Institute of the Pacific School of Religion; New Haven: ASOR, 1947).

[62]J. R. Zorn, *Tell En-Naṣbeh: A Re-evaluation of the Architecture and Stratigraphy of the Early Bronze Age, Iron Age, and Later Periods* (Ph.D. dissertation, University of California, Berkeley; Ann Arbor, Mich.: UMI, 1993). For further bibliography cf. J. R. Zorn, "Tell En-Naṣbeh," *NEAEHL* (ed. E. Stern; New York: Macmillan; Jerusalem: Israel Exploration Society, 1993) 1098-1102.

[63]Zorn, *Tell En-Naṣbeh: A Re-evaluation*, 73.

[64]Cf. McCown, *Tell En-Naṣbeh I*, 151-53.

[65]B. Halpern, "Jerusalem and the Lineages in the Seventh Century BCE: Kingship and the Rise of Individual Moral Liability," *Law and Ideology in Monarchic Israel* (eds. B. Halpern and D. W. Hobson; JSOTSup 124; Sheffield: JSOT Press, 1991) 36.

[66]These verses discussed in more detail below in the following paragraph.

Sennacherib's campaign. The principal evidence is that the general architectural plan of the site remains intact through most of the Iron Age, indicating that the site was never destroyed. Zorn emphasizes this point and states, "It is important to note that for a period of at least four hundred years the town was never destroyed. This means that its overall plan changed little in the Iron Age II."[67] Zorn is even more explicit in his dissertation, where he reexamines the stratigraphy and architecture of Tell en-Naṣbeh. He states, "The excavators found no signs of fiery destruction in any of the Stratum 3 [the Iron Age II stratum] buildings. Badè's team knew what destruction debris looked like, and would not have missed it."[68] He adds that the site grew to its largest size by the late 8th century (Stratum 3A) and that the town continued at the large size until the fall of the Judean kingdom. However, even with the construction that took place in the second half of the 8th century, substantial additions were made on top of a town that had not been destroyed.[69]

In light of Zorn's analysis, Halpern's reconstruction must be modified. Halpern's position rests or falls on the evidence from Isa 10:27b-32, yet those verses do not necessitate that the itinerary of the aggressor belongs to Sennacherib. The verses merely detail the attack of an enemy coming from the north to Jerusalem. As H. Wildberger points out, attributing the itinerary to Sennacherib "is impossible...since that offensive against Jerusalem did not come from the north, but from the southeast, from the coastal region."[70] It seems most probable that in its original setting the itinerary describes an attack from the Syro-Ephraimatic War led by Rezin. This is the only known attack from the north on Jerusalem during the 8th century. Moreover, a plan of attack that bypasses the major fortifications of Tell en-Naṣbeh (Mizpah) and Tell el-Jib (Gibeon) makes perfect sense for a quick attack during the Syro-Ephraimatic War. It is unclear, however, why any Assyrian army would have cowered away from these fortifications.[71] It is also possible, though less likely,

---

[67]Zorn, "Tell En-Naṣbeh," 1099.

[68]Zorn, *Tell En-Naṣbeh: A Re-evaluation*, 161.

[69]Zorn, *Tell En-Naṣbeh: A Re-evaluation*, 91, 151, 161-62, 331.

[70]H. Wildberger, *Isaiah 1-12: A Commentary* (trans. T. H. Trapp; Continental Commentaries; Minneapolis: Fortress Press, 1991) 451.

[71]So H. Donner, *Israel und den Völkern* (VTSup 11; Leiden, 1964) 30-38; H. Donner, "Der Feind Aus dem Norden: Topographische und Archäologische Erwägungen Zu Jes. 10:27b-34," *ZDPV* 84 (1968) 46-54. I am indebted to J. J. M. Roberts for discussing Isa 10:27b-34 with me, for pointing out Donner's work, and for sharing his arguments for a setting during the Syro-Ephamatic War. Roberts' arguments will appear in his forthcoming commentary on Isaiah.

that the itinerary describes an attack by Sargon II designed solely to warn Judah against involving itself in defense of Israel,[72] or that it describes an otherwise unknown Scythian attack as evidenced by some rare arrowheads at Gibeon.[73] In any case, it is clear that the original setting of the poem was not Sennacherib's campaign, and the lack of destruction debris from 701 BCE accords well with this interpretation.

By combining data from Badè's excavations at Tell en-Naṣbeh with archaeological surveys in the Benjamin Hill Country,[74] Finkelstein makes a case for interpreting the 7th century as the peak of settlement at Tell en-Naṣbeh.[75] Such a conclusion must be tentative, however, due to the methological problems from Tell en-Naṣbeh discussed above. In summary, Tell en-Naṣbeh is an example of a site in the hill country surrounding Judah that at the very least does not suffer significantly in terms of settlement following the campaign of Sennacherib and that may have even experienced some limited growth during Josiah's reign.

c. Gibeon (el-Jib)

Gibeon (el-Jib) is another extensively excavated site just north of Jerusalem. Gibeon contained a major production facility for wine during the 8th and 7th centuries BCE.[76] In addition, it had substantial fortifications. There is evidence that this industrial center existed in both the late 8th and late 7th centuries. 95 *lmlk* impressions were discovered in a fill, indicating settlement during the late 8th century. In assigning a date to the defenses of Gibeon in the Iron II period, Pritchard stated the following:

> From the general picture of occupation of the site in the Iron II period it would seem that the city enjoyed one of its major periods of prosperity toward the end of the seventh century. There was an abundance of jar handles stamped with the royal stamp (*Hebrew Inscriptions*, pp. 18-26) and the Iron II pottery forms found within living areas correspond to those from the latest period of occupation at Tell Beit Mirsim A.[77]

---

[72] So Wildberger, *Isaiah 1-12*, 451-54.

[73] J. B. Pritchard, *Winery, Defenses, and Soundings at Gibeon* (Museum Monographs; Philadelphia: University Museum, University of Pennsylvania, 1964) 162.

[74] Cf. I. Finkelstein and Y. Magen, eds. *Archaeological Survey in the Hill Country of Benjamin* (Publications of the Israel Antiquities Authority; Jerusalem: Israel Antiquities Authority, 1993).

[75] Finkelstein, "Days of Manasseh," 174.

[76] See discussion in Chapter 3.

[77] Pritchard, *Winery, Defenses, and Soundings*, 39.

Noting that Pritchard was writing at a time when both the *lmlk* jars and the pottery from Tell Beit Mirsim were thought to come from the 7th century instead of the late 8th, one may modify his conclusions to provide evidence for the extensive occupation of Gibeon during the late 8th century.

Occupation during the 8th century would have fit well into Ofer's thesis if the occupation died off in the 7th century, but Finkelstein argues that is not the scenario found at Gibeon. Pritchard does not report signs of destruction during Sennacherib's invasion or any other invasion in the Iron Age. He states, "No evidence has appeared thus far for a general destruction by fire within either the Iron I or the Iron II periods. Apparently the city continued to grow and develop throughout these two ages of its history without any marked disruption of its normal life."[78] Moreover, in addition to pottery examples comparable to those at Lachish Level III, Gibeon also contains examples comparable to those at Lachish Level II. One example is an ovoid jar with a plain collar rim.[79] Other examples from the winery are also comparable to those at Lachish Level II and Ramat Raḥel Level VA.[80] In addition, the burial caves surrounding Gibeon are dated to the late 7th century.[81] Thus, it seems that Gibeon continued to thrive as an industrial center throughout the 7th century. Similar to the situation at Tell en-Naṣbeh, there is no evidence that it was destroyed until the Babylonian invasion of 586 BCE. Some scholars even conclude that Gibeon reached its settlement peak during the late 7th century. In light of these considerations, Finkelstein argues that Gibeon serves as another example that calls Ofer's thesis into question.[82] On the other hand, the counterargument to Finkelstein is that Tell en-Naṣbeh is a site north of Jerusalem that Sennacherib may not have destroyed. If this is the case, the only area with decreased settlment may be the area to the south of Jerusalem, so the sites north of Jerusalem would not call Ofer's conclusions into question.

---

[78]J. B. Pritchard, *Gibeon, Where the Sun Stood Still: The Discovery of the Biblical City* (Princeton: Princeton University Press, 1962) 161.

[79]Pritchard, *Winery, Defenses, and Soundings*, 21, fig. 32:4.

[80]Pritchard, *Winery, Defenses, and Soundings*, fig. 34:1-15.

[81]H. Eshel, "The Late Iron Age Cemetery of Gibeon," *IEJ* 37 (1987) 1-17.

[82]Finkelstein, "Days of Manasseh," 174. Halpern ("Jerusalem and the Lineages," 35) argues for a major contraction at Gibeon following Sennacherib's invasions; however, his argument is based on the assumptions that the itinerary in Isa 10:27b-32 describes Sennacherib's campaign and that both Gibeon and Mizpeh suffered adverse consequences. As shown in this section, however, the archaeological data do not support his interpretation in either case.

d. Ramat Raḥel

Ramat Raḥel is another site near Jerusalem where extensive excavations have taken place. This site has greater bearing on Ofer's thesis than the sites north of Jerusalem because it is located to the south, adjacent to the area surveyed by Ofer. It is clear that the stratigraphy of Ramat Raḥel continues into the 7th century BCE in Level VA, so the site also might support Finkelstein critique of Ofer's thesis. The particulars of this stratigraphy are complicated and warrant a special discussion.

The existence of Ramat Raḥel during the 8th century is suggested by Level VB, which contained many pottery fragments similar to those from Lachish Level III that were found in fills sealed beneath the floors of Ramat Raḥel Level VA. The pottery in these sealed fills did not contain examples of pottery from Lachish Level II, whereas the pottery from Level VA did have such parallels. Thus, Aharoni postulated that the pottery from this fill area came from a stratum that predated Level VA, and he dated that stratum to a destruction some time during the late 8th century.[83] The problem is that this level is "hypothetical." That is, its existence is indicated only by the fact that pottery fragments similar to Lachish Level III came from a fill layer below the floors of Level VA. Yet, Aharoni found very little or no architecture in Level VB. He found only a few remains of casemate walls, which he attributed to Level VB, but he did not find any buildings. In light of this situation, Aharoni concluded that the late 8th-century fortress was relatively small and was almost completely destroyed during the construction of the Level VA fortress.[84]

In 1984, Barkay returned to the site and excavated several squares and trenches to check the size of Ramat Raḥel and to locate some architecture from Level VB. By excavating several trenches to the north and west of the acropolis, he discovered that the site was much larger than Aharoni had realized. Aharoni's excavation concentrated on the central, fortress area of the site, but it failed to locate a developed area west of the acropolis. Barkay located a wall in that area. He also located several *lmlk* impressions that suggested that the wall should be dated to the late 8th century or earlier. Further, Barkay discovered some building remains in the central courtyard sealed below the floor of Aharoni's Level VA, and thus revealed architecture from the level predating VA. The pottery found in the areas of these building remains was parallel solely to Lachish Level III without any examples parallel to Lachish Level II[85]

---

[83]Cf. Aharoni and Aharoni, "Stratification of Judahite Sites."

[84]Y. Aharoni, "Ramat Raḥel," *NEAEHL* (ed. E. Stern; New York: Macmillan; Jerusalem: Israel Exploration Society, 1993) 1263.

[85]Barkay, personal communication. Barkay and the I are in the process

Barkay concluded that the presence of these remains, coupled with the fact that the site was larger than realized by Aharoni, suggested that Ramat Raḥel Level VB was utilized by Hezekiah in the late 8th century. Because there was no pottery corresponding to the 9th century, the site must have been constructed sometime in the 8th century as well, possibly also by Hezekiah. Barkay explains the homogeneity in many pottery remains in Levels VA and VB with a theory that Hezekiah rebuilt Ramat Raḥel almost immediately after Sennacherib withdrew. The construction of Level VA during the earliest part of the 7th century is also suggested by the pottery finds of the floor makeup of the plaster floor in the palace courtyard of Level VA. The pottery from this floor makeup is parallel exclusively to Lachish Level III with no parallels to Lachish Level II. It thus seems that the site was rebuilt by either Hezekiah or his son Manasseh shortly after Sennacherib campaign in 701 BCE.[86] Moreover, as is shown below, the isolated *lmlk* and official seal impressions found in the fills of Ramat Raḥel Level VA should not be taken as evidence that the *lmlk* or official impressions were used beyond the kingdom of Hezekiah.

It can be concluded that Barkay's excavations prove that Ramat Raḥel was a major fortress during the late 8th century. His findings also indicate that the site prospered and was completely resettled during the 7th century. Whether this rebuilding was conducted by Hezekiah or by Manasseh is not vital for the purposes of the current study. In either case, Ramat Raḥel is another site that was settled during both the 8th and the 7th centuries. This site sits on the border of the Judean Hill Country south of Jerusalem, so this continued settlement during the 7th century again calls Ofer's thesis into question. On the other hand, most of Ofer's survey was conducted further away from Jerusalem, so one must investigate the possibility that the reconstruction and new settlement during the seventh century BCE was more extensive close to Jerusalem and in the areas not destroyed by Sennacherib to the north of Jerusalem

e. Khirbet Rabûd

Perhaps the two most important sites that have a bearing on Ofer's thesis are Khirbet Rabûd and Beth-Zur, because they are excavated sites directly within the boundaries of the Judean Hill Country. M. Kochavi conducted two seasons of excavations at Khirbet Rabûd in 1968 and 1969. Those excavations established that Khirbet Rabûd should be identified with biblical Debir, whereas Albright had previously suggested that Tell

---

of publishing the Iron Age areas from Barkay's 1984 excavation, and this publications should appear during the 2000-2001 academic year.

[86]Barkay, personal communication.

Beit Mirsim was Debir. Both scholars identified two distinct levels from the Iron II period at Khirbet Rabûd. Two trenches (A and B) were dug on the western edge of Khirbet Rabûd. Trench B revealed signs of Iron Age II occupation in both the late 8th century (Level B-2) and the late 7th century (Level B-1). In trench A, the signs of the 8th-century layer were clearly wiped away by the 7th-century layer found in Level A-2. The pottery from the 8th-century layer (B-2) was found in a storehouse (Locus 109) and was similar to examples from Lachish Level III. Several *lmlk* and official impressions were also discovered in this storehouse, confirming the late 8th-century date.[87]

Evidence of occupation in the late 7th century was found in both trenches. In Trench B, the 7th-century layer (B-1) was built directly on top of the layer destroyed in the late 8th century (B-2). This rebuilding obviously included a strengthening of the settlement, since the wall from the late 8th century (W7) was widened from 4 to 7 m. In addition, a tower (W9) was added to the 7th-century fortifications.[88] In Level A-2 of Trench A, there was more evidence of fortifications and settlement during the 7th century.[89] Further signs of development and growth at the site during the 7th century appeared with the discovery of an extramural settlement established during the 7th century on a lower "step" of the tel (Kh. Rabdeh). This settlement was unfortified and contained pottery with parallels to Lachish Level II.[90]

The fact that Khirbet Rabûd was resettled during the 7th century raises questions about Ofer's conclusions. However, the expansion and strengthening that takes place at the site raises even more doubts. If Ofer's thesis that there was even a slowing of settlement in the Judean Hills were true, one would not expect resettlement to involve the strengthening of fortifications and the establishment of extramural settlements.

f. Beth Zur (Khirbet et-Tubeiqa)

Whereas the evidence from the above sites may raise some questions about Ofer's conclusions, the evidence from Beth Zur may support it. Reexamination of the Iron II period at Beth Zur is difficult to accomplish due to the extensive excavations carried out at the site in 1931. These excavations exposed more than two acres at the center of the

---

[87]Moshe Kochavi, "Khirbet Rabûd = Debir," *Tel Aviv* 1 (1974) 13-18.

[88]Kochavi, "Khirbet Rabûd," 13-14.

[89]Kochavi, "Khirbet Rabûd," 6-12.

[90]Kochavi, "Khirbet Rabûd," 6.

mound down to bedrock but failed to establish a clear stratigraphy.[91] The same expedition team returned to the site in 1957 to clarify the stratigraphy and concluded that during the Iron Age II the site was not fortified.[92] The expedition reports from both digs also concluded that the site was sparsely settled in the Iron Age II until the latter half of the 7th century, and the 1931 expedition found scattered signs of destruction that were attributed to Nebuchadnezzar's campaign in 586 BCE.[93] However, mistaken assumptions concerning the dating of Tell Beit Mirsim, Beth Shemesh, and Lachish Level III caused some errors in these conclusions, so the results must be reexamined.

The excavators found little evidence of settlement in the Iron I period. They concluded, "The Iron II remains in Field II of the 1957 campaign cannot be earlier than ca. 650 B.C., and there is no evidence in Fields I and III for any extensive occupation earlier in the Iron II period."[94] However, this conclusion is seen to be in error when the reasons for this dating of Field II are reexamined. In discussing the pottery from Field II, P. Lapp states that "the homogeneity of the pottery, its close parallels in TBM [Tell Beit Mirsim] A2 and ᶜAin Shems [Beth Shemesh] IIc, and the two winged *lmlk* handles confirm the attribution of this destruction to the campaign in which Nebuchadnezzar destroyed Jerusalem."[95] In another instance, P. W. Lapp and N. L. Lapp conclude that the pottery from the other two fields is similar to finds from Field II and that all of the Iron II pottery came from Stratum III. Thus, "The closest parallels to Stratum III pottery come from the neighboring towns of ᶜAin Shems [Beth Shemesh] (Stratum IIc) and Tell Beit Mirsim (Stratum A2)."[96] As was shown above,

---

[91]Cf. O. R. Sellers, *The Citadel of Beth-Zur: A Preliminary Report of the First Excavation Conducted by the Presbyterian Theological Seminary, Chicago and the American School of Oriental Research, Jerusalem, in 1931 at Khirbat et Tubeiqa* (Philadelphia: Westminster Press, 1933).

[92]Cf. discussion in Chapter 3 for the importance of the lack of fortifications for the use of the *lmlk* jars.

[93]R. W. Funk, "Beth-Zur," *NEAEHL* (ed. E. Stern; New York: Macmillan; Jerusalem: Israel Exploration Society, 1993) 261.

[94]R. W. Funk, "The History of Beth-Zur with Reference to Its Defences," *The 1957 Excavation at Beth-Zur* (eds. O. R. Sellers, R. W. Funk, J. L. McKenzie, P. W. Lapp, and N. L. Lapp; AASOR 38; Cambridge, MA: ASOR, 1968) 8.

[95]P. W. Lapp, "The Excavation of Field II," *The 1957 Excavation at Beth-Zur* (eds. O. R. Sellers, R. W. Funk, J. L. McKenzie, P. W. Lapp, and N. L. Lapp; AASOR 38; Cambridge, MA: ASOR, 1968) 28-29.

[96]P. W. Lapp and N. L. Lapp, "Iron II-Hellenistic Pottery Groups," *The 1957 Excavation at Beth-Zur* (eds. O. R. Sellers, R. W. Funk, J. L. McKenzie, P. W. Lapp, and N. L. Lapp; AASOR 38; Cambridge, MA: ASOR, 1968) 54.

both sites were destroyed by Sennacherib in 701 BCE and were not resettled. The discussion below (see Chapter 3) builds on the work of Ussishkin[97] and shows that both the two-winged and four-winged *lmlk* impressions come solely from the late 8th century. The pottery parallels cited by the excavators of Beth Zur must be pushed back. They suggest a date for the earliest settlement of Stratum III in the 8th century.

In light of this redating of Stratum III to the 8th century, it seems probable that the site was destroyed by Sennacherib in 701 BCE. It is hard to envision Sennacherib bypassing this site as he moved from Lachish to besiege Jerusalem, and scattered signs of violent destruction were found in the 1931 excavations. The fact that no signs of fortifications were discovered from the Iron II period would explain why only limited destruction debris was found. The excavators posit that the site was occupied prior to destruction, but the citizens of Beth Zur likely fled to a fortified town before the conqueror destroyed deserted town.[98]

The question remains whether there was a significant occupation of the site in the 7th century BCE. The question is difficult to answer because the excavators only point to one Iron II stratum that was unfortified (Stratum III), and most of the pottery parallels from that level are comparable to Tell Beit Mirsim Level A2 and Beth Shemesh IIc. More important, I was unable to locate, in all the pottery plates, even one cooking pot with the flaring, ridged rim that is diagnostic of pottery with parallels in Lachish Level II and Ramat Raḥel Level VA.[99] On the other hand, there were five handles with rosette impressions that are commonly dated to the 7th century, so there seems to have been some 7th-century settlement at Beth Zur even if the site did not reach the peak of settlement known from the late 8th century.[100]

In summary, it seems that Beth Zur was occupied but not fortified during the reign of Hezekiah. The site seems to have been destroyed by Sennacherib in 701 BCE. Further, the signs for occupation during the 7th century indicate that resettlement was not on as large a scale as the 8th-century settlement. Therefore, Beth Zur may be seen as a site that provides corroboration of Ofer's survey conclusions.[101]

---

[97]Cf. Ussishkin, "Destruction," 50-54.

[98]Cf. Funk, "History of Beth-Zur," 8; Funk, "Beth-Zur," 261.

[99]Aharoni and Aharoni, "Stratification of Judahite Sites," 86.

[100]Sellers, *The Citadel of Beth-Zur*, 52-53, fig. 44.

[101]Contra Finkelstein, "Days of Manasseh," 174.

Summary

The more extensive excavations conducted in the suburbs of Jerusalem to the north and in the Judean Hill Country may call into question the precision of Ofer's survey conclusions. As Finkelstein rightly points out, the limited number of pot sherds that allow for dating a survey site to the 8th or the 7th century may introduce error.[102] Thus, in the case of Ofer's surveys where his conclusions only show a decrease of 20% in the built-up area in the Judean Hill Country as compared with the 76% drop found in Dagan's surveys, the possible range of error raises concern with an attempt to draw decisive conclusions about whether the built-up area was greater in one period than the other. Ofer's statistics must be taken seriously, but they are not foolproof. On the other hand, the sites north of Jerusalem did not seem to experience destruction during 701 BCE, while the sites south of Jerusalem did. Therefore, contra Finkelstein, these findings might support Ofer's conclusion that the decrease of population was greater in the southern part of Judah.

In any case, Ofer's surveys and the more extensive excavations provide important data that suggest that the ecomonic buildup and civil strength in the towns north of Jerusalem and the Judean Hill Country was not markedly greater during Josiah's reign than during Hezekiah's reign. First, the fact that Ofer's surveys pointed to a decline in the settlement during the 7th century suggests that the region was nearly as builtup and developed during Hezekiah's reign as in Josiah's reign even if it is impossible to determine precisely which king had the greatest buildup. Further, all of the sites with extensive excavations discussed exhibited settlement in both the late 8th and the late 7th centuries. All of these factors indicate that the development of the Judean Hills during Hezekiah's reign rivaled the development during Josiah's reign.

The three sites south of Jerusalem (Ramat Raḥel, Khirbet Rabûd, and Beth Zur) all showed signs of being destroyed by Sennacherib in 701 BCE and then being resettled, and in some cases, refortified. However, the sites north of Jerusalem showed signs of occupation in both the late 8th and the 7th centuries, but they did not exhibit signs of destruction in 701 BCE.[103] This scenario suggests that Sennacherib moved from Lachish to Jerusalem in 701 BCE and destroyed all of the sites along the way. Yet, after turning back from his siege of Jerusalem, he apparently did not destroy the suburbs to the north. This situation would contribute to a positive evaluation of Hezekiah, because some of his cities, in addition to Jerusalem, were saved from destruction by Sennacherib.

---

[102]Finkelstein, "Days of Manasseh," 174-75.

[103]Contra Halpern, "Jerusalem and the Lineages," 34-37.

In summary, a dramatic decrease in settlement or in population cannot be maintained for the Judean Hills from the late 8th century (the period of Hezekiah) to the late 7th century (the period of Josiah). In fact, it does not appear that there was a large variance between the two periods. Thus, one cannot say that Hezekiah was either greater or weaker than Josiah by comparing the settlement patterns in the Judean Hills and Jerusalem. This conclusion is important because it seems unlikely that the Dtr. historian invented the powerful status of Josiah. From the data presented in this section, it appears that both Hezekiah and Josiah had a large amount of economic buildup and civil strength in the Judean Hills and towns surrounding Jerusalem.

3. The Negeb

a. General discussion

Unlike the Shephelah and the Judean Hills, no extensive archaeological surveys from the Negeb[104] are available for comparing settlement there during the late 8th and the late 7th century. There is one limited survey of the Naḥal Yattir area,[105] but the majority of the Negeb has not been adequately surveyed. Thus, the few published excavation reports from the area must be relied upon exclusively. Utilizing the available data, Finkelstein noted that presently five sites are believed to have been occupied during the late 8th century while the number grows to seven sites during the late 7th century. He concludes that "when fully surveyed, the Beer-sheba valley will yield more 7th-early 6th-century sites [than 8th-century sites]."[106] Some other indications must be taken into account which question the significance of any increased Judean settlement during Josiah's reign as compared with Hezekiah's reign. In analyzing the situation in the Negeb, it is important to examine each of the major sites.

---

[104]The biblical use of "Negeb" corresponds roughly to the Beersheba Valley (cf. Y. Aharoni, "The Negeb of Judah," *IEJ* 8 [1958] 26-27; A. F. Rainey, "Early Historical Geography of the Negeb," *Beersheba II: The Early Iron Age Settlements* [ed. Z. Herzog; Tel Aviv: Institute of Archaeology, Tel Aviv University, 1984] 90).

[105]Y. Govrin, *Archaeological Survey of Israel: Map of Naḥal Yattir (139)* (Jerusalem: Israel Antiquities Authority, 1991).

[106]Finkelstein, "Days of Manasseh," 176.

b. Beersheba

One of the most important sites for comparing Hezekiah's and Josiah's influence in the Negeb is Beersheba.[107] There was a much larger settlement at the site during the late 8th century than during the late 7th. Stratum II of Beersheba was destroyed by Sennacherib in 701 BCE.[108]

---

[107]Naʾaman has questioned the identification of Tel Beersheba with biblical Beersheba because there are few remains from the end of the Bronze Age and the end of the Iron Age. Naʾaman thus proposes Bir es-Sabaᶜ as the location of biblical Beersheba. Bir es-Sabaᶜ does contain remains dating to the last days of the Judean kingdom (N. Naʾaman, "The Inheritance of the Sons of Simeon," *ZDPV* 96 [1980] 149-51). However, this interpretation is not convincing, because it fails to explain the central location of the mound at Tel Beersheba and its large fortifications that were capable of supporting an administrative center. It seems most probable that, just as Arad in Shishak's inscriptions seems to refer to two separate sites, Beersheba was a name identified with two separate sites (cf. A. F. Rainey, "Early Historical Geography of the Negeb," *Beersheba II: The Early Iron Age Settlements* [ed. Z. Herzog; Tel Aviv: Institute of Archaeology, Tel Aviv University, 1984] 102; Z. Herzog, "Tel Beersheba," *NEAEHL* [New York: Macmillan; Jerusalem: Israel Exploration Society, 1993] 168).

[108]A. F. Rainey ("Hezekiah's Reform and the Altars at Beer-sheba and Arad," *Scripture and Other Artifacts: Essays on the Bible and Archaeology in Honor of Philip J. King* [eds. M. D. Coogan, J. C. Exum, and L. E. Stager; Louisville: Westminster/ John Knox Press, 1994] 335) points out that K. M. Kenyon (Kenyon, "The Date of the Destruction of Iron Age Beer-sheba," *PEQ* 108 [1976] 63-64) first raised the question of whether the pottery from Beersheba predated Lachish Level III by about a decade. She based this conclusion on the mistaken assumption that Lachish Level III predated Lachish Level II by only 10 years. Noting the differences between the pottery of these two levels, she concluded that since there was a slight variation in some forms from Beersheba Stratum II and Lachish Level III, Beersheba Stratum II must have been destroyed a decade or so before Lachish Level III. According to her, this was some time around 615 BCE. She further concluded that the lack of a historical context for this destruction was a problem for historians to argue about, but that the pottery readings suggested this destruction. N. Naʾaman ("The Brook of Egypt and Assyrian Policy on the Border of Egypt," *Tel Aviv* 6 [1979] 82-83, esp. n. 20; N. Naʾaman, "Sennacherib's Campaign to Judah and the Date of the *lmlk* Stamps," *VT* 29 [1979] 74-75) developed Kenyon's idea, but he rightly utilized the correct destruction date of Lachish Level III as 701 BCE. Whereas Kenyon did not have a historical setting for a destruction around 615 BCE, Naʾaman postulated that Beersheba was destroyed by Sargon and not Sennacherib, and thus explained the difference in pottery noted by Kenyon.

However, this conclusion that there was variance in the pottery from Beersheba II and Lachish III must be called into question. First, the existence of a variance came into place due to the way in which Kenyon analyzed the pottery from Lachish Level III. Many of the loci that have now been firmly identified

This level contained remains of an extensive fortified city. There was a casemate wall with a thickness of 1.60 m for the outer wall and 1.05 m for the inner wall. The fortification walls were also supplemented by a glacis.[109] The pottery remains from Level II were comparable to those from Lachish Level III and revealed that Beersheba was heavily occupied during that period.[110] There are also remains of storehouses that served as an administrative center.[111] On the other hand, Stratum I of Beersheba shows signs of very limited occupation and little or no fortification. In summary, Beersheba is a site that functioned as an important administrative center during Hezekiah's reign, but it was almost nonexistent during Josiah's reign.[112]

---

from Level III, Kenyon interpreted as being from Level II. Thus, Kenyon's conclusions that the pottery from Beersheba was earlier than Lachish Level III are skewed. Moreover, it is very hard to specify pottery changes within ten years. It is more plausible to follow the interpretation of the excavator of Beersheba, Aharoni, who concluded the following: "The pottery found in the stores and in the western living quarters, including rooms of the casemate wall, contains a large sampling of Stratum II. Its types are virtually identical with those of Level III at Lachish" (Y. Aharoni, "Beersheba—The Stratification of the Site," *Beersheba I: Excavations at Tel Beer-sheba 1969-1971 Seasons* [ed. Y. Aharoni; Tel Aviv: Institute of Archaeology, Tel Aviv University, 1973] 5). Finally, there is no indication that Hezekiah or any . part of the Judean kingdom took part in the rebellion against Sargon, so one would not expect Sargon to destroy Beersheba.

[109]Y. Aharoni, "Beersheba—The Fortifications," *Beersheba I: Excavations at Tel Beersheba 1969-1971 Excavations* (ed. Y. Aharoni; Tel Aviv: Institute of Archaeology, Tel Aviv University, 1973) 10-11.

[110]Aharoni, "Beersheba—The Stratification," 4-6.

[111]Z. Herzog, "The Storehouses," *Beersheba I: Excavations at Tel Beersheba 1969-1971 Excavations* (ed. Y. Aharoni; Tel Aviv: Institute of Archaeology, Tel Aviv University, 1973) 23, 28-30.

[112]An example of Hezekiah's involvement in Beersheba can be seen in the dismantling of an altar. Aharoni ("The Horned Altar of Beer-sheba," *BA* 37 [1974] 2-6) drew on biblical references of Hezekiah's reforms (2 Kgs 18:4 and 2 Chr 31:1) and first made the suggestion that the dismantled altar from Beersheba was an example of one of Hezekiah's reforms. Yadin ("Beer-sheba: The High Place Destroyed by King Josiah," *BASOR* 222 [1976] 5-17) questioned this identification and suggested that the altar was dismantled by Josiah. However, the dismantled altar comes from Stratum II (destruction date of 701 BCE), so the identification with Hezekiah seems correct. Cf. Rainey, "Hezekiah's Reform," 333-354; O. Borowski, "Hezekiah's Reform and the Revolt Against Assyria," *BA* 58 (1995) 150-51.

c. Arad

Arad is another site in the Judean Negeb that was important during Hezekiah's and Josiah's reigns. Unfortunately, due to the excavator's (Aharoni's) untimely death, much of the material remains unpublished. Futhermore, the excavations were conducted on such a large scale, without reporting proper sections, that it is difficult if not impossible to check the stratigraphy of Arad from existing reports and notes or from further excavations.[113] In light of these factors, it is difficult to compare in detail the respective strata from the periods of Hezekiah and Josiah. Nevertheless, general observations can be made.[114]

Strata X-VIII are the levels with possible bearing on Hezekiah's influence. The excavators reported that Stratum X was destroyed in the middle of the 9th century, Stratum IX was destroyed by Tiglath-Pileser III, while Stratum VIII was destroyed by Sennacherib at the very end of the 8th century, in 701 BCE. Further, the excavators found that a cultic shrine was established at Arad during Stratum X, and that the altar for that shrine was put out of commission by burying it in a 1-m fill during Stratum VIII.[115] This abolishing of the altar has been interpreted, in conjunction with the dispersal of the previously mentioned altar at Beersheba, as support for cultic reforms undertaken by Hezekiah.[116]

However, one cannot simply estimate Hezekiah's presence at Arad by looking at Stratum VIII and the demolition of the altar in the shrine of this level, because the stratigraphic scheme presented by the excavators has been challenged on several fronts. In separate studies, Zimhoni, A. Mazar with E. Netzer, and Ussishkin have all challenged the dating of these three levels. Zimhoni, in her study of the assemblages of pottery from Lachish, Tel ʿEton, Tell Beit Mirsim, and Arad, points out that the pottery from Strata X-VIII at Arad is very similar to that from Lachish Level III and the parallel strata from the other sites. Thus, she considers it highly unlikely that these three strata are separated by more than fifty

---

[113]Ussishkin, "Judaean Shrine at Arad," 156-157. Cf. also the analysis of various controversies on Arad research found in Manor and Herion's survey article of Arad (D. W. Manor and G. A. Herion, "Arad," in *The Anchor Bible Dictionary of the Bible* [ed. D. N. Freedman; New York: Doubleday, 1992] 331-36, esp. 335-36).

[114]Zeʾev Herzog is reexamining the records from the Arad excavations. His work will result in a final publication that establishes new loci for the entire site, and many of the stratigraphic questions will doubtlessly be solved. In light of this situation, the observations made in this section must be considered tentative until Herzog's final report is published.

[115]Herzog et al., "Arad," 8-23.

[116]Rainey, "Hezekiah's Reform."

years.[117] Mazar concurs that the pottery is similar and states, "It appears that Strata X-VIII are in fact one major building phase of the fortress, with a series of floor raisings and interior alterations."[118] Ussishkin builds on both these arguments to argue that the founding of the cultic shrine at Arad must have taken place at a much later date.[119]

In light of these objections, it seems most prudent to look at Strata X-VIII and VII-VI as a type of composite. Whatever their origin, during the late 8th century Stratum VIII contained a citadel that was constructed on top of the remains of Strata X and IX. The conclusions of Zimhoni, Mazar, and Ussishkin are compelling, but even if the opposing view is accepted, Arad is seen as a well fortified city during Hezekiah's reign.

Indifference cannot be claimed with respect to the sacrificial altar, however. It seems from a typological parallel with Beersheba that the altar at Arad probably would have been dismantled during Hezekiah's reign at the end of the 8th century.[120] On the other hand, such an interpretation presumes an establishment of the shrine at least by the last quarter of the 8th century. Ussishkin concludes that this is possible, but he prefers to assign a date in the first part of the 7th century, but at the same time he acknowledges that it is impossible to prove one interpretation over the other.[121] In light of this situation, it seems most prudent to use the dismantled altar as suggestive of Hezekiah's influence at Arad, but it must be acknowledged that at present the data are not conclusive.[122]

Turning to the late 7th century, Mazar, Ussishkin, and others make convincing arguments for combining Strata VII and VI. The Arad expedition mistakenly attributed a casemate wall to Stratum VI although it actually came from the Hellenistic period.[123] This mistake caused them to classify two separate rooms with epigraphic finds mentioning the official Eliashiv to different strata. Since this official could not have ruled for more than 100 years, they postulated two destructions—one in 597 BCE and one in 586 BCE.[124] In light of these objections to the Arad report, it

---

[117]Zimhoni, "Pottery of Tel ᶜEton," 89-90.

[118]Mazar and Netzer, "Arad," 89.

[119]Ussishkin, "Judaean Shrine at Arad," 149.

[120]Rainey, "Hezekiah's Reform," 338-39.

[121]Ussishkin, "Judaean Shrine at Arad," 151-52, 154.

[122]Borowski, "Hezekiah's Reform," 151, 154 n. 10.

[123]Cf. Yadin, "Stratigraphy of Arad," 180; Nylander, "Stonecutting and Masonry," 56-59.

[124]Cf. Ussishkin, "Judaean Shrine at Arad," 151-52; Mazar and Netzer, "Arad," 87-89.

seems prudent to postulate that Arad experienced one destruction, around 586 BCE.

In summary, Arad was a restrengthened fortress in the Judean Negeb during Josiah's reign, and the numerous ostraca from Strata VII and VI point to its importance as an administrative center.[125] This does not necessarily mean, however, that Arad was stronger in Josiah's reign than in Hezekiah's reign: it is difficult to determine if either monarch had a stronger presence. The fortress was fortified during both periods, and in both periods it functioned as an administrative center. Finally, though typological parallels suggest Hezekiah dismantled the altar, this conclusion cannot be proven.

d. So-Called "New" Seventh-Century BCE Settlements

Finkelstein has pointed out that there are seven sites with a combined built-up area of just less than 100 dunams identified in the Negeb area with late 7th-century occupation, compared to five such sites totalling about 40 dunams from the late 8th century.[126] This increase is due to five sites in the Negeb region that were reported as unsettled in the late 8th century but as containing new settlement in the 7th century, These sites are Aroer, Ḥorvat ʿUza, Ḥorvat Radom, Tel ʿIra, and Tel Masos. The addition of so many new sites in the period roughly corresponding to Josiah's reign might seem at first glance to indicate much more influence and power on Josiah's part as compared with Hezekiah, but several factors mitigate against drawing dramatic conclusions.

First, some signs of occupation during the late 8th century at several of these sites are dismissed by their excavators. Second, there are signs at many of the sites that they were settled or influenced by the Edomites in the late 7th century. If this latter scenario is confirmed at many sites, the additional builtup area of Edomite sites during Josiah's reign could point to weakness in the kingdom's defense system. Finally, the total amount of additional builtup area is very small compared with the large areas of settlement in the Shephelah and the Judean Hills. It is instructive to consider each of these sites individually.

α. Aroer

Aroer is located on a mound near Naḥal Aroer in the Negeb about 22 km southeast of Beersheba. It is mentioned in 1 Sam 30:28 and in the Greek version of Jos 15:22. Despite the early references, the excavators

---

[125]Cf. Herzog et al., "Arad," 22-29.
[126]Finkelstein, "Days of Manasseh," 176.

report no finds earlier than the 7th century. The pottery reported from the earliest stratum (IV) paralleled Ramat Raḥel VA and En Gedi V.[127] On the other hand, three *lmlk* impressions were found on isolated jar handles,[128] so one should question whether or not some settlement at Aroer dated to at least the late 8th century.

The archaeological context of these *lmlk* impressions is inconclusive, but habitation in the late 8th century is corroborated by a large number of complete and restorable vessels from a silo in Area B (Locus 62), which the excavators assigned to Stratum III. These vessels contain parallels with levels commonly dated to the late 8th century. One of the most recognizable pottery forms from this locus is a complete *lmlk*-type jar without any seal impressions.[129] Biran and Cohen explain the presence of this jar by referring to the existence of an unstamped *lmlk* type jar found in Locus 4084 of Lachish Level II (late 7th century). They add that Ussishkin concluded that this unstamped form at Lachish showed "that the tradition of using storage jars of that shape persisted until the end of the Judean monarchy."[130]

Biran and Cohen's citation of Ussishkin is misleading. Zimhoni points out that this particular *lmlk*-type jar from Lachish Level II (Locus 4084) is from a different "production line" than the classic *lmlk* jar. It contains a plain, rounded rim and its fabric is coarser and more pink than the *lmlk* jars.[131] In contrast, the *lmlk* jars commonly have a reddish-brown ware that is well fired and less coarse. The neck is either straight or sloping inward, and the rim is thickened and often protrudes outward. The base is rounded. Many of these jars were not stamped.[132] Zimhoni thus concludes that the "storage jar [from Locus 4084]...should not be considered as a late example of this type of jar type."[133]

The example from Aroer (reg. no. 110/20) is of the *lmlk* type from Lachish Level III, not Level II. The jar is described as having a reddish brown ware, a gray core, and white grits, similar to the jars from Lachish Level III. The drawing and photograph of the jar show that the neck is

---

[127]A. Biran, "Aroer (in Judea)," *NEAEHL* (ed. E. Stern; New York: Macmillan; Jerusalem: Israel Exploration Society, 1993) 90.

[128]Biran, "Aroer," 90-91.

[129]Reg. no. 110/20; A. Biran and R. Cohen, "Aroer in the Negev," *EI* 15 (1981) 259, fig. 8:2, pl. 3:מ (Hebrew).

[130]Ussishkin, "Destruction," 57; cf. Biran and Cohen, "Aroer," 259, n. 38.

[131]O. Zimhoni, "Two Ceramic Assemblages from Lachish Levels III and II," *Tel Aviv* 17 (1990) 30-31.

[132]Zimhoni, "Two Ceramic Assemblages," 15.

[133]Zimhoni, "Two Ceramic Assemblages," 31.

straight and the rim is thickened and protrudes outward, also similar to the jars from Lachish Level III.[134] In light of all these considerations, it is reasonable to view this jar as paralleling the examples from Lachish Level III.

Another clear type of pottery vessel with parallels to the late 8th century is a deep cooking pot with a grooved rim. The deep cooking pot in the 7th century has only one ridge and the ware is thinner and more metallic.[135] The cooking pot from the silo is this earlier type with multiple ridges.[136] It is clearly typologically identical to late 8th-century forms found in Arad Stratum VIII,[137] Beersheba Stratum II,[138] and Lachish Level III.[139]

Biran and Cohen admit that the other cooking pots from this silo have parallels in the 8th century. They point out that reg. nos. 110/2 and 110/30 have parallels with Beersheba Stratum II and Lachish Level III.[140] Further, the lamp from this silo is described as a "flat-based" lamp,[141] while Aharoni and Aharoni note that during the 7th century the bases on these lamps became higher and thicker.[142]

In summary, the complete vessels from the silo in Locus 62 and the three *lmlk* impressions suggest late 8th-century occupation at Aroer. It appears that this occupation was less extensive than during the 7th century, but these material remains do support the biblical references for occupation at Aroer prior to the 7th century. For the purposes of the present study, these finds suggest that Hezekiah and the Judean kingdom had some presence at Aroer, but that the more significant settlement took place during the 7th century.

Another factor with bearing on Josiah's influence at Aroer during the late 7th century is the relatively high proportion of Edomite-type finds. In Locus 124 of Stratum III, there was an Edomite seal with the

---

[134]Biran and Cohen, "Aroer," 258-59, fig. 8:2, pl. 3מ.

[135]Aharoni and Aharoni, "Stratification of Judahite Sites," 76.

[136]Reg. no. 110/1; Biran and Cohen, "Aroer," 259, fig. 7:4-5, pl. 3מ.

[137]Aharoni and Aharoni, "Stratification of Judahite Sites," fig. 3:4.

[138]Aharoni and Aharoni, "Stratification of Judahite Sites," fig. 4:4.

[139]Zimhoni, "Two Ceramic Assemblages," figs. 5:5-6.

[140]Biran and Cohen, "Aroer," 259, fig. 7:4-5; Y. Aharoni, ed., *Beersheba I: Excavations at Tel Beersheba 1969-1971 Seasons* (Tel Aviv: Institute of Archaeology, Tel Aviv University, 1973) pl. 43:1-6; and Tufnell, *Lachish III*, pl. 93:440-42.

[141]Reg. no. 110/21; Biran and Cohen, "Aroer," 1981:259, fig. 7:11.

[142]Aharoni and Aharoni, "Stratification of Judahite Sites," 84.

theophoric name קוס.[143] There was also a large amount of Edomite pottery with Edomite-style painting[144] in Stratum II in Loci 102, 104, 105, 125, 133, and 136.[145] These finds point at least to Edomite influence in Aroer during during the 7th century, if not to actual Edomite occupation of the site.

β. Ḥorvat ʿUza

At Ḥorvat ʿUza, it is again difficult to check the excavator's results because only preliminary publications have appeared, and there are no extensive pottery plates from which comparisons can be made. It is clear from the published preliminary reports that Ḥorvat ʿUza functioned as an important military outpost during the late 7th century and early 6th centuries. The site itself is located about 8 km southeast of Arad and controls the road linking Edom and the Arabah. The 7th-century fortress is large, measuring 51 x 42 m, with a settlement on the bank of the adjacent wadi. The excavator states that "pottery characteristic of the Negev at the end of the First Temple period was found both in the fortress and in the settlement."[146]

Ḥorvat ʿUza seems to represent a move by Josiah to secure this important trade passage in the Negeb region; however, there are indications that the site may not have been ruled by Judeans. Some of the pottery is characteristically Edomite and, more important, several ostraca written in the Edomite dialect have been found. One of them seems to indicate that, at some point in the late 7th or early 6th century, the commander of the fortress was an Edomite official. The letter is addressed to an official with an Edomite name and requests a shipment of food and other supplies.[147]

γ. Ḥorvat Radum

Ḥorvat Radum is in very close proximity to ʿUza. It lies about 2 km south of ʿUza and functioned as some sort of outpost fort. Because the view south of ʿUza into Naḥal Qinah is obstructed, it seems that Radum functioned as a lookout station to the south. Excavations at the site were carried out by Beit-Arieh at the same time that he excavated at

---

[143]Biran and Cohen, "Aroer," 264, pl. 4:טו.

[144]Cf. E. Mazar, "Edomite Pottery at the End of the Iron Age," *IEJ* 35 (1985) 261-263, figs. 4-7.

[145]Biran and Cohen, "Aroer," 265, fig. 14:1-11; cf. Biran, "Aroer," 91.

[146]I. Beit-Arieh, "Ḥorvat ʿUza," *NEAEHL* (ed. E. Stern; New York: Macmillan; Jerusalem: Israel Exploration Society, 1993) 1496.

[147]I. Beit-Arieh and B. Cresson, "Horvat ʿUza, A Fortified Outpost on the Eastern Negev Border," *BA* 54 (1991) 126-35.

ᶜUza. The fort is very small, measuring only 25 x 21 m, and the site has only one stratigraphic level with two or three phases. Various types of pottery remains including bowls, jar, jugs, juglets, cooking pots, and lamps all point to a 7th-century date. Edomite ties are again suggested by the presence of Edomite cooking vessels.[148]

Radum provides evidence of strengthening the position at ᶜUza during the late 7th century, supposedly by Josiah. Once again, it is difficult to draw many conclusions about Josiah's influence in the area from this little outpost. It is too small to have functioned as more than an observation station, and the Edomite finds may suggest Edomite influence, if not control. Evidence from Radum and ᶜUza indicates an effort to control this important passageway during the 7th century, but the presence of Edomite pottery suggests that this was not solely a Judean endeavor.

δ. Tel ᶜIra

Tel ᶜIra is midway between Arad and Beersheba. It is about 9 km directly north of Aroer on the southern spur of the Hebron Hills. The site is strategically located at the top of a large hill and controls a passageway from the Negeb to Hebron. Once again, the inability to check the excavators' results impedes an effort to check the stratigraphy. Only brief preliminary notes have been published. The most extensive of these prelimary publications are three overview articles, and even these are contradictary in certain aspects.[149] In 1985, both Beit-Arieh and Biran concluded that there was only 7th and early 6th-century occupation at Tel ᶜIra. Biran's excavations pointed to one destruction in *ca.* 586 BCE, while Beit-Arieh's continued excavations distinguished two separate levels for the 7th century (Strata VII and VI). Both excavators found signs of an Edomite presence, especially in Stratum VI, through the pottery and one ostracon.[150]

Beit-Arieh's attribution of two levels is certain because there were two distinct destruction layers. Further, the rebuilding of the casemate walls in Area E from Stratum VI followed a different line from the Stratum VII walls.[151] Beit-Arieh intially dated the earlier stratum (VII) to the first

---

[148]I. Beit-Arieh, "A Small Frontier Citadel at Ḥorvat Radum in the Judean Negev," *Qad* 24 (1991) 87-89 (Hebrew); cf. Aharoni and Aharoni, "Stratification of Judahite Sites," 84-86.

[149]Cf. I. Beit-Arieh, "Tel ᶜIra—A Fortified City of the Kingdom of Judah," *Qad* 18 (1985) 17-25 (Hebrew); A. Biran, "Tel ᶜIra," *Qad* 18 (1985) 25-27 (Hebrew); I. Beit-Arieh, "Tel ᶜIra," *NEAEHL* (ed. E. Stern; New York: Macmillan; Jerusalem: Israel Exploration Society, 1993) 642-46.

[150]Biran, "Tel ᶜIra," 26-27; Beit-Arieh, "Tel ᶜIra-- A Fortified City," 18-19.

[151]Beit-Arieh, "Tel ᶜIra," 643-644; cf. also Beit-Arieh, "Tel ᶜIra-- A Fortified City," 19-20.

half of the 7th century, and the later one to the end of the 7th century.[152] Later, he contradicts this earlier dating without explanation and lists a date of "late 8th-early 7th cent. BCE" for Stratum VII.[153]

One of the problems with dating both Strata VII and VI to the 7th century is that it is difficult to posit a historical cause for the two destructions in the late 7th century and early 6th centuries. By studying Babylonian docusments and relating them to geographic features in Israel, Rainey has shown that the Babylonian attack in 596 BCE was solely on Jerusalem.[154] Thus, the only remaining historical cause for a destruction in the Negeb would be Nebuchadnezzer's campaign in 586 BCE or perhaps a later Babylonian campaign in 582 BCE. The difference of four years in between these two dates is not enough to allow for the variance in the pottery styles found in Strata VII and VI. Moreover, it is also difficult to posit such an extensive rebuilding effort in a short period of time. However, if Stratum VII were dated to the 8th century, this problem is alleviated.

There is other evidence of late 8th-century occupation at ʿIra, much of it unpublished. The tel is located atop a high hill, the summit of which is comprised of flint bedrock. In many of the strata, most or all the debris from the summit was removed and thrown over the steep embankment. This practice accounts for the limited architecture found for Stratum VIII. The existence of Stratum VIII is indicated by a fill in Stratum VII and by pottery from some burials.[155] There was one locus near the gate area that did contain pottery from Stratum VII with clear parallels to Lachish Level III, thus suggesting a date in the late 8th century.[156] Another indication of occupation during the reign of Hezekiah is the discovery by Aharoni of a *lmlk* impression.[157] Given these indications of settlement during the late 8th century and Beit-Arieh's revised estimate of occupation from Stratum VII in the late 8th century, one may reasonably posit that the historical cause for the conflagration of Stratum VII was the campaign of Sennacherib in 701 BCE.

---

[152]Beit-Arieh, "Tel ʿIra—A Fortified City," 19; I. Beit-Arieh, "An Early Bronze Age III Settlement at Tel ʿIra in the Northern Negev," *IEJ* (1991), 2.

[153]Beit-Arieh, "Tel ʿIra," 642.

[154]A. F. Rainey, "The Fate of Lachish During the Campaigns of Sennacherib and Nebuchadrezzar," *Lachish V: Investigations at Lachish—The Sanctuary and the Residency* (ed. Y. Aharoni; Tel Aviv: Institute of Archaeology, Tel Aviv University, 1975) 53-59.

[155]Cf. Beit-Arieh, "Tel ʿIra—A Fortified City," 18-19; Beit-Arieh, "Tel ʿIra," 642-43.

[156]A. F. Rainey, personal communication.

[157]Y. Aharoni, "The Negeb of Judah," *IEJ* 8 (1958) 36, pl. 16:D.

In summary, even if this redating of Stratum VII is not accepted (and it cannot be proved until more data are published from ʿIra), the evidence suggests that there was some type of Judean settlement at ʿIra in the late 8th century BCE. This conclusion is important because ʿIra obviously served as a vital fortress along a major trade route from the Negeb to Hebron. This fortress seems to have been occupied during both Hezekiah's and Josiah's reigns. Given the strong evidence of an Edomite influence at ʿIra during the late 7th century, one might even suggest that Hezekiah had a stronger influence in this part of the Negeb than Josiah. In any case, it is clear that ʿIra should not be singled out as an example of stronger Judean strength in the Negeb during the late 7th century than during the late 8th century.

ε. Tel Masos

Turning to the final site noted by Finkelstein as an example of a new settlement in the Negeb during the 7th century BCE, one observes that the situation at Tel Masos is not as ambiguous concerning settlement during the late 8th century as the other sites. The site has been published,[158] so more information is available. It also supports Finkelstein's conclusion of settlement in the 7th century but not in the 8th.

Although the excavations have been published, the extent of the 7th-century fortress is still not entirely clear. The excavations focused on the part of the tel with Chalcolithic, Middle Bronze, and Iron I settlement. The excavators only dug a probe on the mound about 200 m from the Iron I settlement, where there are Iron II remains. Enough data were recovered to distinguish four phases. The size of the entire mound is relatively small, so the fortress could not have been large. The pottery also contained much Edomite material as well as three ostraca with Edomite PNN.[159]

Masos thus seems to be an example like Ḥorvat Radum that contains a small fortress from the late 7th century and shows no signs of occupation in the late 8th. However, Tel Masos is a small site so it is unclear how much importance one can draw from its occupation during Josiah's reign as compared to occupation during Hezekiah's reign. Finally, like Radum, there are many signs of Edomite influence at Masos, so it is unclear how completely Josiah actually controlled the site.

---

[158]V. Fritz and A. Kempinski, *Ergebnisse der Ausgrabungen auf der Hirbet El-Masas (Tel Masos) 1972-1975*, 3 vols., (Abhandlungen des deutschen Palästinavereins; Wiesbaden: Harrassowitz, 1983).

[159]A. Kempinski, "Tel Masos," *NEAEHL* (ed. E. Stern; New York: Macmillan; Jerusalem: Israel Exploration Society, 1993) 989.

e. Ḥorvat Qitmit

Ḥorvat Qitmit is *ca.* 10 km south of Arad. It contains signs of settlement from the late 7th century, but has no occupation evidence for the late 8th century. The pottery consists of two groups. The first is similar to other Judean pottery from the late 7th century (Lachish Level II and Arad VII-VI), and a large second group contains typical Edomite pottery. In addition, there are six inscriptions that contain a writing style typical of Edom rather than of Judah. One of these inscriptions contains the Edomite DN קוס. The site seems to have functioned almost solely for cultic purposes. The layout is centered on an open sacred area and a platform for sacrifices. Remains of many cult objects and sacrifices were also found. In light of these data, the excavator concludes:

> It appears that Qitmit was the site of an Edomite
> shrine within the Judean kingdom at the end of the First
> Temple period. Its existence in this region attests to the
> strengthening of Edomite influence in the eastern Negev then,
> or even to territorial acquisitions by the Edomites just before or
> soon after the destruction of the First Temple.[160]

Summary

In contrast to the Shephelah and the Judean Hill Country, it appears that Josiah had a greater amount of economic buildup and civil strength in the Negeb than Hezekiah. Hezekiah, however, is not totally absent from this region. Previous treatments[161] tend to emphasize the near total absence of Judean influence in the Negeb until the 7th century. As shown above, areas in the Negeb were settled during Hezekiah's reign even if less significantly than during Josiah's reign. Thus, Judean activity in the Negeb during Hezekiah's reign was not completely eclipsed by Judean activity during Josiah's reign. This point is especially important because the Negeb served as a critical trade route for the Judean kingdom.

According to Finkelstein's calculations, the combined built-up area in the Negeb more than doubles from Hezekiah's time to Josiah's (from about 40 to about 100 dunams); however the actual increase may be somewhat smaller in light of the evidence presented above pointing to at least limited 8th-century settlement at sites Finkelstein considers to have been unoccupied during the late 8th century. Moreover, even if Finkelstein's numbers are correct, the total additional built-up area is only about 60 dunams. This number is very small when compared to the

---

[160]I. Beit-Arieh, "Ḥorvat Qitmit," *NEAEHL* (ed. E. Stern; New York: Macmillan; Jerusalem: Israel Exploration Society, 1993) 1233.

[161]For example, Finkelstein, "Days of Manasseh."

roughly 4,651 dunams of builtup area in the Shephelah during Hezekiah's reign and even 1,124 dunams during Josiah's reign.[162] Thus, even if Josiah is seen to have a much wider presence in the Negeb than Hezekiah, one must question the importance of a difference of merely sixty dunams in the larger scheme of the kingdom. Moreover, Herzog has shown that increases in settlement in the Negeb from the 3rd millennium BCE through the modern era have been tied to climatic conditions as much as to political conditions.[163] It is possible that this increase in settlement may simply indicate more consistent rainfall during the late 7th century than in the late 8th.

Related to the total size of increased settlement is the question of the kingdom-wide significance of Josiah's increased presence in the Negeb. As Dagan's survey work showed, Judean settlement in the 7th century was almost wiped out in many parts of the Shephelah, and overall Judean settlement in the Shephelah dropped to a quarter of the size known from the late 8th century. Further, the coastal plain site of Ekron prospered as an Assyrian (or possibly later as an Egyptian) province. The Judeans seem to have been pushed out of the Shephelah into what had previously been considered marginal areas. Thus, the increase in settlement during the 7th century in the Negeb probably reflects the necessity of the Judean government to seek economic growth and development in an area that previous regimes would have regarded as too marginal to warrant as great an investment of resources.

---

[162]The measurements are those of Dagan cited above. Finkelstein lists somewhat smaller figures for the Shephelah: 250 hectares (= 2,500 dunams) during the late 8th century and 80 hectares (= 800 dunams) during the late 7th century.

[163]Z. Herzog, "The Beer-sheba Valley: From Nomadism to Monarchy," *From Nomadism to Monarchy: Archaeological and Historical Aspects of Early Israel* (eds. I. Finkelstein and N. Naʾaman; Washington: Biblical Archaeology Society; Jerusalem: Israel Exploration Society, 1994) 122-24.

4. Jerusalem

a. Introduction

One of the most important questions regarding the size and strength of Jerusalem during the reigns of Hezekiah and Josiah was whether Jerusalem spread beyond the boundaries of the City of David before the Hasmonean period. The existence of urban development beyond the City of David is hinted at during the first century CE by Josephus, who makes comments that suggest settlement on two hills during the First Temple period. He says, "The city was built upon two hills, which are opposite to one another, and have a valley to divide them asunder.... Of these hills, that which contains the upper city is much higher, and in length more direct.... The other hill...sustains the lower city, (and) is of the shape of the moon when she is horned."[164]

Scholars identify the two hills as the Lower City in the City of David (on the Eastern Hill) and as the Upper City (on the Western Hill). However, the question remains as to whether Josephus' comments accurately describe Jerusalem during the First Temple period or if they reflect Jerusalem as Josephus knew it during the first century CE. Scholarly opinion on Josephus' comments was divided during the majority of the 20th century. One side became known as the Minimalist School and held that Josephus' comments were anachronistic. For those scholars, First Temple Jerusalem was a small town that did not exceed the boundaries of the City of David. The other side, the Maximalist School, held that Jerusalem grew to the boundaries that Josephus mentions during the First Temple period. For those scholars, Jerusalem was a major city as one would expect for the capital of Judah.

b. Minimalist/Maximalist Debate Before Avigad's Excavations

The size and role of the capital city Jerusalem during the reigns of both Hezekiah and Josiah is important for an understanding of the economic buildup and civil strength of each monarch. The minimalist interpretation was first suggested by A. H. Sayce in 1883.[165] Among others, A. Alt developed the minimalist position and pointed out its ramifications for the role Jerusalem played in the reigns of David and

---

[164]Flavius Josephus, *The Works of Josephus: New Updated Edition* (trans. W. Whiston from *War of the Jews V*, 4, 1; Peabody, MA: Hendrickson Publishers, 1987); quoted by N. Avigad, *Discovering Jerusalem* (Nashville: T. Nelson, 1983) 27; G. Barkay, "Northern and Western Jerusalem in the End of the Iron Age," (Ph.D. dissertation, Tel Aviv University, 1985) 501 (Hebrew).

[165]A. H. Sayce, "The Topography of Pre-exilic Jerusalem," *PEFQSt* (1883) 215-23.

Solomon as well as later kings. Alt's interpretation of the biblical texts held that Jerusalem was established solely as an administrative center by David. He held that the general populous remained in the lands of their inheritance throughout the First Temple period. Jerusalem was inhabited only by the king, the royal family, and the royal guard or mercenaries.[166] M. Noth developed Alt's position and also held that although Solomon expanded the size of the City of David as he increased in military power, Jerusalem did not expand to the Western Hill.[167]

The maximalist position has also existed since the turn of the century with the work of Bliss and Dickie[168] and was adopted by many other scholars.[169] However, as M. Avi-Yonah pointed out in 1954, up until that point in time there were no archaeological data to confirm either interpretation. In light of this situation, Avi-Yonah joined other scholars in asserting that the written sources of Nehemiah supported accepting the minimalist interpretation of Jerusalem.[170]

The archaeological support that Avi-Yonah rightly desired was found in Kathleen Kenyon's excavations during the 1960s. Kenyon conducted excavations in the garden of the Armenian Monastery and in the Christian Quarter of Jerusalem. In these digs, "Kenyon claimed to have found no occupation remains outside the walls earlier than the time of Herod Agrippa (1st century A.D.)."[171] Further, although she found potsherds and other small finds dating from the First Temple period at various places on the Western Hill, she concluded that these came from

---

[166]A. Alt, "Das Taltor von Jerusalem," PJb 24 (1928) 83-84; A. Alt, "The Formation of the Israelite State in Palestine," Essays of Old Testament History and Religion (trans. R. A. Wilson; New York: Doubleday, 1967) 285.

[167]M. Noth, The History of Israel (New York: Harper and Row, 1958) 207.

[168]F. J. Bliss, Excavations at Jerusalem, 1894-1897 (London: Committee of the Palestine Exploration Fund, 1898) 290, 320-22, pl. 29, map 3, quoted in Barkay, "Northern and Western Jerusalem," 451.

[169]Cf. bibliography cited in Barkay "Northern and Western Jerusalem," 458, including: G. A. Smith, Jerusalem, The Topography, Economics and History from the Earliest Times to A.D. 70, Vols. I-II (London, Hadler & Stoughton, 1907) 195-204, 207, 217-18; G. Dalman, Jerusalem und Sein Gelände (BFCT 4; Gütersloh: Bertelsmann, 1930); J. Simons, Jerusalem in the Old Testament: Researches and Theories (Leiden: E. J. Brill, 1952) 437; L. H. Vincent, Jérusalem de L'ancien Testament: recherches d'archeologie et d'histoire, Vol. I (Paris: J. Gabalda, 1954) 64-72.

[170]M. Avi-Yonah, "The Walls of Nehemiah—A Minimalist View," IEJ 4 (1954) 240. Cf. Avi-Yonah ("Walls of Nehemiah," 239-40) for a brief history of interpretation to 1954. Cf. Barkay ("Northern and Western Jerusalem," 451-58) for a more recent history of interpretation.

[171]Avigad, Discovering Jerusalem, 29.

backfill that originated from a place other than the Western Hill. Therefore, "Kenyon arrived at the far-reaching conclusion that there had been no settlement on the Western Hill during the Israelite period."[172] At the time of her discoveries, Kenyon's findings seemed conclusive. Yet, in retrospect it has been seen that the conclusions were based on too limited a sample since her digs were confined to trial pits and trenches.

c. Avigad's Excavations in the Jewish Quarter

Kenyon's methodological error was rectified by Avigad in his excavations of the Jewish Quarter from 1969-1978. It is unfortunate that the final publication of the excavations has yet to appear. Avigad died before publishing or adequately distributing the information to others so that it might be published. However, since the question of the settlement of the Western Hill was a focus of the preliminary reports, enough information can be gleaned from these publications to link occupation on the Western Hill positively to the Iron II period.

The most dramatic discovery with relevance to settlement during the First Temple period was an extremely wide Israelite fortification wall in the northern part of the modern Jewish Quarter and in Area A of Avigad's excavations. The date of this wall was confirmed by the pottery and small finds in the fills above the wall and by the pottery along its western face as well as a clear floor on the eastern face. The western face of the wall contained more than twelve stratigraphic layers of fill which were 3.3 m deep and consisted of purely Iron II deposits. There was a floor running up to the eastern face of the wall, and "the pottery above the floor and in the fill beneath was pure Iron Age II."[173] Notable Iron II small finds included 15 *lmlk* seal impressions and one official seal impression (לצפן א/במעץ) found above the wall and along its base.[174] Avigad summed up the dating of this wall as follows: "Nowhere did we encounter any evidence which might have caused doubt of its Israelite origin."[175]

Isolated signs of Iron Age fortifications were also found just north of this broad wall in Areas W, C, and X-2. In Area W, two distinct Iron Age phases were identified. The lower level contained clear residential signs with Iron II pottery found above and below the floors. These floors were cut by a massive building with walls measuring about 4.5 m in

---

[172]Avigad, *Discovering Jerusalem*, 30.

[173]N. Avigad, "Excavations in the Jewish Quarter of the Old City, Jerusalem, 1970 (Preliminary Report II)," *IEJ* 20 (1970) 130, fig. 2.

[174]Avigad, "Jewish Quarter, 1970," 131, pl. 30:C-D; cf. Barkay ("Northern and Western Jerusalem," 447-48) for the specific find nos. of these impressions.

[175]Avigad, *Discovering Jerusalem*, 47.

thickness. This building also dated to the Iron II period. Since the building cut the floors and dated to the Iron II period, the floors must have been from an earlier phase of that period. Avigad concluded that the building "obviously belonged to the northern defense line of Jerusalem during the later Judean monarchy," but he held that it was unclear if the building dated to the 8th or the 7th century.[176] Avigad also proposed that this building was part of a gate structure that might have connected with the Broad Wall discussed in the preceding paragraph, but this proposal should be seen as tentative since there was no clear archaeological connection found between the two structures.[177]

Numerous residential buildings inside the fortification line of the Western Hill offered other important signs of First Temple settlement. One of the areas with residential finds, Area F, contained the largest amount of Iron Age material from any area in Avigad's excavations. Much of the pottery and small finds from Area F came from clear contexts.[178] Futher, a pre-exilic Hebrew inscription containing the phrase ...קנ ארץ [ואל] was found in this area. The absence of the *he* mater following the *nun* in the word *qōnē* and the paleography of the letters have clearly dated this inscription to the pre-exilic period.[179]

In summary, it became clear from Avigad's excavations that Jerusalem was settled on the Western Hill by at least the late 8th century. However, the question of how extensive the 8th-century settlement was, remained unanswered. The key question is whether the extensive settlement and buildup of the Upper City on the Western Hill took place during or before Hezekiah's reign, or whether it began only with Manasseh or Josiah. Even if the settlement of the Western Hill had begun by the time of Hezekiah's reign, it would also be important for the purposes of the investigation presented here to determine if the Upper City was more developed during Hezekiah's reign or during Josiah's reign.

---

[176]N. Avigad, "Jerusalem, the Jewish Quarter of the Old City, 1975," *IEJ* 25 (1975) 260-61.

[177]Avigad, *Discovering Jerusalem*, 59, fig. 30.

[178]N. Avigad, "Excavations in the Jewish Quarter of the Old City of Jerusalem, 1971." *IEJ* 22 (1972) 194-95.

[179]Avigad, "Jewish Quarter, 1971," 195-196, pl. 42:B; Avigad, *Discovering Jerusalem*, 41; cf. also P. D. Miller, "El, The Creator of Earth," *BASOR* 239 (1980) 43-46.

d. Comparison of Economic Development by Hezekiah and Josiah

The archaeological data from Avigad's excavations in Jerusalem are ambiguous for the purposes of comparing the economic development of Hezekiah's and Josiah's reigns. The Broad Wall shows definite signs of dating from the Iron II period, and it seems to come from at least the late 8th century because much of the pottery surrounding it has parallels with Lachish Level III. However, the fact that the excavations in the Jewish Quarter were broken up by modern buildings made the intricate chronological association of various features impossible. Indeed, even with regard to the Broad Wall, it was impossible to establish a positive chronological connection with the tower found just to the north.[180]

In most instances, the limited chronological clarity seen with the Broad Wall and the tower to the north was almost completely absent. The continual rebuilding of Jerusalem over thousands of years resulted in at least 10 m of built-up debris. Each time the city was rebuilt, the remains below were further disturbed. Avigad stated, "[Jerusalem's] builders were often no less destructive than the warriors who razed it. This cyclic process [of building and destruction] has left only a few early remains intact, and those still extant are often covered by huge accumulations of debris."[181] Stratigraphic investigations in Jerusalem are hampered further by modern structures that cover almost the entire city. In light of all these hindrances, it is often impossible to establish a precise chronology.[182]

This ambiguity does not mean that it is impossible to prove that the Western Hill was settled during both Hezekiah's and Josiah's reigns. Avigad's excavations unearthed pottery and small finds that date to both the late 8th and late 7th centuries. These finds from Avigad's excavations in the Jewish Quarter have since been corroborated by other excavations on the Western Hill and outside the Western Hill. Avigad rightly stated:

> There is no doubt whatsoever that all these finds point to a permanent settlement on the Western Hill. And even though their distribution is rather sparse, the fact that such remains have been found scattered throughout the Jewish Quarter indicates that we are not dealing with mere isolated houses, but rather an extensive settlement.[183]

---

[180]Avigad, "Jewish Quarter, 1975," 260-61; Avigad, *Discovering Jerusalem*, 59, fig. 30.

[181]Avigad, *Discovering Jerusalem*, 13.

[182]Cf. Barkay, "Northern and Western Jerusalem," 488-92.

[183]Avigad, *Discovering Jerusalem*, 45.

On the other hand, the isolated nature of the finds makes it impossible to speak with assurance about the size and scope of the development in Hezekiah's reign versus that in Josiah's reign.

e. Date of First Settlement on the Western Hill

Similarly, it is difficult to determine exactly when the expansion of Jerusalem to the Western Hill began. Avigad was justifiably cautious and concluded that the Western Hill was settled at least by the late 8th century with the founding of the Broad Wall. At the same time, he held forward several signs of earlier settlement outside the City of David as suggestive of an earlier date for the nonfortified settlement of the Western Hill. B. Mazar identified several installations outside the Temple Mount but within the defense lines of the Upper City on the Western Hill as 8th-century tombs. If these installations were indeed tombs, they would not have been used once the Upper City was enclosed by the Broad Wall as they would have then contaminated the city. Avigad thus suggested that the development of the Western Hill began in the early 8th century, but that the fortifications were not constructed until the late 8th century, probably by Hezekiah.[184]

Broshi presented an opinion in 1974 that provided a historical reason for this development of the Western Hill. He posited that the settlement on the Western Hill was a direct result of immigration by refugees from the fallen northern kingdom of Israel after 722 BCE. He also posited that a second wave of refugees came on the scene following Sennacherib's devastation of the Shephelah in 701 BCE.[185] Even though a later article made it clear that Broshi should not be misunderstood as stating that no limited settlement took place outside the City of David before the fall of the northern kingdom, he held (with Finkelstein) that the first significant move to settle the Western Hill came after 722 BCE.[186] This hypothesis has been generally accepted in studies presenting an overview of research concerning Jerusalem.[187]

---

[184]Avigad, *Discovering Jerusalem*, 55-56.

[185]M. Broshi, "The Expansion of Jerusalem in the Reigns of Hezekiah and Manasseh," *IEJ* 24 (1974) 23, 25.

[186]M. Broshi and I. Finkelstein, "The Population of Palestine in Iron Age II," *BASOR* 287 (1992) 52.

[187]Cf. Halpern, "Jerusalem and the Lineages," 48; Y. Shiloh, "Jerusalem: The Early Periods and the First Temple Period," *NEAEHL* (ed. E. Stern; New York: Macmillan; Jerusalem: Israel Exploration Society, 1993) 700.

This hypothesis, however, seems a little too simple. Since Judah experienced prosperity and growth during the reigns of kings prior to Hezekiah, it seems surprising that the expansion of Jerusalem would take place only after the fall of the north. Keeping this question in mind, one should look at three objections that Barkay[188] raises to the interpretation that Jerusalem expanded its boundaries only after 722 BCE: a) the script of the קן ארץ [אל] inscription is dated by Aharoni to around 800 BCE instead of about 700 BCE;[189] b) the identified tower has a typological parallel to a tower found in Lachish Level IV; c) pottery sherds and other small finds have parallels to Lachish Level IV.

The criticism raised about the dating of the קן ארץ [אל] ostracon is important, because if the inscription dates from the early 8th century, the dating of other small finds and pottery from a substantial settlement previous to 722 BCE would be possible. Aharoni compares the script on the ostracon from the Jewish Quarter to the script from ostraca from Level X at Arad which he dates to ca. 800 BCE.[190] Before proceeding further, one should recall that many scholars challenge Aharoni's dating of Arad Stratum X to ca. 800. Those scholars date Strata X-VIII to the last half of the 8th century.[191] If this interpretation is valid, the fact that the ostracon from the Jewish Quarter has parallels to ostraca from Arad Level X would say nothing about dating the ostracon to the first half of the 8th century.

It is still helpful to look at Aharoni's proposal for the ostracon from the Jewish Quarter. He draws attention to "the early *kaph* and *qoph*, the angular verticals of the *kaph*, *mem*, and *nun*, and the great length of the verticals."[192] However, none of the ostraca that are clearly from Stratum X have a *kaph* or *qoph* that is comparable to the ostracon from the Jewish Quarter.[193] From Aharoni's script charts, it seems that the Stratum X ostraca he refers to are nos. 72 and 74. These ostraca do not come from a clear stratigraphic context, and they are identified as "Stratum X ostraca" by their paleographic character.[194] Thus, the argument is clearly circular.

---

[188]Barkay, "Northern and Western Jerusalem," 490-492.

[189]Aharoni, *Arad Inscriptions*, 132; cf. Avigad, "Jewish Quarter, 1971," 195-196, pl. 42:B; Avigad, *Discovering Jerusalem*, 41; P. Miller, "El," 43-46.

[190]Aharoni, *Arad Inscriptions*, 132.

[191]Zimhoni, "Pottery of Tel ʿEton," 89-90; Mazar and Netzer, "Arad," 89; Ussishkin, "Judaean Shrine at Arad," 149.

[192]Aharoni, *Arad Inscriptions*, 132.

[193]Aharoni, *Arad Inscriptions*, 93-94, nos. 67-70.

[194]Aharoni, *Arad Inscriptions*, 96-97, 137.

In spite of this circular argument, several characters highlighted by Aharoni are indeed archaic and deserve special treatment. The *kaph* in the ostracon from the Jewish Quarter contains a head with three distinct bars that intersect at the vertical shaft. This form is clearly more archaic than early 6th-century *kaph*s from Arad and Lachish, which contain a head with only two bars. In one version of the later form a horizontal bar of the head joins the vertical shaft, while the second bar is vertical and parallel with the vertical shaft and joins the horizontal bar (cf., among others, Lachish Letters II and III and Arad Letters I and II). In other instances, such as Lachish Letter IV, the vertical and horizontal bars of the head merge into one fluid stroke that joins the vertical shaft. The *kaph* from the Jewish Quarter ostracon is more like *kaph*s found in the Samaria ostraca (cf. nos. 27, 44, 48, and 49) and on two pithoi from Kuntillet ʿAjrûd.[195] As both the ostraca from Samaria and from Kuntillet ʿAjrûd date from approximately the middle of the 8th century, these data can be used as support for Aharoni's proposed date of the early 8th century for the Jewish Quarter ostracon.

These limited parallels do not seal the case for an early date. One notices the same type of head with three distinct bars as in the *kaph* from the Jewish Quarter ostracon on Arad Ostracon no. 40 from Stratum VIII (late 8th century).[196] The vertical shaft does have a greater slope than the one on the ostracon from the Jewish Quarter, but another *kaph* that contains a vertical shaft with very little slope is found on the Siloam Tomb (אשר על הבית) inscription republished and deciphered by Avigad.[197] Although this tomb inscription is incised instead of inked like the ostracon from the Jewish Quarter,[198] the presence of such a *kaph*—in light of so few parallels of other late 8th-century inked ostraca—should give one pause in dating the Jewish Quarter ostracon solely on the letter *kaph*. In short, there are not enough clear parallels to establish that the vertical shaft of a *kaph* with little slope is diagnostic of the early 8th century. It may be that the head of the *kaph* from the Jewish Quarter Ostracon is indeed archaic,

---

[195]For photographs cf. Z. Meshel, "Kuntilat ʿAjrûd—An Israelite Site on the Sinai Border," *Qad* 9 (1976) 122; and S. Aḥituv, *Handbook of Ancient Hebrew Inscriptions. From the Period of the First Commonwealth and the Beginning of the Second Commonwealth (Hebrew, Philistine, Edomite, Moabite, Ammonite, and the Bileam Inscription)* (Biblical Encyclopedia Library; Jerusalem: Bialik Institute, 1992) 155, 157 (Hebrew).

[196]Aharoni, *Arad Inscriptions*, 70.

[197]Avigad, "Epitaph," 137-52, pls. 8-10.

[198]See discussion in A. G. Vaughn, "Palaeographic Dating of Judean Seals and Its Significance for Biblical Research," *BASOR* 313 (1999) 43-64, for the problems in drawing paleographic conclusions from inscriptions on different media.

but even here there are parallels from the late 8th century that seem as likely as the early 8th century. This same sort of argument holds true for the vertical shafts of the *mem* and the *nun* that contain very little slope. Aharoni attempts to date these as features pointing to an early 8th-century date,[199] but they could very well be found in the late 8th century.

The other letter from the Jewish Quarter ostracon emphasized by Aharoni is the *qoph*. Unfortunately, Aharoni does not specify the characteristics that make this letter "early."[200] The letter consists of a vertical shaft that does not extend to the top of the head. The head is composed of an "S" stroke that leaves a small opening above the vertical shaft. This form is comparable to *qophs* found in Lachish Letter IV and in an ostracon from Meṣad Hashavyahu.[201] The former ostracon dates to the early 6th century, while the latter comes from the 7th. Both attestations clearly show that, although the letter in question on the ostracon from the Jewish Quarter may come from the 8th century, it also has paleographic parallels in the 7th and early 6th centuries.

Aharoni probably refers to a closed head of the letter *qoph* in the Jewish Quarter ostracon instead of an open head described in the preceding paragraph. In the closed form, the head begins with a horizontal bar starting from vertical shaft and extends to the left, and this stroke continues in a clockwise, circular motion around to the other side of the downward shaft below the starting horizontal bar to form a three-quarter, pie-shaped head. As the head of the *qoph* in the Jewish Quarter ostracon is blurred, it is easy to mistake the open head for a closed head, especially in several of the published photographs.[202] However, close examination of the published photographs[203] and the ostracon itself (now on display in the Israel Museum) reveal that the head definitely contains an opening, albeit a slight one.

In summary, none of the letters are clearly diagnostic of the early 8th century. A separate study by the present author that was referenced in Chapter 1 has presented a detailed analysis of the paleographic dating of Hebrew seals and demonstrated the difficulty in dating precisely with a small sample of inscriptions.[204] Although caution should be exercised

---

[199]Aharoni, *Arad Inscriptions*, 132.

[200]Aharoni, *Arad Inscriptions*, 132.

[201]J. Naveh, "A Hebrew Letter from the Seventh Century B.C.," *IEJ* 10 (1960) 129-39, pl. 17.

[202]Cf. photographs in Aharoni, *Arad Inscriptions*, 132; and Miller, "EI," 43-46.

[203]Cf. esp. Avigad, "Jewish Quarter, 1971," pl. 42:B.

[204]Vaughn, "Palaeographic Dating," 43-64.

in drawing conclusions for the dating of inked ostraca from a study on the paleographic dating of seals, the same problems surface with regard to the inked ostraca. It is possible to take a few isolated letters and find parallels from the mid-8th century all the way down to the early 6th century. It seems from the archaic character of the *kaph* that the ostracon should indeed be dated to at least the late 8th century, but the evidence is too meager to argue compellingly for an earlier date. Consequently, the first objection raised by Barkay to Broshi's view that the development of the Western Hill first began in full force after the fall of Samaria in 722 BCE is not convincing.

Barkay's second objection is that typological parallels between the tower just north of the Broad Wall in the Jewish Quarter and the southwest corner of the palace in the fortress from Lachish Level IV suggest a date in the early 8th century for the Jewish Quarter tower.[205] The parallels exist between these two buildings, but it is not convincing in the absence of other data that the tower and gate from the Jewish Quarter *must* date from the early 8th century as Lachish Level IV. At best, these typological parallels are only suggestive of an early date.

Barkay's third and final objection is more convincing. He highlights the parallels of pottery and other small finds to materials from Lachish Level IV. He says that "different elements in the Iron Age pottery from Avigad's excavations, like the emergence of lug handles and bar handles on bowls and the types of polishing, recall the general characteristics of Level IV at Lachish."[206] Avigad's excavations have not been published, so it is impossible to verify Barkay's observations. Barkay admits that this is a problem and makes the following disclaimer in a footnote: "I saw the pottery from the excavations of the Jewish Quarter thanks to the generosity of Prof. N. Avigad. It is self-evident that [my] impression [of the pottery] is only limited, and it is necessary to wait for the analysis and publication of the material."[207] Since Avigad unfortunately died before his findings were published, for the foreseeable future, Barkay's comments must suffice.

In light of Barkay's observations, it is helpful at this point in the discussion to return to the refutation of Alt and Noth's position on Jerusalem. Both Alt and Noth held that Jerusalem was merely an administrative center, and that most of Judah continued to live and make a livelihood in the lands of their inheritance. According to Alt and Noth, Jerusalem was inhabited only by the king, the king's family, and the

---

[205]Barkay, "Northern and Western Jerusalem," 490.

[206]Barkay, "Northern and Western Jerusalem," 490.

[207]Barkay, "Northern and Western Jerusalem," 490, n. 6.

royal guard or mercenaries. The recent excavations in the Jewish Quarter showed that Alt and Noth were wrong in this aspect of their argument. Jerusalem developed into a thriving capital with extramural settlements by at least the late 8th century BCE. It is thus seen that the Judean monarchs did not make it a policy to prohibit settlement and development of the area, at least during the latter half of the monarchy.

It does not seem reasonable to suppose that, if settlement had been prohibited in areas other than the lands of the old Judean inheritance, the situation would have changed only after the fall of the north. On the other hand, if Alt and Noth had been correct about the sole administrative function of Jerusalem, then one would expect that any refugees from the north would have been forced to settle in the inheritance lands of Judah along with the other Judeans. It is unclear why an exception would have been made only for the northern Israelites.

The converse position is more logical. The archaeological evidence of settlement on the Western Hill proves that Alt and Noth's theories about the sole administrative character of Jerusalem are in error, and that the settlement of the area around Jerusalem was permitted from the beginning of the monarchy. Jerusalem did not grow overnight from the time David established the monarchy to include the Western Hill, but it also seems reasonable from a historical standpoint to interpret the ceramic evidence of late 9th and early 8th-century life as evidence that the extramural settlements began gradually by at least the beginning of the 8th century. Indeed, this is the same picture of development that occurs in the Shephelah. In the Shephelah, Dagan showed that settlement grew steadily throughout the Iron Age with a peak in the late 8th century. It is reasonable to assume that when refugees came south after the fall of Israel, many of them settled in Jerusalem. However, this new influx of settlers should not be taken, as Broshi argues, as the primary cause for the settlement and development of the land around the old City of David.

f. Extent of Extramural Settlements Around Jerusalem.
The case for the gradual development of the extramural settlements is supplemented by a study of the extent of this settlement during Iron Age II. Barkay's dissertation research shows that many burials were located far north and west of the Western Hill. It is commonly accepted that burial caves were constructed just outside inhabited areas,[208] so it seems reasonable to conclude that unfortified extramural settlements would have existed north and west of the fortified areas of the City of David and the Western Hill. This theory is corroborated by the existence

---

[208] Avigad, *Discovering Jerusalem*, 55-56.

of the remains of much fragmented Iron Age architecture and Iron Age pottery in the areas to the north and west. Barkay's research also reveals a wide area in Jerusalem where Iron II residential remains and pottery have been found.[209] From Iron Age remains in the modern Christian and Muslim Quarters of the Old City, as well as just outside the modern Damascus gate, it seems the extramural settlements of Iron Age II Jerusalem expanded far beyond the confines of the Western Hill and the City of David. Coupling this tendency for Iron Age II Jerusalem to grow beyond the confines of its borders with the evidence of extramural settlement dating back to at least the start of the 8th century, one may interpret these extramural settlements as growing gradually over several centuries and not merely springing up overnight with the arrival of refugees.

It is helpful at this point to refer to what Barkay has labeled the "supermaximalist" approach for the settlement of Jerusalem. Both at the 1984 International Congress on Biblical Archaeology[210] and in his dissertation,[211] Barkay has presented a proposal for understanding the growth of Jerusalem as not being limited to just the Western Hill and the City of David. Barkay's suggestion that Iron II Jerusalem included extramural settlements north and west of the Western Hill is the most probable position. It should also be noted that just as the Western Hill had not been thoroughly excavated before Avigad's excavations, the modern areas of the Christian and Muslim Quarters in the Old City have not been excavated because of dense modern building.

Summary

All these factors point to Iron Age Jerusalem during the reigns of Hezekiah and Josiah as a city that served much more than an administrative role. Unfortunately, it is impossible at this time to determine precisely the comparable size and strength of Jerusalem in Hezekiah's reign as compared with its size during Josiah's reign. It is possible (but not necessary) that Josiah's city was larger than Hezekiah's. However, the data show that Hezekiah's Jerusalem had already become a thriving capital city and was not simply an administrative center (contra Alt and Noth). These data indicate that, at the very least, the area of Jerusalem encompassed by fortifications was not significantly less during Hezekiah's reign than during Josiah's reign. In terms of the present investigation,

---

[209]Barkay, "Northern and Western Jerusalem," fig. 167.

[210]G. Barkay, "Response to 'Revealing Biblical Jerusalem,'" *Biblical Archaeology Today: Proceedings of the International Congress on Biblical Archaeology. Jerusalem, April 1984* (ed. J. Amitai; Jerusalem: Israel Exploration Society, 1985) 476-77.

[211]Barkay, "Northern and Western Jerusalem," 451-58.

this conclusion adds further credence to the position set forward by Rosenbaum that the high status of Hezekiah gave Dtr a reason to omit some specifics of Hezekiah's economic buildup and political strength.

5. The Judean Desert

a. Introduction

In Finkelstein's survey article, he uses only three sentences to describe the situation in the Judean Desert with regard to settlement in the 8th and 7th centuries. He categorically claims, "Permanent 8th-century BCE sites have not been recorded in the Judean desert (with the possible exception of Ein-Gedi...). All late Iron II sites found in the region date to the 7th/early 6th centuries BCE."[212] E. Stern presents a more detailed discussion of the area and draws a similar conclusion:

> Even more impressive are Josiah's accomplishments along his eastern border, in the region extending from Jericho down to En-gedi, which recently have been clarified. We can state with confidence that during the entire Iron Age this whole area was not settled (except perhaps the town of Jericho itself) until the arrival of Josiah.[213]

In spite of these sweeping evaluative comments by prominent archaeologists like Finkelstein and Stern, the situation is not as clear as their treatments suggest. Perhaps the first clue to the ambiguity can be found in the fact that both Finkelstein and Stern state that all settlement in the Judean Desert dates to the late 7th century with the possible exception of one site; however, each names a different site. Actually, there are possible exceptions at multiple sites, but unfortunately the present poor state of publication of these areas does not allow for a definitive analysis.

b. Ḥorvat Shilḥah

Ḥorvat Shilḥah is the site with the highest probability of sole 7th-century settlement. This site is a small fort or outpost building on the road between Jerusalem and Jericho. The fort likely facilitated travel and provided protection for travelers. The excavators report that all of "the pottery is most homogeneous, and it is typical of the end of the Iron Age

---

[212]Finkelstein, "Days of Manasseh," 175.

[213]E. Stern, "The Kingdom of Judah in Its Last Days," *Scripture and Other Artifacts: Essays on the Bible and Archaeology in Honor of Philip J. King* (Louisville: Westminster/ John Knox Press, 1994) 399.

during the Judean monarchy."[214] Further, all of the floors at Shilḥah, whether they be earthen, plaster, or stone pavement, show signs of a short life. They were all thin and none were repaired.[215] Thus, the excavators conclude that the site was probably founded by Josiah to provide protection for the road from Jerusalem to Jericho, and it was destroyed or abandoned near the fall of Jerusalem in 586 BCE.[216]

Even though this site is probably to be dated to the late 7th century, the ambiguity arises with the occurrence of a *lmlk* stamped jar-handle fragment among the pottery. At other sites in the discussion presented above, similar occurrences of *lmlk* stamped handles are cited as suggestive that some sort of settlement, even if limited, might have taken place during the late 8th century. It is tempting to posit the same type of phenomenon at Ḥorvat Shilḥah; however, none of the published pottery plates support such a claim.[217] Moreover, A. Mazar informed the author during a conversation (August 6, 1995) that among the pottery from Shilḥah "there is not one 8th-century sherd other than the *lmlk* impression."

In light of all these factors, the *lmlk*-stamped handle most probably represents an isolated find discovered out of context and has no chronological significance for the *lmlk* phenomenon. Less likely, the stamped handle could represent the only clear evidence of a very limited reuse of royal-stamped jars in the 7th century. Finally, the isolated *lmlk*-stamped handle might suggest the earlier establishment of the building, but this interpretation must also be considered less likely since the excavator does not report any other late 8th-century pottery. It thus seems most prudent to conclude that Ḥorvat Shilḥah was probably established by Josiah.

c. Tel Goren (En-Gedi)

Tel Goren (En-Gedi) is the site noted by Finkelstein as a possible exception to the lack of settlement during the late 8th century. Finkelstein[218] calls attention to B. Mazar's publication of a tomb adjacent to Tel Goren that contains many parallels to Lachish Level III, Tell Beit Mirsim Stratum A, and Beth Shemesh Stratum IIc.[219] All of these layers date to the late

[214]A. Mazar, D. Amit, and Z. Ilan, "The 'Border Road' Between Michmash and Jericho and the Excavations at Horvat Shilḥah," *EI* 17 (1984) 243.

[215]A. Mazar, Amit, and Ilan, "Horvat Shilḥah," 238.

[216]A. Mazar, Amit, and Ilan, "Horvat Shilḥah," 248.

[217]A. Mazar, Amit, and Ilan, "Horvat Shilḥah," figs. 3-5.

[218]Finkelstein, "Days of Manasseh," 175.

[219]B. Mazar, T. Dothan, and I. Dunayevsky, *En-Gedi: The First and Second*

8th century and do not continue into the 7th century. The parallel references to Lachish, Tell Beit Mirsim, and Beth Shemesh found in the publication are too numerous to recount, but it is useful to highlight the cooking pots with multiple ridges on the neck.[220]

Settlement from the late 8th century is confirmed by several other small finds at Tel Goren, all of which are related to the *lmlk* jar phenomenon. The excavators discovered a stamped *lmlk zyp* jar handle in Locus 241 of Building 234.[221] Another jar handle with an official seal impression of a prancing horse figure instead of a PN was also found in an area adjacent to the *lmlk* handle in Locus 212. This jar handle belongs to a reconstructable Lachish Type 484 storage jar. The jar is now exhibited in the Israel Museum (I.A.A. no. 67-422). Barkay has presented a compelling argument for interpreting these iconographic seal impressions on *lmlk* jars as variants of the official seal impressions with PNN also found on *lmlk* jars.[222] An official seal impression (עבדי / לנחם) with a PN was also found at nearby Naḥal Arugot.[223] Finally, Barkay has shown that a two-winged stamped handle (also of Lachish Type 484), previously regarded as from the Babylonian period, belongs to the *lmlk* phenomenon of the late 8th century. It contains an enlarged two-winged emblem with the PN נרא. It seems that this seal impression represents a combination of an official seal impression and the two-winged *lmlk* emblem.[224]

In summary, signs of 8th-century life in and around Tel Goren are not isolated as they are at Ḥorvat Shilḥah. Whereas the latter site has only one isolated *lmlk* seal impression, the En-Gedi area has much pottery of varied types that is dated to the late 8th century. In light of all of these considerations, it seems certain that some sort of settlement at En-Gedi existed during Hezekiah's reign. Unfortunately, it is impossible to compare this settlement with the later town from Josiah's period. Moreover, it even seems logical to assume that the dearth of finds of late 8th-century origin in comparison to those from the late 7th-century point to a larger settlement at En-Gedi during Josiah's reign than during Hezekiah's. On

---

Seasons of Excavations, 1961-1962 (ᶜAtiqot [English Series] 5; Jerusalem: Israel Exploration Society, 1966) 53-58, figs. 29-33.

[220]B. Mazar, Dothan, and Dunayevsky. *En-Gedi*, 54, figs. 29:19, 29:21.

[221]B. Mazar and I. Dunayevsky, "En-Gedi: Fourth and Fifth Seasons of Excavations—Preliminary Report," *IEJ* 17 (1967) 137.

[222]G. Barkay, "'The Prancing Horse'—An Official Seal Impression from Judah of the 8th Century B.C.E." *Tel Aviv* 19 (1992) 124-29.

[223]G. Hadas, "Naḥal ᶜArugot, Seal Impression," *ESI* 2 (1983) 77.

[224]G. Barkay, "The King of Babylonia or a Judean Official?" *IEJ* 45 (1995) 41-47.

the other hand, the position espoused by Stern, that no settlement at all took place in the Judean Desert during Hezekiah's reign, is in need of correction with respect to the En-Gedi region.

d. Jericho (Tell es-Sultan)

Jericho is the site singled out by Stern as a possible exception to the lack of settlement during the late 8th century. Stern calls attention to Kenyon's final publication of Tell es-Sultan where there are several strata reported from the Iron Age. Kenyon's excavation of Trench I is the most relevant, because in this area there were two distinct building plans from separate Iron Age II strata. The second building was built on top of the ruins of the first, and each was destroyed by fire. It is thus impossible that they were contemporaneous.[225]

The architectural evidence is confirmed by the pottery. In the publication of the pottery from Trench I,[226] there is a recognizable difference between the forms of the two strata. Unfortunately, the excavators do not provide parallel references with pottery from other sites, but several distinctive 8th-century forms are noticeable. Finally, the presence of 8th-century pottery is confirmed by a two-winged *lmlk* handle from the earlier stratum from Trench I.[227]

Due to Kenyon's method of excavating in only narrow trenches, it is difficult to assess whether the settlement was greater during Hezekiah's or Josiah's reign. The evidence leans towards a more significant settlement during Josiah's reign, because the only other trench excavated with Iron Age remains (Trench II) has only one clear stratum. This stratum seems to be placed at the end of the Iron Age, and there was no sign of an earlier stratum in Trench II.[228] Coupling this evidence with the fact that other sites in the Judean desert have a greater settlement rate during Josiah's reign than Hezekiah's, one judges that Jericho was likely settled during Hezekiah's reign, but that Josiah had a more significant presence.

---

[225]K. M. Kenyon and T. A. Holland, *Excavations at Jericho, Volume 3: The Architecture and Stratigraphy of the Tell* (London: British School of Archaeology at Jerusalem, 1981) 111-13.

[226]K. M. Kenyon and T. A. Holland, *Excavations at Jericho, Volume 5: The Pottery of Phases at the Tell and Other Finds* (London: British School of Archaeology at Jerusalem, 1983) 58-84.

[227]K. M. Kenyon and T. A. Holland, *Excavations at Jericho Volume 4: The Pottery Type Series and Other Finds* (London: British School of Archaeology at Jerusalem, 1982) 537, 539.

[228]Kenyon and Holland, *Jericho, Volume 3*, 171-73.

e. Buqê^{c}ah Sites[229]

The last set of sites to be analyzed in this section is a group of three fortresses (Khirbet Abū Ṭabaq, Khirbet es-Samrah, and Khirbet el-Maqari) in the Buqê^{c}ah valley. Once again, the question of settlement during Hezekiah's and Josiah's reigns is not as clear as one might assume. Finkelstein[230] and Stern[231] both refer to the unpublished dissertation of L. Stager[232] and a later article by Stager[233] as support for their separate conclusions that the establishment of the Buqê^{c}ah sites took place in the second half of the 7th century; however, a reexamination of the pottery plates, the historical analysis, and the excavation descriptions from Stager's dissertation reveals signs of settlement during the late 8th century at the Buqê^{c}ah sites.[234]

A review of Stager's historical analysis shows that he assumes the destruction of Lachish Level III in 596 BCE. He also follows Lance in affirming the similarity of pottery from Ramat Raḥel Strata VA and VB,[235] and he holds that Ramat Raḥel Stratum VB could not have been established before 650 BCE.[236] These presuppositions are central reasons that Stager concludes that the Buqê^{c}ah sites were established in the late 7th century

---

[229]Throughout this section on the Buqê^{c}ah sites, I am indebted to James Hardin for sharing his analysis of the pottery plates from Stager's dissertation and for providing a detailed critique of an earlier version my treatment of these sites.

[230]Finkelstein, "Days of Manasseh," 176.

[231]Stern, "Kingdom of Judah, 402-4.

[232]Cf. L. E. Stager, "Ancient Agriculture in the Judaean Desert: A Case Study of the Buqê^{c}ah Valley in the Iron Age" (Ph.D. dissertation, Harvard University, 1975) esp. 249-50, 257-58.

[233]Cf. L. E. Stager, "Farming in the Judean Desert During the Iron Age," *BASOR* 221 (1976) 145.

[234]The articles by Finkelstein and Stern should not be enlisted as support that the details from Stager's dissertation preclude settlement at the Buqê^{c}ah sites during the late 8th century. Even though both Finkelstein and Stern refer to Stager's dissertation, neither scholar provides precise citations. Finkelstein ("Days of Judah," 176) merely cites Stager's entire thesis without listing specific pages. Stern ("Kingdom of Judah," 402-4) refers only to the large block of pages (171-267) that was listed in Stager's 1976 article (cf. Stager, "Farming in the Judean Desert," 145 n. 4). It seems that both scholars concentrated on Stager's general historical conclusions listed in his 1976 article and did not reexamine the details in his unpublished dissertation.

[235]Lance, "Royal Stamps," 320 n. 26, quoted by Stager, "Agricultute in the Judaean Desert," 249.

[236]Stager, "Agriculture in the Judaean Desert," 249-50.

and only experienced a short lifespan. He says, "It is difficult to see how the shallow-deposits in the Buqêᶜah, especially, could represent such a lengthy span. The same argument could be made for the shabbily built houses of Lachish, Level II."[237] As subsequent research has disproven these presuppositions,[238] one must reexamine the specifics of Stager's data to determine if his arguments for the absence of late 8th-century settlement at the Buqêᶜah sites are still valid.

The detailed descriptions of the excavations at Khirbet Abū Ṭabaq reveal signs of settlement during the late eight century. In Area 3 at Khirbet Abū Ṭabaq, there were seven Iron II phases.[239] The earliest phase (Phase 1) contained a fragment of a rilled-rim cooking pot that was found on Floor .020.[240] This rim fragment is comparable to pottery forms from Lachish Level III and Ramat Raḥel Stratum VB.[241] In a later phase (Phase 3), Iron II sherds included a bowl rim[242] that is comparable to examples from Lachish Level II and Ramat Raḥel Stratum VA.[243] Phases 4-7 contained pottery that was also similar to forms from the late 7th century.[244] Stager summed up Phases 1-7 of Area 3 as follows: "Thus from bottom to top, Phases 1-7, we have a cycle repeated several times of primary deposits of bricky material used as a living surface whose organic remains—mostly dung and chaff—were then burnt off."[245] Building on the parallels from Lachish Level III and noting Stager's presuppositional error in dating Lachish Level III to the late 7th century, the investigator should date the earliest phase as Khirbet Abū Ṭabaq to the late 8th century. The presence of 7th-century pottery forms in the later phases shows that the site continued in usage throughout the 7th century. Similarly, Phase 2 of Area 4 at Ṭabaq contains several pottery sherds found in an occupational debris layer that are characteristic of the late 8th century.[246]

---

[237]Stager, "Agriculture in the Judaean Desert," 250.

[238]Cf. esp. the work of Ussishkin ("Destruction," 50-54) supporting Tufnell's thesis for a 701 BCE destruction date of Lachish Level III (see detailed commentary below in Chapter 3). Cf. esp. the work of M. Aharoni and Y. Aharoni ("Stratification of Judahite Sites") for the establishment of the differences in the pottery of Ramat Raḥel Strata VB and VA.

[239]Stager, "Agriculture in the Judaean Desert," 52-59.

[240]Cf. Stager, "Agriculture in the Judaean Desert," pl. 1:1.

[241]Cf. Aharoni and Aharoni, 76, figs. 2:4, 3:4.

[242]Stager, "Agriculture in the Judaean Desert," 55, pl. 1:2.

[243]Cf. Aharoni and Aharoni, 84, pl. 6:3.

[244]Stager, "Agriculture in the Judaean Desert," 56-59.

[245]Stager, "Agriculture in the Judaean Desert," 59.

[246]James Hardin has drawn my attention to the plate drawings of three

The discovery of two *lmlk* impressions at Khirbet es-Samrah provides additional evidence of settlement at the Buqêᶜah sites during the late eight century. In Area B, a *lmlk* stamp was discovered that probably contains the GN מנשה. The handle was found in the gate area, and Stager states that "the rest of the pottery from ashy debris in the gate was uniformly Iron II."[247] The second *lmlk* impression was located in Phase 2 of a storage magazine in Area 8-9. The handles contained a two-winged *lmlk* impression with incised concentric circles. It was found in the occupational debris, so it clearly dates Phase 2 to the late 8th century.[248] This same phase also contained three rilled rim pot sherds[249] that have parallels to Lachish Level III.[250] Thus, just as with Khirbet Abū Ṭabaq, there was at least some settlement at Khirbet es-Samrah during the late 8th century.

In light of all these factors, it is instructive to include the historical assessment of the Buqêᶜah sites found in a survey article of these sites published in 1993 by Cross. In that article, Cross dates the establishment of these sites to either the 8th or the 7th century. He draws attention to a *lmlk* jar handle found at Khirbet es-Samrah and states that another site (Khirbet el-Maqari) experienced two violent destructions.[251] Cross concludes that "Hezekiah or Josiah may have been responsible for settling and developing the Buqeiᶜa. Both kings are credited with building operations."[252] Given the indicators of settlement during the late 8th century cited in the preceding paragraphs, it seems safe to conclude that the Buqêᶜah sites were established at least by Hezekiah's time, and that the sites continued in use during the 7th century. Further, the presence of two *lmlk* impressions at Khirbet es-Samrah and two *lmlk* impressions

---

bowls from Phase 2 of Area 4 at Ṭabaq (pls. 1:20, 24, 29) that are characteristic of the late 8th century. For a description of this phase, cf. Stager, "Agriculture in the Judaean Desert," 71-75.

[247]Stager, "Agriculture in the Judaean Desert," 140. Stager also states ("Agriculture in the Judaean Desert," 169 n. 55) that he only located the *lmlk* impression at the Albright Institute. The rest of the pottery from the gate area was missing, so his dating had to be based on the pottery plates.

[248]Stager, "Agriculture in the Judaean Desert," 147, 149.

[249]Stager, "Agriculture in the Judaean Desert," 143, pls. 3:6-8.

[250]James Hardin has called my attention to a cooking pot (pl. 3:36) with strong parallels in the late 8th century and many sherds that are typical of the transition from the late 8th to the 7th century (cf. pls. 3:33-35, 4:21-25, and 4:27-28).

[251]F. M. Cross, Jr., "El Buqeiᶜa," *NEAEHL* (ed. E. Stern; New York: Macmillan; Jerusalem: Israel Exploration Society, 1993) 268.

[252]Cross, "El Buqeiᶜa," 269.

at Jericho indicates that the Buqê°ah region was used by Hezekiah as a supply route to send royal goods to the Judean Desert region.[253]

Summary

The situation is the same in almost all of the major sites in the Judean Desert. Hezekiah seemed to have some settlement, but the extent of his settlement is uncertain. Horvat Shilhah is the only possible case of sole 7th-century settlement. Even there, however, a *lmlk* handle raised the question of late 8th-century settlement, but the absence of any other late 8th-century pottery mitigated against an interpretation of settlement at Horvat Shilhah during the earlier period. In each of the other locations (En-Gedi, Jericho, and the Buqê°ah sites), there is scattered evidence of 8th-century settlement, but the more significant settlement seems to come from the period of Josiah.

Josiah had a more significant presence than Hezekiah in the Judean Desert. However, two additional observations are important. First, there are signs of Hezekiah's influence and settlement of the Judean Desert, so he should not be viewed as totally absent from the region. Second, even though Josiah is seen to have a greater role in the Judean Desert, one must question how significant this greater role was to measuring the economic buildup and civil power of Hezekiah and Josiah. All of the Judean Desert sites are limited in size due to the arid climate, thus a greater presence by Josiah in the region is not nearly as significant as a greater presence by Hezekiah in the Shephelah. Likewise, the Judean Desert was a marginalized part of Judah. Just as increased settlement in the marginal area of the Negeb by Josiah might reflect the inability to settle other areas, the same sort of factors likely operated in the Judean Desert. On the other hand, Stern convincingly shows that the Judean Desert played an important role in international commerce—probably in the trade of spices and perfumes.[254] Thus, a stronger role by Josiah in the region can also be taken as evidence of international ties with the nations on the eastern border of Judah, primarily Edom.

---

[253]Stager ("Agriculture in the Judaean Desert," 227-28) uses the presence of *lmlk* handles at Jericho and Khirbet es-Samrah as evidence of Josiah's use of the Buqê°ah as a royal supply route. Since the *lmlk* jars were used during Hezekiah's reign instead of Josiah's reign as Stager argued, the same criteria support a royal trade route in the Judean dessert during the reign of Hezekiah.

[254]Stern, "Kingdom of Judah."

C. Conclusions

The Shephelah experienced four times more settlement and development of resources during the reign of Hezekiah than during that of Josiah. Further, settlement of Jerusalem, the towns surrounding it, and the Judean Hills was at least not significantly greater during Josiah's reign than during Hezekiah's. The only areas where Josiah had a greater presence were in the marginal areas of the Judean Desert and the Negeb.

Several points are relevant to the investigation presented here, which analyzes the regimes of Hezekiah and Josiah. First, the archaeological data point to a reign with much economic buildup and great civil and administrative power for Hezekiah. Moreover, this economic buildup and civil strength exceeds that of Josiah in some areas and may rival Josiah's economic buildup and civil strength in other places. Second, Josiah seems to have had a greater presence in terms of settlement and development only in areas that were regarded as marginal during Hezekiah's reign.[255] This fact should not detract from the importance of Manasseh and Josiah utilizing these areas, but it does indicate that the devastation suffered at the hands of Sennacherib forced later Judean monarchs to develop less productive areas than Hezekiah originally had at his disposal.

In conclusion, the archaeological data support Rosenbaum's explanation for the omission by Dtr of specifics regarding the economic buildup and civil strength of Hezekiah.[256] Moreover, these data also corroborate the specific details concerning Hezekiah's economic and civil strength given in 2 Chr 32:27-30. The discussion on the *lmlk* jars, which follows in Chapter 3 will supplement these data and further corroborate the positive account of Hezekiah by the Chronicler.

---

[255]Cf. Finkelstein, "Days of Manasseh," 176-80.

[256]These archaeological data also make it necessary to reevaluate the scholarly preference for the greater political power of Josiah over Hezekiah. For instance, F. L. Moriarty wrote the following more than 30 years ago: "Some [of Hezekiah's] reform activities seem to have been carried out in the north by fervent Yahwists returning from the Passover in Jerusalem. But it is most unlikely that Hezekiah gained any real political hold over the northern provinces even though he may have dreamed of some kind of restoration of the Davidic empire. A century later Josiah had far greater success in acheiving this aim even while Judah was under nominal Assyrian suzerainty" (F. L. Moriarty, "The Chronicler's Account of Hezekiah's Reform," *CBQ* 27 [1965] 399-406).

THREE

THE *LMLK* JARS: THEIR BEARING ON THE REIGN OF HEZEKIAH

A. Preliminary Issues and History of Research

1. Introduction

The *lmlk* (= [belonging] to the king) jars are some of the most abundant historical data available from the late 8th century. Although scholars have known about the seal impressions on these jars for more than 100 years, and although more than 1000 *lmlk* seal impressions have been listed in various corpora, there is still much that is not understood about their function and origin. The situation is further complicated by the fact that many scholarly opinions on the *lmlk* jars were originally presented as hypotheses but are now cited by biblical scholars as fact, almost without qualification. The appendices to this monograph present new data on the *lmlk* and official impressions to provide a basis from which to clarify some of the issues surrounding these jars. While these new data clarify some of the issues, they do not solve all of the problems. Many questions will remain unsolved until still further data are brought forward. However, we can now determine partial answers to some of the historical questions, and these clarifications prove helpful in interpreting the Chronicler's account of Hezekiah.

Before these conclusions can be demonstrated, one must first survey the history of scholarship surrounding the *lmlk* jars. This survey not only reveals unresolved issues but also shows that several unproven hypotheses about the *lmlk* phenomenon are often presupposed as fact in the scholarly debate. After identifying these key issues, one can proceed into a discussion of how the phenomenon of the *lmlk* jars is helpful in understanding the kingdom of Hezekiah. At the same time, it is important to discuss how the seal impressions of private individuals, found on the same type of jar handles, are related to the phenomenon of the royal seal impressions.

2. Previous Arguments for the Dating of the *lmlk* Jars

Since the earliest discoveries, the inscription למלך made it apparent that the jars associated with the *lmlk* seal impressions were somehow associated with a royal function, even if the exact nature of that function was uncertain. It has been widely debated in which kingdom or kingdoms these jars were used. Part of the ambiguity regarding the dating of these jars was due to the wide variation in the paleographic style of the letters found on the impressions. Albright interpreted this variation as evidence that the impressions dated from the late 8th century to the beginning of the 6th century BCE.[1] In Albright's scheme, Class I seals were used during the reign of Hezekiah, Class II seals were used during Manasseh's kingdom, and Class III seals were used by Josiah and subsequent Judean kings until the first Babylonian deportation in 597 BCE.[2] Diringer followed Albright in this conclusion, so his interpretation also had ramifications for the dating of various Judean stratigraphic levels.[3]

These paleographic arguments were confirmed initially by C. L. Starkey's stratigraphic investigation at Lachish. In an article that appeared shortly before he was murdered, Starkey claimed that there was not sufficient variation in the pottery of Levels II and III to justify a large chronological difference in the occupation of those levels. Thus, he postulated that Level III had a destruction date during Nebuchadnezzar's campaign in 597 BCE, while Level II was destroyed in 586 BCE.[4] As a result of this interpretation, the use of the *lmlk* jar handles was seen as material evidence for the reforms of Josiah.[5]

After the publication of Starkey's excavations in 1953, the synthesis presented by Starkey and Albright was almost immediately challenged by O. Tufnell who argued that Level III should be dated to 701 BCE. Tufnell reported that the excavations subsequent to Starkey's death

---

[1]Albright, *Tell Beit Mirsim III*, 74.

[2]Albright, *Tell Beit Mirsim III*, 74. The use of subdivisions or "classes" was developed by Diringer (D. Diringer, "On Ancient Hebrew Inscriptions Discovered at Tell Ed-Duweir (Lachish)—II," *PEQ* [1941] 91-101). Class I refers to four-winged impressions of the styled type. Class II refers to four-winged impressions that contain more square and formal-looking letters. Class III refers to all the two-winged impressions.

[3]D. Diringer, "The Royal Jar-Handle Stamps of Ancient Judah," *BA* 12 (1949) 84-86.

[4]J. L. Starkey, "Excavations at Tell Ed Duweir," *PEQ* (1937) 236.

[5]J. L. Starkey, "Lachish as Illustrating Bible History," *PEQ* (1937) 175; Albright, *Tell Beit Mirsim III*, 74-75.

resulted in the definition of two phases for a central road of Level II (1072).[6] She attributed these two phases to occupations with destructions in 597 and 586, respectively. Further, the continued excavations produced pottery from Level II that exhibited a wide variation from that of Level III. She saw no reasonable way to account for this variation with only a ten-year difference in occupation; thus, she concluded that Level III must have been destroyed by Sennacherib in 701 BCE. She said that Starkey's evaluation "was made in 1937 before the discovery of the Level II rooms, which were only excavated after his death. If he had had this evidence to consider, I feel sure that his conclusion would not have differed from my own."[7]

The problem of these conflicting reports was compounded by Tufnell's conclusions which, if valid, necessitated redating strata at almost every other major archaeological site in Judah.[8] All of the levels that needed to be redated exhibited a high level of growth and activity; thus, many scholars were inclined to associate these levels with Josiah's rule which is described in great detail in Kings. The net result was that British and American scholars tended to side with Starkey and date Lachish Level III to 597 and interpret the *lmlk* jars as evidence of Josiah's reform.[9] On the other hand, Israeli scholars in general sided with Tufnell and held that Lachish Level III was destroyed in 701 by Sennacherib.[10] For the purposes of the present study, the issues at stake are whether the more highly populated and active Lachish Level III is to be associated with Hezekiah or with Josiah, and whether the related phenomenon of the *lmlk* jars is associated with Hezekiah's or Josiah's reign.

---

[6]Tufnell, *Lachish III*, 56-58, 95-98.

[7]O. Tufnell, "Hazor, Samaria, and Lachich: A Synthesis," *PEQ* (1959):90-105, 103; cf. Ussishkin, "Destruction," 32.

[8]Aharoni and Aharoni, "Stratification of Judahite Sites."

[9]Cf. F. M. Cross, Jr., "Judean Stamps," *EI* 9 (1969) 20-21; P. Lapp, "Late Royal Seals," 16-18; Lance, "Royal Stamps," 321-329; W. F. Albright, "Some Recent Publications," *BASOR* 132 (1953) 46; W. F. Albright, "Recent Progress in Palestinian Archaeology: Samaria-Sebaste III and Hazor I," *BASOR* 150 (1958) 24; G. E. Wright, "Review of *Lachish III*," *VT* 5 (1955) 100-104.

[10]Cf. Y. Aharoni and R. Amiran. "A New Scheme for the Sub-Division of the Iron Age in Palestine," *IEJ* 8 (1958) 182 n. 42; Y. Aharoni, *The Land of the Bible, A Historical Geography* (Philadelphia: Westminster, 1967) 341-342; Aharoni, "Beersheba—The Stratification," 5-6; Aharoni, *Lachish V*, 15-16; Aharoni and Aharoni, "Stratification of Judahite Sites;" B. Mazar, "The Campaign of Sennacherib in Judaea," *The Military History of the Land of Israel in the Biblical Times* (ed. J. Liver, Tel Aviv, 1964) 295 n. 18 (Hebrew); Rainey, "Fate of Lachish."

The renewed excavations of Lachish by Ussishkin clarified the debate over Lachish Levels II and III. Many of the problems were resolved by excavating areas that were not completely understood by Starkey. One such key area was the "upper house" in area S. Ussishkin showed that the habitation units located at various elevations actually belonged to the same stratigraphic unit.[11] In area S, important buildings linked to occupation during Level III include the "government storehouse" and a series of rooms just to the south of this storehouse.[12]

Although these clarifications confirmed Tufnell's conclusion that the pottery from Level III was different from that of Level II, Ussishkin did not take this confirmation as conclusive. Rather, he realized that the debate had resulted from the use of "indirect" data such as historical references and pottery. He aimed to present a more comprehensive picture by connecting these stratigraphic clarifications from Level III with all the other strata down to the Late Bronze level. He stated:

> It seemed . . . that a satisfactory and conclusive solution to our problem would be found only by means of direct stratigraphic evidence recovered from the mound. By learning the stratigraphy down to the Late Bronze Age levels, it would become apparent or not if there exists another Iron Age level under Level III which may be identified with the city destroyed in 701 BCE.[13]

Ussishkin's excavations revealed that there were only three Iron Age strata that could possibly be associated with the stratum destroyed by Sennacherib in 701 BCE—Levels III, IV, and V. Level V showed some signs of destruction by fire, but the pottery was a red-slipped, hand-

---

[11]Ussishkin, "Destruction," 42-44.

[12]Ussishkin, "Destruction," 46. The clarification of area S is also important from a paleographic point of view, because one of these rooms (1003) contained a bulla sealed by destruction debris. Tufnell published this room as belonging to either Level II or III (Tufnell, *Lachish III*, 104, 106-108). With dating of this room secured to the late 8th century by Ussishkin, this bulla becomes important paleographically, because it contains a script that is characteristic of what has previously been identified as late 7th-century script. Of particular importance is the *samek* that exhibits a tick-stroke on the lowest horizontal bar which connects this bar with the vertical shaft. To date, this *samek* joins only one other example of this type from a clear late 8th-century context. Moreover, the other example is dated because it is found on a *lmlk* type jar, but it comes from an illicit dig. Thus, although this is a rare form in the 8th century, it provides continued evidence that it is very difficult to date seals based on their paleographic character alone.

[13]Ussishkin, "Destruction," 36.

burnished type common in the Iron I period and was not found during the Iron II period (the time of Sennacherib's campaign). There is a clear separation between Levels IV and III, but there is no indication that Level IV was destroyed by fire. In addition, all of the significant Level III buildings either reused the walls or the foundation walls from Level IV, so it seemed that the transition from Level IV to Level III was not caused by a military defeat.[14] Level III, on the other hand, did exhibit a violent destruction and pottery consistent with the Iron II period. Thus, Level III was the only candidate for the stratum destroyed by Sennacherib.[15]

Further confirmation was obtained through the excavation of the siege ramp. Ussishkin was able to show that the construction of the ramp was identical with pictorial depictions of the siege of Lachish by Sennacherib found on the Assyrian reliefs from Ninevah. Moreover, battering rams were located that matched the type shown on these same reliefs.[16] Finally, Ussishkin drew attention to Starkey's discovery of a mass burial of about 1500 people in a tomb associated with Level III as further evidence of killing on the magnitude depicted in the Assyrian reliefs from Ninevah.[17]

In light of Ussishkin's work, one sees that Level III was the only possible candidate for destruction by Sennacherib in 701 BCE. No *lmlk* impressions were found in Level II, while both the two-winged and four-winged varieties were found in Level III. Thus, at least at Lachish, both the two- and four-winged types of *lmlk* impressions were used before the destruction of Lachish in 701 BCE, but no *lmlk* impressions were found in the stratum that was destroyed in 586 and had a minor destruction in 597. These findings suggest that the *lmlk* impressions (both the two- and four-winged types) were used during Hezekiah's reign, but that neither type was used during Josiah's reign.

Ussishkin's arguments to associate the stamped *lmlk* jars solely with Hezekiah have received general acceptance; however, A. D. Tushingham challenged part of his conclusions as recently as 1992. Tushingham reopened the argument that the two-winged impressions are later than the four-winged variety. Instead of stressing the earlier

---

[14]Ussishkin postulated that the cause for the end of Level IV may have been an earthquake during the reign of Uzziah, such as the one described in Amos 1:1. However, Ussishkin ("Destruction," 52) admitted that this hypothesis was impossible to prove.

[15]Ussishkin, "Destruction," 50-53.

[16]D. Ussishkin, "Excavations at Tel Lachish (1973-1977): Preliminary Report," *Tel Aviv* 5 (1978) 67-74.

[17] Tufnell, *Lachish III*, 193-196; pl. 4:3-6; Ussishkin, "Destruction," 53.

paleographic arguments,[18] Tushingham presented a reinterpretation of stratigraphic conclusions from Jerusalem. He admitted that in some cases two- and four-winged types were found in the same stratum (as at Lachish), but he argued that this did not preclude the use of the two-winged stamps after Hezekiah because there was a large occupation gap at Lachish between Levels III and II. More important for Tushingham, he held that the two-and four-winged stamps were never used together inside Jerusalem proper. Further, he reinterpreted the data from Kenyon's excavations in Jerusalem to point towards the existence of the two-winged impression after the period of Hezekiah, although it went out of existence during the reign of Josiah and seemed to be replaced by the rosette stamp.[19]

It will be shown below in a discussion of the PNN found on seal impressions on *lmlk* jar handles that Tushingham's arguments are not convincing. There is little evidence for a large-scale usage of the *lmlk* impressions past the time of Hezekiah. It is sufficient at this point in the discussion to point out that Tushingham ignores the evidence of Avigad[20] and Barkay[21] that Jerusalem had extended its boundaries during the late 8th century, so his attempt to exclude the discovery of both the two-winged and four-winged types outside of the City of David is questionable. Moreover, two-winged and four-winged impressions have been found in the same stratum at Ramat Rahel and Tel Batash (Timnah), both of which have a destruction date of 701 BCE. Both the two-winged and four-winged stamps were thus used during Hezekiah's reign. This point will be clarified further below in the discussion surrounding the official seal impressions where the issue of the variance in the paleographic style of the *lmlk* impressions will also be addressed.

A more nuanced position for the continued use (even if limited) of the *lmlk* jars has been presented by A. Mazar. As noted in Chapter 2, A. Mazar published an isolated two-winged *lmlk* impression from the 7th-century site of Horvat Shilhah.[22] Mazar stated that "this *lmlk* impression joins a small number of *lmlk* handles that were found in a sufficient 7th-century B.C.E. context."[23] He pointed out that even if the jars originated

---

[18]Cf. P. Lapp, "Late Royal Seals," 19-21; Albright, *Tell Beit Mirsim III*, 74; Diringer, "Royal Jar-Handle Stamps," 76-77, 79, 84-86; Lance, "Royal Stamps," 317, 322, 329.

[19]A. D. Tushingham, "New Evidence Bearing on the Two-Winged *LMLK* Stamp," *BASOR* 287 (1992) 61-65.

[20]Avigad, *Discovering Jerusalem*, 23-60.

[21]Barkay, *Northern and Western Jerusalem*, esp. 451-458.

[22]A. Mazar, Amit, and Ilan, "Horvat Shilhah," 247-248, fig. 5:22.

[23]A. Mazar, Amit, and Ilan, "Horvat Shilhah," 248.

during Hezekiah's reign, the fact that Jerusalem was not destroyed by Sennacherib (many jars would have been stored there) allows for the possibility that at least some *lmlk* jars could have continued to be used well into the 7th century.[24]

In summary, both the two- and four-winged type impressions date from the time period of Hezekiah and obviously carry some sort of royal function. A. Mazar's observations about the possibility for the continued limited use of the *lmlk* jars are important and highlight an area of the discussion that still needs to be addressed even though most scholars have tended to ignore this possibility and focused instead on Ussishkin's studies. The function of the *lmlk* jars is another area in which a consensus has not been reached. It will thus be instructive to rehearse briefly the history of research.

3. Previous Arguments for the Function of the *lmlk* Jars

As noted above, Albright and Diringer developed the interpretation that these jars were used by Josiah as part of his reform, and they argued that the *lmlk* impressions could be divided into paleographic groups. The two-winged impressions were in the latest group chronologically and corresponded roughly to the reign of Josiah. They interpreted the switch from the four-winged to the two-winged symbol as related to Josiah's cultic reform and the removal of pagan symbols. The four-winged symbol was interpreted as an Egyptian flying scarab that carried "pagan" connotations. Albright interpreted the two-winged symbol as representing a flying scroll.[25] Diringer made the same basic argument, but instead of pressing the flying scroll interpretation, he admitted that this interpretation was uncertain even if compelling. Diringer concluded that Josiah opted for a bird instead of a scarab to do away with "pagan" symbols, and that this bird probably represented a flying scroll.[26] Later, Cross developed an argument for understanding the *lmlk* jars as being used as part of Josiah's reform to develop a standardized system of measures.[27]

With the renewed excavations of Lachish by Ussishkin, it was shown that the *lmlk* jars were all dated to the period of Hezekiah, so all the theories about their relationship to Josiah's reform were nullified.

---

[24] A. Mazar, Amit, and Ilan, "Horvat Shilhah," 248, 250, n. 46.

[25] Albright, *Tell Beit Mirsim III*, 74.

[26] Diringer, "Royal Jar-Handle Stamps," 74-75.

[27] Cross, "Judean Stamps," 22.

However, since Hezekiah, like Josiah, was also described as a great reformer of the cult, it was possible to transfer many of the general understandings of how the *lmlk* jars functioned during Josiah's reign to Hezekiah. It is at this point that Ussishkin's investigations at Lachish again refuted the popular theory that the *lmlk* jars functioned as a standard measurement. Ussishkin reconstructed as many *lmlk* jars as possible and showed that the jars themselves were not of a uniform volume, so the function of the seals could not have been to signify a standardized volume.[28] This being the case, N. Na³aman developed the argument that the jars related to Hezekiah's reform not as a standardized measure for trade, but rather as a means of political and military reform. By looking at the distribution of the *lmlk* stamps, Na³aman argued that they showed the extent of Hezekiah's siege preparation for the eminent campaign of Sennacherib.[29]

A. F. Rainey presented another important proposal concerning the function of the *lmlk* jars.[30] Rainey built on Na³aman's arguments but differed in a few key places. Na³aman interpreted the distribution of the *lmlk* jars as suggesting that Hezekiah did not have much influence in the Negeb or the Hill Country. Rainey questioned Na³aman's interpretation by alluding to several instances in those areas where *lmlk* impressions were found; Na³aman had either failed to mention these cases or had glossed over them. Rainey also explained that the Negeb would have had its own system of taxation for supplying of troops and government officials, so one would not expect large quantities of tax goods originating from the Negeb. Finally, by building on geographical lists in the Bible and the four GNN on the *lmlk* jars, Rainey posited that the jars were used for production of wine at royal wineries and the designation *lmlk* simply meant the property of the King. He concluded that Na³aman was probably correct in interpreting the distribution of the *lmlk* jars as an indicator of the extent of Hezekiah's siege preparation.

Although the arguments presented by Na³aman and Rainey are insightful and contain many elements that are doubtless correct, the present state of the data is such that it is impossible to substantiate that the jars were used solely for siege preparation or for wine. That is, these theories were logical in light of the data that were available, but they were far from being authenticated. It is probably due to this sort of "impasse" in data that most scholars take a minimalist position and generally summarize

---

[28]Ussishkin, "Lachish (1973-1977)," 77, 80; D. Ussishkin, "Excavations at Tel Lachish 1978-1983: Second Preliminary Report," *Tel Aviv* 10 (1983) 162-163.

[29]Na³aman, "Sennacherib's Campaign," 73-76. 85-86.

[30]A. F. Rainey, "Wine From the Royal Vineyards," *BASOR* 245 (1982) 57-62.

that the *lmlk* jars come from the time of Hezekiah, indicate something of the extent of Hezekiah's siege resistance, and may have been used for wine or other food supplies.[31] The tendency to interpret the *lmlk* jars as having been used solely for military means can be seen clearly in Halpern's recent thorough treatment of Judah during the time of Hezekiah and Sennacherib. Halpern modifies the siege preparation theory to specify that the jars were used solely for professional soldiers. He states:

> Scholars have long linked the large pithoi with Hezekiah's preparations for siege.[32] However, the exiguous numbers of jars and fragments so far recovered suggest rather that their use was restricted to the professional soldiery.[33]

This consensus interpretation that the jars had some sort of military function is actually fairly empty; it fails to say concretely how the jars actually functioned in Hezekiah's kingdom. M. S. Moore summarizes the situation well in a survey article that addresses some of the issues that remain unclarified. He says, "Though some opinions based on this seductive, highly fragmentary evidence may seem more acceptable than others, they remain simply that—opinions."[34] Building on Moore's observations, one notices that the opinions have not moved far away from the original proposals that the *lmlk* jars were used as part of Josiah's reform. In light of this situation, it seems prudent to review all of the relevant clues as well as to include new data that might help lead to some new conclusions. One of the most relevant clues available is the relationship of the official seal impressions to the *lmlk* jar phenomenon, so it is instructive at this point to review briefly the history of discussion on this topic.

---

[31]Y. Garfinkel, "2 Chr 11:5-10 Fortified Cities List and the *lmlk* Stamps—Reply to Nadav Naʾaman," *BASOR* 271 (1988) 69; D. Ussishkin, *The Conquest of Lachish by Sennacherib* (Tel Aviv: Institute of Archaeology, Tel Aviv University, 1982) 47; A. Mazar, "The Northern Shephelah in the Iron Age: Some Issues in Biblical History and Archaeology," *Scripture and Other Artifacts: Essays on the Bible and Archaeology in Honor of Philip J. King* (eds. M. D. Coogan, J. C. Exum, and L. E. Stager; Louisville: Westminster/John Knox Press, 1994) 258.

[32]See Naʾaman, "Sennacherib's Campaign," with references.

[33]Halpern, "Jerusalem and the Lineages," 23.

[34]M. S. Moore "The Judean *lmlk* Stamps: Some Unresolved Issues," *ResQ* 28 (1985/86) 25-26.

4. Relationship Between Official and *lmlk* Seal Impressions

The relationship between the *lmlk* and the official seal impressions was evidenced from the beginning of their discovery because both types were discovered on the same type of jar. This relationship was confirmed with the British excavations at Lachish, where separate reconstructable jars were found with *lmlk* impressions and with official seal impressions.[35] Later, at Ramat Raḥel, a jar handle was found with both a Type HIIb *lmlk* impression and the official impression, לגרא / שבנא, on the same handle.[36] Recently, another jar handle was published that contained both the official impression, לגרא / שבנא, and a Typle HIIa *lmlk* impression on the same handle. This new handle contained the same name as the one from Ramat Raḥel (נרא [בן] שבנא), but the impression was made by a different seal.[37] Both handles contained a two-winged *lmlk* impression, but one was Type HIIa while one was Type HIIb.

Further evidence came to light when the renewed excavations at Lachish uncovered two *lmlk* jars with *lmlk* and official seal impressions on different handles from the same jar. Both jars came from clear stratigraphic contexts and were found *in situ* in Level III.[38] Thus, these jars with both the lmlk and official seal impressions clearly came from the period of Hezekiah. One jar contained an official impression published as "unreadable" on one handle and a two-winged *lmlk* on two other handles.[39] The second jar contained a two-winged *lmlk* impression on two handles (Lemaire Type SIIa) and an impression of the official משלם אחמלך (בן) on the other two.

Ussishkin also compared the ware of handles found in the same locus from the previous excavations at Lachish and from other sites to see if additional jars could be located that contained both *lmlk* and official seal impressions. He discovered that two other jar handles containing the impression משלם / אחמלך were found in Room 1089, together with a handle of identical ware that contained a Lemaire Type SIIa impression. He concluded that these three handles likely belonged to the same jar. It is also interesting to note that this jar was found about 20 m from the reconstructed jar; yet both contained the impression of the same individual

---

[35]Cf. Diringer, "Royal Jar-Handle Stamps," 71, 73, figs. 2, 3.

[36]Aharoni, *Ramat Raḥel, Seasons 1959 and 1960*, 16-17, fig 14:2, pl. 6:2.

[37]R. Deutsch and M. Heltzer, *Forty New Ancient West Semitic Inscriptions* (Tel Aviv-Jaffa: Archaeological Center Publication, 1994) 33-34.

[38]Ussishkin, "Royal Judean Storage Jars," 1-3, figs. 1-4.

[39]The correct reading is now found in G. Barkay and A. G. Vaughn, "An Official Seal Impression from Lachish Reconsidered," *Tel Aviv* 22 (1995) 94-97.

and at least one SIIa Type *lmlk* impression.[40] In addition, Ussishkin was able to locate two sets of handles from Tell Beit Mirsim where the ware of an official seal impression on one handle was identical to the ware of other handles with *lmlk* impressions. All the handles from each respective set were found in the same locus on the same day, or on successive days. Each set contained an impression of the official אליקם / נער יוכן and at least one HIIa *lmlk* impression. Again, the same official had his stamp on different jars with the same type of *lmlk* stamp (Type HIIa).

Y. Garfinkel further develops Ussishkin's work by adding other reasons to associate the official seal impression with the *lmlk* impressions. Although his larger argument for a specific hierarchy for Hezekiah's officials is refuted below with additional data not available to Garfinkel, his arguments for the association of the official and *lmlk* seal impressions as well as his attempt to make sense of the distribution of the official seal impressions are important and deserve attention.[41] First, Garfinkel notes that the official impression לצפן א/במעץ is found at Tel Batash (Timnah) on the same floor with many royal (*lmlk*) seal impressions (Squares J30-32). Although the jar handle with the official seal impression is not part of a restorable jar, it adds more evidence for the association of the *lmlk* and official seal impressions.[42]

In a different type of argument, Garfinkel drew attention to an archaeometric analysis conducted on jar handles with *lmlk* and official seal impressions. This analysis showed that handles with the following official seal impressions were manufactured out of clay identical to the clay analyzed from jar handles with *lmlk* seal impressions: לתנחם / מגן, יהוחל / שחר, מנחם / ויהבנה, לאליקם / נער יוכן. Further three of four of these official seal impressions were found in the same locus with royal seal impressions on jar handles with the same chemical makeup of the clay.[43] לאליקם / נער יוכן, as Ussishkin pointed out, was found in the same locus with two HIIa Type handles. מנחם / ויהבנה was found on the same floor of a courtyard with a jar handle of the same fabric containing a למלך / זף (Type ZIIb) impression.[44] Finally, יהוחל / שחר (Lachish No.

---

[40]Ussishkin, "Royal Judean Storage Jars," 6.

[41]Y. Garfinkel, "A Hierarchic Pattern in the 'Private Seal Impressions' on the *lmlk* Jars," *EI* 18 (1985) (Hebrew) 108-109.

[42]Kelm and Mazar, "Three Seasons," 29.

[43]Garfinkel ("Hierarchic Pattern," 108) listed one of these impressions incorrectly as מנחם / יובנה. He also incorrectly identified לתנחם / מגן (Lachish No. 11205/1) from a locus with *lmlk* impressions, but this official seal impression was actually a surface find (cf. Ussishkin, "Lachish [1973-1977]," 81).

[44]Aharoni, "Ramat Raḥel, 1954," 144-145, pl. 25:1, 3.

10622/1) was found in Locus 4014 of Area G at Lachish together with two handles with Type HIa stamps (Lachish No. 10624/1 and 10629/1).[45] Despite Garfinkel's intimation, the official impression and the two *lmlk* impressions were of different fabric and did *not* seem to originate from the same jar. Nevertheless, Garfinkel was correct in drawing attention to the association of separate jars with *lmlk* and official seal impressions in the same locus.[46]

Garfinkel presented a similar third type of argument by drawing attention to stratified archaeological contexts where both *lmlk* and official seal impressions have been found, but the handles have not been tested archaemetrically. Room number 1089 from Lachish Level III contained the impressions עבדי / לנחם (No. 7168) and עזריהו/צפן (No. 7166) together with למלך / חברן and למלך / שוכה impressions.[47] Similarly, the handles with the impressions הושע / צפן and לשבנא/א. שחר were found on the floor of the palace in area K.14 / J.14 AG (Level 271.60) together with *lmlk* impressions that contain the GNN Sokoh, Ziph, and Hebron.[48] At Khirbet Rabûd, two impressions of לשלם / אחא (188/1 and 188/2) were found in Locus 107 together with a למלך / חברן impression.[49] Garfinkel concluded his argument with numerous instances in which official and royal seal impressions are found together in fills or in early excavations where loci were not recorded, so these examples were only suggestive and did not present any additional concrete data.[50]

In summary, in two instances there were jar handles with both *lmlk* and official seal impressions on the same handle. The royal seal impressions were both Type HIIa, but the official impressions, although they contained the same name, were made from different seals. There were two examples from Lachish of reconstructed jars containing official and royal seal impressions on separate handles from the same jar. Ussishkin also presented strong arguments for interpreting two jars from Tell Beit

---

[45]Ussishkin, "Lachish (1973-1977)," 80-81.

[46]Garfinkel ("Hierarchic Pattern," 108) also argued that three *lmlk* impressions should be associated with this official impression. He was correct that three impressions came from this general area, but one of the royal impressions (Lachish No. 11207/1) was discovered as a surface find in this locus several years after the discovery of the others. It seems prudent to exclude this additional handle from association with the official impression (cf. Ussishkin, "Lachish [1973-1977]" 81).

[47]Tufnell, *Lachish III*, 124-125.

[48]Tufnell, *Lachish III*, 341-342.

[49]Kochavi "Khirbet Rabûd," 11.

[50]Garfinkel, "Hierarchic Pattern," 108-109.

Mirsim as containing both royal and official seal impressions. If Ussishkin is correct, both jars contained the official impression לאליקם / נער יוכן and at least one Type HIIa royal impression. Finally, Garfinkel presented various arguments that showed that handles with the official and *lmlk* impressions were made of the same type of clay and found in the same stratified archaeological contexts. All these data show that the official seal impressions are to be understood as related to the phenomenon of the *lmlk* seal impressions and that both of these impressions were used at the same period on jars used for the same purpose.

B. Date of the *lmlk* and Official Impressions Revisited

1. Introduction: Possibilities Raised by Tushingham and A. Mazar

It was shown above that the *lmlk* impressions were clearly used at Lachish during the late 8th century BCE and not during the 7th. However, because of the occupation gap at Lachish following Level III, if there were no other evidence, it would be possible to conclude that the *lmlk* jars experienced widespread use after the reign of Hezekiah but fizzled out by the reign of Josiah when the full scale resettlement of Lachish took place. As noted, Tushingham employed this type of theory to conclude that the *lmlk* jars continued in use during the 7th century in Jerusalem.

Tushingham presents this scenario in an effort to attribute the four-winged symbol as the seal of the northern kingdom of Israel, while the two-winged symbol was the seal of the southern, Judean kingdom. He argues that after the fall of Israel, the four-winged emblem was used initially to bring northern Israelite support to Judah. However, he holds that this four-winged emblem was not used in the City of David due to its northern character. His arguments are not convincing for several reasons. First, there are very few royal impressions in the north. He dismisses the four-winged impressions found on the Western Hill of Jerusalem as not coming from the heart of Jerusalem and thus not representing Judean policy. It seems strained to say that because a jar was found several hundred meters outside the old City of David, the jar reflects northern influence and not Judean policy. Many of his arguments are based on silence, and it is difficult (and unneccessary) to refute them. However, his point that there is a possibility for continued production of *lmlk* jars is an important issue to address.

In presenting a similar but more nuanced argument that was also noted above, A. Mazar calls attentions to a *lmlk* impression from Horvat Shilḥah that was found in a 7th-century context.[51] Mazar posits that there is a strong possibility that some (many?) of the *lmlk* jars left in Jerusalem after Sennacherib's invasion found their way to these 7th-century sites. There is an important difference between this and Tushingham's proposals. Whereas Tushingham argues for the continued production of *lmlk* jars into the 7th century, Mazar presents the possibility for the continued usage in the 7th century of jars produced in the late 8th century. Mazar lists the following sites where such continued use is evidenced by what he terms a "sufficient 7th-century [archaeological] context": Arad, Ramat Raḥel, Ein Gedi, Khirbet es-Samrah, and Tel ʿIra.[52] However, he also finesses this possible 7th-century usage with the following qualification:

> Only at isolated sites is it permissible to separate out *lmlk* impressions with a sufficient seventh-century B.C.E. context. Moreover, with regards to the question of the chronological relationship of these impressions, it is a difficult situation, for at most of these sites, eighth-century finds also exist. And due to this it is possible to ask if the origin of the impressions is not eighth-century jars.[53]

Both Tushingham and A. Mazar have presented possible exceptions to the sole late 8th-century context of the *lmlk* jars, and these possibilities must be addressed before conclusions concerning the administration of Hezekiah can convincingly be drawn from the data. The sites that need to be examined for possible widespread 7th-century use of the jars are · Jerusalem, Ramat Raḥel, and Arad. Several smaller sites (Ein Gedi, Khirbet es-Samrah, and Tel ʿIra) named by A. Mazar as containing more limited *lmlk* data also need to be examined.

Despite the possibilities raised by both scholars, there is other evidence at almost all of the above-mentioned sites that suggests that the jars were not manufactured after the reign of Hezekiah. This evidence is based on new finds and rereadings of official impressions first published as "uncertain" or "unreadable," so the new data have not been factored into past discussions of the royal jars. An examination of these official seal impressions establishes that neither Jerusalem nor Ramat Raḥel supports a theory for the widespread continued use of the *lmlk* jars into

---

[51]A. Mazar, Amit, and Ilan, "Horvat Shilḥah," 248.

[52]A. Mazar, Amit, and Ilan, "Horvat Shilḥah," 250, n. 46.

[53]A. Mazar, Amit, and Ilan, "Horvat Shilḥah," 250, n. 46.

the 7th century as Tushingham suggests. It is more difficult to arrive at such a conclusive evaluation regarding Mazar's more nuanced proposal, so his suggestion will need to be kept in mind as an evaluation is made on the bearing of the *lmlk* data for the kingdom of Hezekiah.

2. Role of Official Seal Impressions in Evaluating the Chronology of the *lmlk* Jars

In light of the connection between the official and royal seal impressions, it is instructive to study the occurrences of these official impressions in various stratified contexts. Starting with a list of the officials whose impressions are found on *lmlk* handles at Lachish, one is able to derive a fairly large list of officials from Hezekiah's kingdom. Lachish is the ideal starting point because it is clear from excavations there that the *lmlk* jars were not used there during the 7th century. With the list of officials whose impressions are found at Lachish, it is possible to date other stratified layers to the late 8th century when impressions of these same officials are found there. Finally, by including additional officials whose impressions are found at Beth Shemesh, Tell Beit Mirsim, Tell ej-Judeideh, and Tell eṣ-Ṣâfi (other sites with no Judean occupation during the 7th century), one can develop a comprehensive list of all the officials known to have seal impressions on *lmlk* jar handles. Thus, any stratified layer containing one of these official seal impressions known from Lachish, Beth Shemesh, Tell Beit Mirsim, Tell ej-Judeideh, or Tell eṣ-Ṣâfi clearly does not date earlier than the late 8th century. Further, in the absence of secondary placement of the jar handle, the stratum would not date from a later period either.

The presupposition lying behind the type of argument presented here is that, unlike a *lmlk* seal for which there is a possibility of using the same royal seal during several reigns, a seal that contained the name of a private individual or the name of an official would only be used during the lifetime of that person. Even the possibility of the seal being passed on to the grandchild is precluded in this situation because there is no evidence for the use of the *lmlk* jars after the reign of Manasseh. Further, the fact that the impressions containing the name of the owner and the patronym were used on a specific type of jar that had some sort of significance in the functioning of the royal kingdom precludes the possibility of two people having the same designation on these seals. In other words, if there had been a possibility of confusing the ownership of a seal used on a specific medium such as these royal jars, some variation would have been made in the seals so that the identification would be certain. These factors lead to the conclusion that if an impression belonging to a particular individual was found at Lachish or at another site that is stratigraphically comparable to Lachish Level III, then all other seals that contain this same official's name would have been used at a time contemporary with the usage at Lachish Level III. Assuming that the official impressions belonged to adults, one can thus limit the possible future use of these seals on this particular type of jar normally to no more than approximately 20 years after the destruction of Lachish Level III.

At Lachish, there are at least nineteen officials represented by the official seal impressions discovered there. This list includes finds from the renewed Lachish excavations,[54] jar handles found in Starkey's excavations that were lost in either the Rockefeller or the British Museum, and rereadings of impressions published incorrectly, as "uncertain," or as "unreadable." Table 3 is a list of officials with at least one impression at Lachish; where more than one seal was used to make these impressions, each seal and the total number of impressions is indicated:[55]

.

---

[54]See D. Ussishkin, "Excavations and Restoration Work at Tel Lachish 1985-1994: Third Preliminary Report," *Tel Aviv* 23 (1996) 57-59; Barkay and Vaughn, "*LMLK* and Official Seal Impressions," 61-74.

[55]Appendix II contains a comprehensive listing of these impressions. A list of the *lmlk* and official seal impressions from Lachish is also found in Barkay and Vaughn, "*LMLK* and Official Seal Impressions," 61-74.

TABLE 3: OFFICALS WITH SEAL IMPRESSIONS AT LACHISH

name of official	list of seal impressions
1. אחזיהו (בן) תנחם	אחזיה/ו. תנחם (2 impressions)[56]
	תנחם / לאחא (1 impression)[56]
2. הושע (בן) צפנ[יהו]	הושו / צפן (4 impressions)
3. יהוחיל (בן) שחר	יהוחל / שחר (1 impression)
	יהוחיל / שחר (1 impression)
4. כרמי (בן) יפיהו	כרמי / יפיהו (2 impressions [may be read as כרמי / אפיהו])
5. מנחם (בן) יובנה	למנחם / יובנה (4 impressions)[57]
6. משלם (בן) אחמלך	משלם / אחמלך (12 impressions)
7. למשלם (בן) אלנתן	למשל/ם אלנתן (1 impression)
8. נחם (בן) הצליהו	לנחם / הצליהו (1 impression)
9. נחם (בן) עבדי	לנחם / עבדי (13 impressions)
10. נרא (בן) שבנא	לנרא / שבנא (1 impression)
11. סמך (בן) צפניהו	לסמך / ב ן / צפניהו (3 impressions)
12. עבדי	לעבד/י (1 impression)
13. צפן (בן) עזריהו	צפן ע/זריהו (5 impressions)
	לצפן / עזר (3 impressions)
14. שבנא (בן) שחר	לשבנ/א. שחר (3 impressions)
15. שבניהו (בן) עזריהו	שבניה / עזריה (1 impression)
16. שוכי (בן) שבנא	לשוכ/י שבנ/א (2 impressions)[58]
17. לשלם / אחא	לשלם / אחא (1 impression)
	לשלם / אחאם (4 impressions)[59]
18. תנחם (בן) מגן	לתנחם / מגן (7 impressions)

Table 4, a continuation of this list, contains the names of officials with impressions found in strata clearly dated to the late 8th century, but whose impressions have not yet been located at Lachish. Table 4 omits identical impressions if an impression was already cited above from Lachish, as well as any impressions found in strata that are not securely dated to the late 8th century. As argued above (Chapter 2), it is assumed that there was no Judean occupation during the 7th century at Beth Shemesh, Tell Beit Mirsim, Tell ej-Judeideh, and Tell eṣ-Ṣâfi.

---

[56]One impression of אחזיה/ו. תנחם is found on the same handle with an impression of לאחא / תנחם, indicating that these impressions belong to the same official.

[57]These impressions were originally published as לפן בן / יחני and תנחם / מגן. The correct reading is presented in Barkay and Vaughn, "New Readings," 35-37, nos. 7-9.

[58]These impressions were originally published as לשוכ/ה שבנ/א. The correct reading is presented in Barkay and Vaughn, "New Readings," 40-41, nos. 11-12.

[59]One of these impressions was published as "unreadable." The correct reading is presented in Barkay and Vaughn, "New Readings," 37-40, no. 10.

TABLE 4: 8TH-CENTURY OFFICALS KNOWN ONLY FROM OTHER SITES

name of official	list of seal impressions
19. אליקם נער יוכן	לאליקם / נער יוכן (2 at Tell Beit Mirsim, 1 at Beth Shemesh)
20. בכי (בן) שלם	לבכי / שלם (1 from Beth Shemesh)
21. בנאי (בן) יהוכל	לבנאי / יהוכל (1 from Tell ej-Judeideh, 1 from Tell eṣ-Ṣâfi)
22. חסדא (בן) ירמיהו	לחסדא / ירמיהו (1 from Beth Shemesh)
23. כסלא (בן) זכא	לכסלא / זכא (2 from Beth Shemesh)
24. עזר (בן) חגי	לעזר / חגי (1 from Tell ej-Judeideh, 1 from Gezer)
25. צדק (בן) סמך	לצדק / סמך (1 from Beth Shemesh)
26. צפן (בן) ובמעץ	לצפן א/במעץ (1 from Tel Batash, 2 from Tell eṣ-Ṣâfi)
27. תנחם (בן) נגב	לתנח/ם. נגב (2 from Beth Shemesh, 1 from Gibeon)

Only eleven of a total thirty-eight known officials do not have at least one impression from a clear 8th-century context. Of the remaining eleven, nine are officials whose impressions are known only from the antiquities market; thus, their existence does not threaten the dating of controlled archaeological strata. The final handles are from Jerusalem and are discussed below.

The official seal impressions are thus clearly dated to the late 8th century. This fact is vital to the paleographical study[60] referred to earlier (Chapter 1), and it is also important for dating any strata where *lmlk* or official impressions are found. Indeed, since it has been shown that the *lmlk* and official impressions are part of the same phenomenon and are often found on the same jar, the conclusive dating of the official impressions to the late 8th century without significant continued use in the 7th suggests that the same scenario is true for the related *lmlk* impressions. A discussion of strata with a possible 7th-century dating where both official and *lmlk* seal impressions are found confirms this conclusion.

3. Refutation of the Possible 7th-Century Use of *lmlk* Impressions in Jerusalem

It is instructive to study Jerusalem first in this examination of official seal impressions and the possibility of 7th-century *lmlk* jars, because this city is the backbone of Tushingham's argument for the continued, widespread use of the royal jars in the 7th century. It is helpful to compare this list of officials from Lachish and other late 8th-century contexts with the list found in Jerusalem. In Avigad's excavations of the present-day Jewish Quarter, forty-four jar handles were found with *lmlk* impressions of both the two- and four-winged varieties. No specific stratigraphic

---

[60]See Vaughn, "Palaeographic Dating," 43-64.

information is given by Avigad, but they are described as being found in the same context as four official stamps: לנרי ב/ן שבניו, לנרא / שבנא לצפן א/במעץ and למנחם / יובנה.[61] The first two impressions are recognized as belonging to the official נרא (בן) שבנא, and another impression of this official is known from Lachish. Although an impression of the second official, צפן (בן) אבמעץ has yet to be discovered at Lachish, an identical impression of this official was discovered at Tel Batash (Timnah) in Stratum III—the stratum that corresponds to Lachish Level III and that experiences a destruction date of 701 BCE.[62] Another identical impression is known from Tell eṣ-Ṣâfi, a site that was not under Judean control after the late 8th century. The fourth impression belongs to the official מנחם (בן) יובנה and is also known from Lachish. Thus, in every case from Avigad's excavations on the Western Hill, the official seal impressions can be matched with a stratigraphically datable impression belonging to the same person. This matching indicates that all of the official and *lmlk* impressions from this excavated area should be seen as being used primarily in the late 8th century and not much later.

Y. Shiloh's excavations of the City of David in Jerusalem uncovered about 50 *lmlk* impressions. Due to Shiloh's unexpected early death, the publication of the dig has been delayed and not many details are presently available. However, the information available suggests that none of the *lmlk* jars from the City of David were used for a substantial time after the period of Hezekiah. Of course, since Jerusalem was not destroyed in 701 BCE, one would expect some continued use of the jars that had already been manufactured. Shiloh summarizes his finds as follows: "In the City of David about fifty stamped *lamelek* handles have been found, only some of them *in situ*, in Stratum 12" (the stratum dating from the reign of Hezekiah). He continues, "The infrequent appearance of this type of jar, or of isolated stamped handles in later strata. . . does not in our opinion provide evidence of the continued official use of these jars."[63]

A comparison of the official seal impressions from the City of David strengthens Shiloh's conclusions and provides concrete support that isolated jar handles found in strata later than Stratum 12 do not point to continued, extensive use of the *lmlk* seals. At least four official seal impressions were found in Shiloh's excavations. Since the jar handles containing these impressions have yet to be published, it is uncertain if

---

[61] Avigad, *Discovering Jerusalem*, 43-44.

[62] Kelm and Mazar, "Three Seasons," 29.

[63] Y. Shiloh, "Judah and Israel in the Eighth-Sixth Centuries B.C.E." *Recent Excavations in Israel: Studies in Iron Age Archaeology* (eds. S. Gitin and W. G. Dever; AASOR 49; Winona Lake, IN: Eisenbrauns, 1989) 104.

there are more impressions exactly where these were found. Shiloh gave the following list Barkay:[64] אלשמע / חשי, צפניהו / ב ן / לסמך, אחא / לשלם, and נגב .לתנח/ם. Comparison of these finds with impressions from clear late eight-century contexts, shows that identical impressions of three of the four were also found at Lachish or Beth Shemesh. The final impression belonging to אלשמע (בן) חשי has parallels at Ramat Raḥel in a sealed stratigraphic context from Stratum VB—the stratum with a destruction date of 701 BCE.[65] Once again, every official seal impression from the City of David excavations can be matched with identical impressions from other stratigraphically dated levels at other sites. This provides another indication that all of these official impressions, together with the *lmlk* impressions discovered in the same context, should be dated in general terms to the reign of Hezekiah and not much after.

Kenyon and Tushingham's excavations in the Armenian Quarter of Jerusalem revealed many *lmlk* impressions and three official seal impressions.[66] Tushingham was involved in both the supervision and publication of this excavation, and the data from this dig supported his theory of the continued usage of the *lmlk* jars into the 7th century. However, none of these official impressions were published as Hebrew impressions by Tushingham. One of the official seal impressions was published as an Arabic [sic!] inscription,[67] but it is actually an official seal impression on a *lmlk*type jar handle. The impression (Reg. no. 5649) is clearly ליהוחיל / שחר, an official whose impressions are also found at Lachish.[68] The third unpublished stamped handle (Reg. no. 267) found in a fill in a 7th-century context contained the inscription כרמי / יפיהו, again with parallels at Lachish. The final official seal impression (Reg. no. 369) was not decipherable from the photograph provided to Barkay and the author by Prag.[69] Thus,

---

[64]I am indebted to Barkay for sharing this list with me.

[65]Aharoni, *Ramat Raḥel, Seasons 1959 and 1960,* 18-19, fig. 14:4, pl. 6:1. It should be noted that this impression was originally published incorrectly by Aharoni as אלשמע / ל....

[66]Prag, personal communication.

[67]Tushingham, *Excavations in Jerusalem,* pl. 69:13.

[68]The correct reading is presented in Barkay and Vaughn, "New Readings," 48-50, no. 21.

[69]I am grateful to K. Prag for the information about these handles, and to G. Barkay who obtained publication rights to these items and allowed me to refer to them in this study. Barkay first recognized that the handle published by Tushingham as an Arabic inscription was in fact an official seal impression. The publication of one of these handles is found in Barkay and Vaughn, "New Readings," 48-50, no. 21. The remaining two handles will be published in a forthcoming article by Barkay and me.

even in one of Tushingham's prime spots for the continued use of the *lmlk* jars into the 7th century, the data support their use only during the late 8th century.

Additional royal and official seal impressions were revealed by of B. Mazar's team near the Temple Mount in Jerusalem. In these excavations, twenty-one handles and handle fragments were found with *lmlk* impressions, but only two handles with impressions came from a clear stratified area; the rest were found in fills. Two official seal impressions were also found in fills. The impression, חגי / הושעם, was found in Locus HJ6, while the impression, הצליהו / לנחם, was found in Locus 12036.[70] Thus far the former impression is unique to the Ophel, but the second impression was also found at Lachish.[71] There is also a third impression on a jar handle fragment from a stratified locus (23041) dated to the middle to late 7th century. The impression belongs to a woman (לחנה ב/ת וזריה),[72] but the handle is not of the *lmlk* type (Lachish Type 484), so it has little bearing on the date of the *lmlk* or official impressions. There were also two *lmlk* impressions on other jar handle fragments from Locus 23041.[73] However, they were not part of a restorable jar and thus seem to be isolated finds. Once again, little evidence is found for the extensive use of the *lmlk* jars past the reign of Hezekiah, and the evidence from an identical official seal impression from Lachish suggests dating all of the *lmlk* and official seal impressions to the late 8th century.

---

[70]Y. Nadelman, "Hebrew Inscriptions, Seal Impressions, and Markings of the Iron Age II," *Excavations in the South of the Temple Mount: The Ophel of Biblical Jerusalem* (ed. E. Mazar and B. Mazar; Qedem 29; Jerusalem: The Institute of Archaeology, The Hebrew University of Jerusalem, 1989) 131.

[71]The date of the impression, הצליהו / לנחם, is thus clearly the late 8th century, despite the claim by Y. Nadelman ("Hebrew Inscriptions," 130-131) in the publication that the shape of the ṣade called for a date of the late 7th century.

[72]Nadelman, "Hebrew Inscriptions," 131; E. Mazar and B. Mazar, *Excavations in the South of the Temple Mount: The Ophel of Biblical Jerusalem* (Qedem Monographs 29; Jerusalem: Keterpress Enterprises, 1989) 18, photo 24; N. Avigad, "A Note on an Impression from a Woman's Seal," *IEJ* 37 (1987) 18-19, pl. 1:A,B.

[73]E. Mazar and B. Mazar, *The Ophel*, 22; Nadelman, "Hebrew Inscriptions," 131.

4. Refutation of the Possible 7th-Century Use of *lml*
Impressions at Ramat Raḥel

Two strata at Ramat Raḥel (VB and VA) contain *lmlk* and official seal impressions. Stratum VB consists of a citadel with very few extant remains, because this layer was almost completely destroyed either before the next layer was built or during the construction process. Most of what remains of Stratum VB is known from a fill found beneath the floors of Stratum VA. Stratum VA was built directly on top of VB after the tell was leveled, and it contains a larger citadel and more extensive fortifications than VB. Most of the *lmlk* handles found at Ramat Raḥel (about 170, including those from Barkay's 1984 excavations) were found in Stratum VB. However, a significant number (the exact count is not given in the site report) were found in Stratum VA, but none were found *in situ*. The majority of official seal impressions were found in VB, but three came from VA. Initially, the discovery of one official seal impression (נער יוכן / לאליקם) in VA caused Aharoni to follow Albright and attribute the name יוכן to King Jehoiachin, the son of Jehoiachim. Aharoni thus argued that VA dated to the end of the Judean monarchy and that some of the *lmlk* and official seal impressions found there came from the late 7th century. Obviously, this interpretation has bearing on the issues being discussed in this chapter and deserves further attention.

There is no debate that Stratum VB predates VA, and that VB contains pottery similar to Lachish Level III.[74] This dating is also confirmed by the fact that eleven of thirteen official seal impressions from Ramat Raḥel found in Stratum VB have parallels from Lachish. Table 5 lists the seal impressions that were found in Stratum VB of Ramat Raḥel and have a parallel at Lachish:

---

[74]Aharoni and Aharoni, "Stratification of Judahite Sites," 73-90.

TABLE 5: RAMAT-RAHEL IMPRESSIONS WITH PARALLELS TO LACHISH

list of seal impressions

1. יהוחל / שחר.[75]
2. ליהוחיל / שחר.[76]
3. למנחם / יובנה.[77]
4. מנחם / ויהבנה.[78]
5. לנחם / הצליהו.[79]
6. לנרא / שבנא.[80]
7. לצפן / עזריהו.[81]
8. לשבנ/א. שחר.[82]
9. לשבנ/א. שחר.[83]
10. לשבנ/א. שחר.[84]
11. לשלם / אחא.[85]

The final two impressions from Stratum VB come from a firm archaeological context. One is the impression לתנח/ם. נגב; however, it

---

[75] Aharoni, Ramat Raḥel, Seasons 1959 and 1960, 44., fig. 31:2, pl. 27:2). Locus 392, Square 19Z, Level 5.20.

[76] Aharoni, Ramat Raḥel, Seasons 1959 and 1960, 44, fig. 31:3, pl. 27:1. Locus 391, Square 17W, Level 6.20. This impression was published without the *lamed* preposition. The correct reading is presented in Barkay and Vaughn, "New Readings," 50, no. 22.

[77] Aharoni, Ramat Raḥel, Seasons 1959 and 1960, 17-18, fig. 14:3, pl. 6:4. Locus 299.

[78] Aharoni, "Ramat Raḥel, 1954," 145.

[79] Aharoni, Ramat Raḥel, Seasons 1961 and 1962, 61, pl. 40:6. Locus 380, Square 17/S, Level 6.60.

[80] Aharoni, Ramat Raḥel, Seasons 1959 and 1960, 16; fig. 14:2, pl. 6:2. Locus 272a.

[81] Aharoni, Ramat Raḥel, Seasons 1959 and 1960," 44. Originally published as "unreadable."

[82] Aharoni, Ramat Raḥel, Seasons 1961 and 1962, 60-1., fig. 37:3; pl. 40:3. Locus 559, Square 13/KK, Level 2.50.

[83] Aharoni, Ramat Raḥel, Seasons 1961 and 1962, 61, fig. 37:2, pl. 40:2. Locus 559, Level 2.15.

[84] Aharoni, Ramat Raḥel, Seasons 1961 and 1962, 19, fig. 14:5, pl. 6:3. Locus 268b. This impression was published incorrectly as ל... /ת ברא. The correct reading is presented in Barkay and Vaughn, "New Readings," 47-48, no. 20.

[85] This handle (excavation no. 8123/1; I.A.A. no. 64-1772) was originally considered unreadable. My reexamination of the handle showed that the end of the frame is visible on the handle. This frame is triangular and unique, so the impression can be identified as לשלם / אחא. No letters are visible.

clearly comes from Stratum VB, so there should be no question that this impression also comes from the late 8th century.[86] Further, two impressions of לתנח/ם. גגב were found at Beth Shemesh, a site with no 7th-century occupation on the tel. Finally, an impression of לחשי / אלשמע was also found under the floor of Stratum VA, so its location in Stratum VB and late 8th-century date is secure.[87] Thus, it is seen that all the official seal impressions in Stratum VB can be dated safely to the late 8th century BCE as one would expect since this level corresponds to Lachish Level III.

A question has been raised about several impressions found in Stratum VA because this stratum dates to the 7th century. The complexity of the situation is compounded by the fact that the crucial comparative level from Tell Beit Mirsim was dated incorrectly at the time of Aharoni's final publication of the Ramat Raḥel excavations.[88] Aharoni initially chose to deal with the problem concerning the official seal impressions in Stratum VA context by assigning them to the late 8th century if the official's impression was also known from Stratum VB. On the other hand, he assigned them to the late 7th century if a parallel was found from Tell Beit Mirsim. If no parallel was found, he left the date open.

A good example of Aharoni's rationale is seen in the impressions belonging to the official, יהוחיל (בן) שחר. The first impression of this official was discovered "in the courtyard (Locus 391, Square 17W), in the filling under the limestone floor (Level 6.20)."[89] Since this handle was found in the filling under Stratum VB, and it had a parallel from Lachish, it is dated to the late 8th century. The second impression belonging to this official was found several years later:

> in the courtyard of the northern building (Locus 468, square 16X, level 7.00). . . . Although the . . . stamp was found on top of the floor of the courtyard, it is clear from the earlier [identical] seal, which was brought to light in the filling under the courtyard, that this later find too belongs to Stratum VB. This is a good illustration of the unreliability of single handles found in higher levels as guides to stratification.[90]

---

[86]Aharoni, *Ramat Raḥel, Seasons 1959 and 1960*, 44, fig. 31:1, pl. 27:3; originally published as שתל / א... The correct reading is presented in Barkay and Vaughn, "New Readings," 45-46, no. 18.

[87]Aharoni, *Ramat Raḥel, Seasons 1959 and 1960*, 18-19; fig. 14:4, pl. 6:1. Locus 310a. Originally published as ל... / אלשמע.

[88]Aharoni, *Ramat Raḥel, Seasons 1961 and 1962*.

[89]Aharoni, *Ramat Raḥel, Seasons 1959 and 1960*, 44; cf. fig. 31:3, pl. 27:1.

[90]Aharoni, *Ramat Raḥel, Seasons 1961 and 1962*, 32-33; cf. fig. 37:1, pl.

With another seal impression that did not have a parallel in Stratum VB, Aharoni concluded that the date of this official impression was uncertain. Aharoni stated that the impression לתנחם / מגן "was found in the eastern room of the northern building (Locus 477, Square 18/X, Level 6.00) in which many objects from stratum VA were unearthed. In spite of this, it cannot be asserted that this particular stamp belongs to the same stratum and not to VB, since the find in question is only a fragment of a handle and not a complete vessel *in situ.*"[91] However, an identical impression is found eight times at Lachish, so it may be safely dated to the late 8th century as well.

The only official seal impression from Ramat Raḥel Stratum VA without a parallel at Lachish is לאליקם / נער יוכן.[92] Aharoni described the find as follows:

> The stamp from Ramat Raḥel was found, together with several holemouth jars, on the floor of the central courtyard in front of the main gate, in a layer showing evidence of fire (locus 420, square 19/V, level 7.00). Once again it must be borne in mind that the find in question is not a whole vessel, but only a fragment of a handle, which makes it difficult to assign it with absolute certainty to a definite Stratum.[93]

Aharoni concluded that the identical impression from Tell Beit Mirsim was from the reign of Jehoiachin. Thus, he argued that some official impressions continued to be used in the 7th century. Subsequent study has made it clear, however, that both Tell Beit Mirsim and Beth Shemesh (where another identical impression לאליקם / נער יוכן was found) were destroyed in 701 BCE and not resettled in the 7th century. So this final possibility from Ramat Raḥel suggesting the continuance of the *lmlk* and official seal impressions into the 7th century is also seen to be without warrant.

40:1.

[91] Aharoni, *Ramat Raḥel, Seasons 1961 and 1962,* 32, fig. 37:5, pl. 40:5.

[92] Aharoni, *Ramat Raḥel, Seasons 1961 and 1962,* 33, fig. 37:6, pl. 40:4.

[93] Aharoni, *Ramat Raḥel, Seasons 1961 and 1962,* 33.

5. Ramifications of These Finds for Tushingham's Proposal

It seems clear that the official seal impressions, as well as the *lmlk* impressions, should be dated to the late 8th century. There is no evidence for their extensive use into the 7th century. Tushingham's hypothesis does not withstand these data. Although there is always a possibility of a limited secondary use of a jar produced in the late 8th century during the first decade or so of the 7th, there is no evidence that these jars were extensively used past the reign of Hezekiah. This conclusion is especially important to the current study, because one may thus be secure in an assessment of the kingdom of Hezekiah by looking at the *lmlk* and official seal impressions without the fear that the data of these jars point to the widespread activity of another Judean king.

6. Discussion of the So-Called Secondary 7th-Century Use of *lmlk* Jars

a. Arad

Arad was the most significant additional site mentioned by A. Mazar for the possibility of continued use of the *lmlk* jars. The site was significant in terms of size and number of total impressions. Following Y. Aharoni's death, M. Aharoni published a catalog of nine *lmlk* impressions found at Arad along with a paragraph description of these impressions.[94] A. Mazar called attention to this catalog which listed nos. 3, 4, and 8 as coming from Stratum VII (a 7th-century stratum).[95]

However, it is doubtful that these three handles point to 7th-century use of *lmlk* jars. One of the three impressions is called into question because M. Aharoni states that *lmlk* impressions "nos. 5-9 are only small fragments of jar handles; none of them were found in stratified context."[96] Clearly, the dating of impression no. 8 by its location in a fill in Stratum VII is not conclusive. A. Mazar himself rightly urges caution and states that "it is difficult to establish whether the impressions from Stratum VII reached the fortress of this stratum during this 7th century, or if their [i.e., the *lmlk* impression's] origin is with the jars from a previous stratum."[97]

---

[94]M. Aharoni, "Weights and Royal Seals," 126-127.

[95]A. Mazar, Amit, and Ilan, "Horvat Shilḥah," 250, n. 46.

[96]M. Aharoni, "Weights and Royal Seals," 126.

[97]A. Mazar, Amit, and Ilan, "Horvat Shilḥah," 250, n. 46.

A. Mazar's caution is given further credence by the evaluation of the editor of the *Arad Inscriptions* volume, A. F. Rainey, who supplements M. Aharoni's brief paragraphs with four paragraphs of analysis on the *lmlk* seal impressions. Rainey states that "none of the *lmlk* inscriptions were found on whole vessels *in situ*."[98] Just like Ramat Raḥel, where it was possible for isolated, stamped jar handles to be discovered in levels above the 8th-century level, the presence of jar handles that are not found *in situ* in Arad Stratum VII mean nothing in terms of dating. This conclusion is further supported by the fact that one of the two *lmlk* impressions in question is a four-winged impression (Lemaire Type SIb), a type that scholars have always dated to the late 8th century.

Finally, the discovery of a previously unreported official seal impression in the stores of the I.A.A. confirms the dating of the *lmlk* impressions at Arad to the late 8th century. With the assistance of B. Brandl, Curator of the State Collection for the I.A.A., the author located a collection card (I.A.A. no. 64-2563) with a photograph of a *lmlk* type handle from Arad with the official impression of לשלם / אחא. The collection specifies that the impressed handle comes from pottery bucket 163 in Locus 3786 during the first season of the Arad excavations. The handle itself has yet to be located, but a photograph on the collection card makes it clear that the handle contained an impression with a triangular frame that matches precisely the unique, triangular frame of the official impression לשלם / אחא. In addition, the word divider following the PN in the first register is clear, and there are traces of a final letter of the PN from the first register. Unfortunately, the rest of the impression is not extant because the handle is broken; but the unique character of the triangular frame for impression of לשלם / אחא makes the decipherment of the impression certain.

Because impressions of לשלם / אחא are found at Lachish and Beth Shemesh,[99] it is certain that this impression from Arad was used during the late 8th century. It is further evidence that at least some royal shipments were sent to Arad during Hezekiah's reign despite challenges raised by Naʾaman that Arad was destroyed by Sargon II.[100] Finally, the I.A.A. collection card lists the dating of the handle to the "Israelite B Period" or to the "Persian Period." While this handle with the לשלם / אחא impression comes from an unstratified context, presumably with other late items

---

[98]Rainey's editorial note in M. Aharoni, "Weights and Royal Seals," 127.

[99]Both impressions are unpublished, but see Appendix II for the identifications.

[100]Naʾaman, "Brook of Egypt," 82-83, esp. n. 20; Naʾaman, "Sennacherib's Campaign," 74-75; cf. above, Chapter 2, for a refutation of this theory.

from the suggestion of the "Persian Period," a late 8th-century dating is made certain by parallels from Lachish and Beth Shemesh. It would clearly be a mistake to date this handle to a later period as suggested on the collection card. In the same way, it would be a mistake to attach significance to the discovery of isolated handle fragments with *lmlk* impressions that are not found *in situ*, whether they were found in a fill layer from Stratum VII or not.

b. Smaller Sites Mentioned by A. Mazar

A. Mazar also mentions four sites that contain *lmlk* impressions in a "sufficient 7th-century context:"[101] Khirbet Shilḥah, Ein Gedi, Khirbet es-Samrah, and Tel ʿIra. The *lmlk* finds from these sites are treated in depth above in Chapter 2. To recall that previous discussion, Khirbet Shilḥah is the only site where a convincing case can be made for the limited, continued use of a *lmlk* jar. At Shilḥah there is no evidence of any 8th-century pottery or settlement, so it must be assumed that the handle found there represents an isolated use of a *lmlk* jar during the 7th century; yet, caution must be exercised in drawing this conclusion because the handle does not come from a restorable vessel. Ein Gedi is the largest site among the four, and the abundant pottery finds in the area and on Tel Goren itself mitigate against interpreting this site as evidence for usage of the *lmlk* jars into the 7th century. Especially helpful is the official seal impression of לנחם / עבדי found in the Ein Gedi area (Naḥal Arugot). Thirteen identical impressions are also found at Lachish, and this find conclusively dates this official seal impression to the late 8th century. At Tel ʿIra, the dating is not as clear, but there does seem to be some occupation during the late 8th century as discussed in Chapter 2 and confirmed in the latest article by the excavator.[102] Similarly, the situation at Khirbet es-Samrah is ambiguous. As described in Chapter 2, Cross,[103] in the most recent survey article on the site, presents the 8th century as a possibility for the establishment of es-Samrah. Stager argued in his dissertation[104] and in a 1976 article[105] for the late 7th-century settlement of the Buqêʿah sites; however, a review of the evidence from Stager's dissertation[106] shows that his incorrect dating of Lachish Level III and Ramat Raḥel Stratum VB caused him to misdate the establishment of

---

[101]A. Mazar, Amit, and Ilan, "Horvat Shilḥah," 250, n. 46.

[102]Beit-Arieh, "Tel ʿIra," 642.

[103]Cross, "El Buqeiʿa," 267-269.

[104]Stager, "Agriculture in the Judaen Desert," esp. 249-250, 257-258.

[105]Stager, "Farming in the Judean Desert," esp. 145.

[106]Cf. above, Chapter 2.

the Buqêᶜah sites. The pottery plates and excavations descriptions from Stager's dissertation show that there is clearly some 8th-century settlement at Khirbet es-Samrah and the other Buqêᶜah sites.

In summary, there is only limited evidence to support A. Mazar's opinion that a few lmlk jars continued to be used during the 7th century, because Jerusalem was not destroyed and an ample supply of jars remained there. At the vast majority of sites, there is no evidence for widespread occurrence of even this limited reuse. It is impossible to refute every possible case, but with only one site of possible continued use into the 7th century, such a phenomenon seems to be isolated indeed.[107] Therefore, it is safe to conclude that lmlk impressions are a strong indication of occupation during the reign of Hezekiah.

7. Earliest Use of the lmlk Jars

All of the previous discussion focuses on the latest use of the lmlk jars, but it is also important to survey briefly why the scholarly consensus generally holds that these jars did not originate before the reign of Hezekiah. As stated above, it is difficult to argue for continued use of official seal impressions beyond the generation of 701 BCE because the owners of the seals would have died before then. A similar rationale can be used to set a limit on the earliest dating of the official seal impression. It is reasonable to assume that an official whose impression was found on a jar handle at the end of the 8th century would not have used that seal for much more than about 20 years prior to 701 BCE.

A second line of argument lies in examining sites where lmlk and official impressions are found that were not part of the Judean kingdom until the reign of Hezekiah. It is widely accepted that Judah benefited politically and economically by being left out of the campaigns of Sargon II. Following Sargon's death in 705, there was a vacuum in Palestine, and the Judean kingdom took advantage of this situation to expand its influence

---

[107]It is probable that at least some lmlk jars located in towns that were not destroyed during Sennacherib's campaign continued to be used in the same context into the 7th century. Such a scenario is supported by ethnoarchaeological studies that show that large storage vessels that were not mobile had a long use life (cf. W. A. Longacre, J. M. Skibo, and M. T. Stark, "Ethnoarchaeology at the Top of the World: New Ceramic Studies Among the Kalinga of Luzon," *Expedition* 33 (1993) 4-15, esp. p. 7. However, this type of continued use does not support an interpretation of secondary shipments of lmlk jars in the 7th century nor their continued production in the same century. I am grateful to J. W. Hardin for discussing these ethno-archaeological studies with me.

west into the coastal plain. Both *lmlk* and official seal impressions have been found in the following sites in or bordering the coastal plain: Tel Erani, Tel Batash, Tel Miqne (Ekron), Tell eṣ-Ṣâfi (Philistine Gath), and Ashdod. None of these sites would have been under Judean influence until the reign of Hezekiah, so the presence of the *lmlk* and official seal impressions is consistent with the earliest usage of the *lmlk* jars during Hezekiah's reign.

C. Conclusions Drawn From the *lmlk* Data

Appendices I and II have systematically set forth much new data relating to the phenomenon of the *lmlk* jars and the related seal impressions found on these jars. The reason that new data are available is that many excavators and historians have not, until now, considered each impression and each detail that corresponds to that impression important enough to warrant discussion. Many scholars feel that the phenomenon is already sufficiently documented, and that an additional impression here or there would not make any difference in the state of knowledge. But, on the contrary, the details presented in the previous sections of this monograph do provide some clues that are significant in interpreting the phenomenon surrounding the *lmlk* jars. They do not answer all the questions, but they do enable a better understanding of the overall phenomenon that in turn allows for several small but important conclusions about the reign of Hezekiah.

1. Identification of the Owners of The Impressions with PNN as Royal Officials

The new data allow for the firm conclusion that the PNN found on the related official impressions actually belong to Hezekian officials and not merely to private individuals or to potters. These names are found on jars marked as belonging to the king; moreover, the stamps with PNN occur in the spot on the jar as the *lmlk* stamps. Therefore, one would not expect these stamps to belong to private individuals or merchants separate from the royal administration. The growing scholarly trend has been to see these individuals as officials,[108] but as recently as 1993 Ussishkin left the question open for debate, stating, "Because the

---

[108]So Garfinkel, "Hierarchic Pattern;" G. Barkay, "A Group of Stamped Handles From Judah," *EI* 23 (1992) 113-28, (Hebrew).

lamelekh stamps and 'private' stamps were impressed on the same jars, the owners of the private stamps may have been officials at the production center, or were potters themselves, as D. Diringer suggests."[109] Obviously, if the new data can secure the identity of the individuals whose names are found on these royal jars, this identification will provide an important clue to the overall phenomenon.

a. Previous Proposals

Diringer made the classic argument for interpreting the PNN found on the *lmlk* jars as belonging to potters.[110] Diringer's noted that many names on these stamps recurred on different seals. He also rightly concluded that orthographic differences in the name of different seals (e.g., שבניה and שבניהו) did not suggest different individuals. He then pieced these two facts together by postulating that the reason so many identical names occurred on the seals in both the first register (the PNN of the seal owners) and in the second registers (the patronymic) was because the seal owners were related. He thus reconstructed a genealogical tree of owners of the seals and theorized that these were the potters who made the royal jars with the *lmlk* stamps.[111]

This theory has been attractive to various scholars, because there is a tendency for several names to reoccur in both the first and second registers. For Ussishkin, this fact is important when combined with a) his observation that many of the jars appear to be carelessly stamped,[112] b) the study by Mommsen, Perlman, and Yellin that suggests that all the jars were made in the same place,[113] and c) the fact the royal stamps and the stamps of individuals occur on the same jars. If it were true that the stamps were applied in such a manner that their reading didn't matter, this would seem consistent with a trademark stamp of a craftsman whose work everyone would recognize. Further, the fact that the jars were made in the same place and the *lmlk* stamps came from a limited number of stamps in six series[114] also plays well with the hypothesis that these stamps are a type of trademark and belong to potters.[115]

---

[109]Ussishkin, "Lachish," 909.

[110]Diringer, "Ancient Hebrew Inscriptions II," 89-91.

[111]Diringer, "Ancient Hebrew Inscriptions II," 89-90.

[112]Ussishkin, "Lachish 1978-1983," 160-164; Ussishkin, "Lachish," 909.

[113]H. Mommsen, I. Perlman, and J. Yellin, "The Provenience of the *lmlk* Jars," *IEJ* 34 (1984) 89-113.

[114]A. Lemaire, "Classification Des Estampilles Royales Judéennes," *EI* 15 (1981) 54*-59*, pl. VIII.

[115]Ussishkin, "Lachish," 906.

The most immediate problem with Diringer's theory is that his genealogical tree is built on many false readings of these impressions. Most of his mistakes were corrected in the subsequent publications of identical impressions,[116] but many more are corrected in an article by Barkay and me.[117] When all of these new readings are taken into account, the genealogical tree presented by Diringer is impossible to construct. There are too many cases in which there are two or three patronyms for one PN. It remains intriguing that so many PNN reoccur on these impressions, but for the present it is simply too speculative (if not impossible) to explain their frequency through a genealogical tree.

b. Method of Application of the Impressions

The seemingly "careless" application of these stamps containing PNN also requires reexamination—exactly what is meant by "careless" needs to be defined. Ussishkin concludes that because the stamps were applied at a variety of angles, the potter applied the stamps in whatever manner was most convenient, rather than worrying about whether all of them were vertical or horizontal. Ussishkin says, "In summary, we see that the seals were applied to the jar in an arbitrary way, probably at the discretion of the potter. This may also explain why so many stamps are applied in such a careless manner—or even upside down."[118] In evaluating Ussishkin's conclusions, it is seen that often it did not seem to matter what angle the stamps were applied, but in many, but not necessarily all, cases there does seem to be a concern to apply the stamps in such a way that they could be read.

Looking more closely at the examples that Ussishkin cites to draw the above conclusion, one sees that he observed several phenomena. One criterion he used was how many stamps a particular jar contained and whether those stamps were found on adjacent handles or on opposite sides of the jars. On jars that contained stamps on all four handles, Ussishkin notes that the person stamping the jar applied the seal stamps at various angles because the vertical or horizontal stance of the stamp obviously did not matter. On jars that only contained two stamps, the stamps are found on adjacent handles, presumably because it was simpler for the person stamping the jars to stamp adjacent handles than to turn the jars around. Further, many of the jars contain stamps that were applied in the area between the dual ridges of the handles so that only part of the stamp can be seen. Other stamps were placed on the edge of

---

[116]Garfinkel, "Hierarchic Pattern"; Barkay, "Group of Stamped Handles."
[117]Barkay and Vaughn, "New Readings."
[118]Ussishkin, "Lachish (1973-1977)," 80.

the handle so that the edge of the stamp was not completely legible. Ussishkin concludes that these types of placement decisions on the part of the stamper are "careless."[119]

Ussishkin is correct in noting that the stamper could exercise discretion in stamping the jars. It is certain that it was acceptable to apply incomplete stamps at a variety of angles, but several factors indicate that the application was not as "careless" as Ussishkin's comments might indicate. Many of the stamps were applied in such a way they could be read even if the impression were not complete. One clear example of this is seen on Ussishkin's Storage Jar VIII (Reg. no. 31266/1). He describes the stamping as follows: "The stamping of this handle was done carelessly on its edge, so part of the seal was not impressed."[120] However, in spite of this "careless" stamping, enough of the impression is readable enough (חן[ב]רן[ן] / למלך) to allow Ussishkin to decipher the stamp and even to give it a specific classification (Lemaire Type HIa). Similarly, Storage Jar VII also contains incomplete stamps that Ussishkin labeled "careless," yet it, too, can be deciphered and classified as Type HIa.[121]

It seems more accurate to conclude in these cases that the aesthetic presentation of the stamp was not always as important as the ability to identify the designations on them. Ussishkin's use of "careless" implies that the ability to read these stamps was not important, but, as will be seen below, the opposite is, in fact, the case. Although it is not certain from the few examples presented here that the stamps' legibility was the primary concern, other factors (below) indicate that this was often so.

One of the most suggestive pieces of data surrounding the importance of the legibility of the stamps to those stamping the vessels is the practise of stamping soft clay that has been added to a leather-hard jar handle. There are multiple examples of jar handles that obviously could not receive an adequate seal impression because the handle had already dried and become leather hard. In those cases, some soft clay added on top of the dried jar handle was stamped. This practise is common on stamped jar handles from controlled excavations, so there is no fear of the stamp's being a forgery. To my knowledge, this phenomenon has not been noted previously.

A four-winged *lmlk* stamp from renewed excavations at Beth Shemesh provides an especially clear example of this type of stamping. The impression is found on a whole jar handle that contains a large

---

[119]Ussishkin, "Lachish (1973-1977)," 76-81; Ussishkin, "Lachish 1978-1983," 160-164; Ussishkin, "Lachish," 909.

[120]Ussishkin, "Lachish 1978-1983," 162.

[121]Ussishkin, "Lachish 1978-1983," 161-162.

portion of the jar fragment. The jar fragment extends for about 2 cm to the right of the upright handle and about 10 cm to the left. The jar fragment and much of the handle contain encrustations, but the stamp itself has been cleared of most of the encrustations. The impression is at the top of the handle in between the dual ridges, but it does not make an indentation into the handle. This fact is important, because it is the first indication that the stamping occurred after the handle had already become leather hard. The next indication is that the lower left portion of the impression has broken off, leaving a clean fracture mark where soft clay was placed on top of a leather-hard handle and then stamped. There is also a difference in the fabric of the clay containing the stamp and the clay of the handle. If the added clay from the impression had not broken off, the impression would have been complete and legible. All of these factors indicate that—at least for this one particular jar—the ability to read the impression was important enough that added soft clay was placed on top of the jar handle to insure a clear stamping.

Since this phenomenon of stamping added soft clay on a leather-hard jar handle has not previously been noted, there are no statistics for how many *lmlk* and official seal impressions exhibit such seals. However, I have compiled a list, while not comprehensive, is suggestive. One example is found on the jar handle from Lachish with the seal impression of אחאם / לשלם (BM 1980/12-14/4156).[122] Another example is an especially clear official seal impression found on a handle from Tell ej-Judeideh:]עْ[זריהו /]שْ[בניהו (I.A.A. P.892). On this example, the added clay is particularly thin and was spread across the complete upper portion of the jar handle. As in the other examples, the impression does not make an indentation into the jar handle; part of the added clay has broken away, making this trait particularly easy for the modern examiner to see. Another example,]עْ[זרייהו / לצפן], is found on a handle from Gibeon (Reg. No. 410/S.146).[123] In conclusion, one notes that at least in these cases, the individual applying the stamp felt that it was necessary to apply additional clay to assure the stamp's legibility.

Another reason for questioning the importance of what Ussishkin labels "careless" stamping is the phenomenon of double stamping—the same seal being applied to the same jar handle at different angles, presumably because the first impression was not clear enough. Like the

---

[122]This impression was originally published as unreadable; the correct reading is presented in Barkay and Vaughn, "New Readings," 37-40, no. 10.

[123]There is no accession number for this handle at the Museum of Archaeology and Anthropology of the University of Pennsylvania. This is probably because the handle is listed in the publication as being stored in Amman, but for some reason it ended up in Philadelphia.

previous phenomenon, this common feature has not been noted previously. One illustrative example is again seen on a restored handle described by Ussishkin as "carelessly" stamped. On Restored Jar III (I.A.A. 75.244) there are three stamps that Ussishkin labels as "carelessly impressed."[124] Two of the impressions are Lemaire type ?II? and cannot be deciphered. The third was not deciphered by Ussishkin because it was stamped twice at opposite angles, but once this feature is noted, the stamp can be deciphered positively as שחר / יהוחיל.[125] On this jar one again observes that all three stamps were applied in a way that is difficult to decipher; however, the crucial stamp with the PN was stamped twice—obviously because the ability to decipher the stamp was considered important. The fact that the *lmlk* stamps were not doubly impressed indicates that whatever identification they were to convey was made clear with the identification of the official impression.

The double-stamped impressions are too numerous to list here, and a comprehensive listing is not available because this feature has not been noted previously. The following list is thus only suggestive of the practice. First, a jar handle from Lachish (Pal Rm AA / L.13 / 273.1) contains two stamps, one on top of the other and at 180 degrees to each other. The first stamp was impressed upside down but was unclear. The second stamp is right side up and clear (HIb). This example indicates that in this instance although the angle of the stamp was not important if the impression could be deciphered, the person who stamped it took the time to change the angle to achieve a stamp that could be deciphered. There are also three examples from Gibeon with double stamping: UPenn reg. nos. 60-13-102, 60-13-121, 60-13-154. Finally, an official impression from Ramat Raḥel (שחר א./לשבנ) that was originally misread because of the double stamping was deciphered in part because the double stamping was recognized.[126]

In summarizing the data concerning the ability to decipher the *lmlk* and official impressions, one notes that two phenomena suggest that the ability to decipher them was important: a) the stamping of added soft clay on the leather-hard handle, and b) double stamping. However, note that hundreds of the *lmlk* impressions are yet indecipherable. This number might be reduced if one were to allow for the blurring that has occurred over several thousand years on many impressions on jar handles, but nonetheless many others were doubtless indecipherable when they

---

[124]Ussishkin, "Lachish (1973-1977)," 77; cf. Ussishkin, "Royal Judean Storage Jars," 1-3, figs. 1-2.

[125]Barkay and Vaughn, "Impression from Lachish Reconsidered," 94-97.

[126]Barkay and Vaughn, "New Readings," 47-48, no. 20.

were originally stamped. The conclusion must be drawn that in some cases the ability to decipher an individual impression was not critical, but that in other cases an added effort was made to insure that the impression could be read (either by double stamping or stamping additional clay).

This observation is especially true regarding the official seal impressions. The fact that twenty-four official impressions previously regarded as unreadable were deciphered in articles by Barkay and Vaughn[127] indicates that many, perhaps most, of the impressions were stamped in such a way that they could be deciphered. The ability to decipher these stamps is made possible by recognizing the phenomenon of double stamping and by having a familiarity with all the identical seals of the same individual. Obviously, the stampers in antiquity knew these things much better than modern researchers; thus, it seems that most if not all of the official impressions were stamped in such a way that they could be deciphered. The *lmlk* impressions that were stamped in such a way that they could not be deciphered were found on jars that also carried a decipherable official seal impression (such as was the case above), or on jars with another decipherable *lmlk* impression, or they were manufactured and shipped with jars containing decipherable *lmlk* impressions.

It is clear that in many cases extra effort was taken to insure that the impressions were decipherable. In light of these data, I prefer to use the term "messy," rather than "careless" with regard to the impression of these seals. The people who applied the stamps often did not seem to care about aesthetic presentation, but they did exercise care—at least on occasion—to make sure that the stamps could be deciphered.

All of this has bearing on the question of the identity of the individuals whose PNN are found on these impressions. If these individuals were potters, as Diringer suggests, one would expect that the application of their names and the *lmlk* stamps would be well known and so these stamps could be carelessly applied. In fact, the opposite is true. Most of the impressions with PNN are decipherable, and probably all of them would be decipherable if more parallels were available. In many cases, it was deemed important to be able to decipher the exact type of *lmlk* impression, and in every case the general two-wing or four-wing genre is decipherable. Regardless of whether the owners of these seals with private names were potters or officials, their identity was often important.

---

[127]See Barkay and Vaughn, "Impression Reconsidered," and "New Readings." Appendix II also contains several additional new readings beyond these 24 that will be published in full in a forthcoming article by Barkay and me.

It thus seems more probable that an official would be more concerned about decipherability than a potter. A potter's stamp would probably just signal that the pot had been completed, but an official's stamp would carry meaning after the jar had been shipped. It is also unclear why care would have been exercised to identify the artisans on these vessels by name since this phenomenon is not known elsewhere. Other factors presented below corroborate this interpretation, but for the present it is sufficient to note that the concern sometimes taken to make the impressions decipherable (especially the impressions with PNN) suggests that the owners of these seals were officials, not potters.

c. Fabric and Makeup of the Seals

A second method of identifying the owners involves examining the fabric of the seals themselves. Unfortunately, to date no actual *lmlk* or official seals have been discovered, so a discussion of the fabric must be limited to clues taken from the seal impressions. This identification of fabric is nevertheless important in determining the owners of the seals because one would not expect potters to own seals found on semiprecious stones, whereas that would not be extraordinary for royal officials.

Even though to date all extant northwest Semitic seals have been found engraved in mediums such as bone, semiprecious gems, or metal, R. Deutsch and M. Heltzer have suggested that the official seal impressions (and by analogy the *lmlk* impressions) were stamped from wooden seals. In support of this claim, Deutsch and Heltzer point to a single seal impression on a *lmlk*type jar handle fragment that possibly shows signs of wood grain.[128] Based on this single impression, they conclude:

> Wooden seals are known from classical archaeology, at least in the region of the Black Sea,[129] and also from Delos and Egypt during the Hellenistic period. Thus, we may conclude that such seals were made especially for the purpose of sealing the *lmlk* jars."[130]

---

[128]R. Deutsch and M. Heltzer, *New Epigraphic Evidence from the Biblical Period* (Tel Aviv-Jaffa, Israel: Archaeological Center Publication, 1995) 45-46, fig. 52.

[129]Deutsch and Heltzer cite two works that were not available to me: J. Braschinsky, "Uspehi keramičeskoi epigrafiki (Progress of Creamic Epigraphics)," *Sovetskaya Archeologiya* (1961) 293-306 (Russian); A. Sardurska, "Stemplowanie imadla amfor, dachowki i inne zabytki epigrafiki ceramiczney (Sealing of the Jar-Handles, Timber, and Other Ancient Finds of Ceramic Epigraphy)," in K. Michalowski, *Mirmeki I* (Warszawa: 1958), 101-116 (Russian).

[130]Deutsch and Heltzer, *New Epigraphic Evidence*, 46.

The impression in question originates from the antiquities market in Jerusalem and presently is found in the private collection of S. Moussaieff, London. The impression is oval in shape and its length is almost twice as long as the width (15.5 x 8.0 mm). It contains two PNN in two registers, separated by a double dividing line. The PN in the upper register is preceded by a *lamed* preposition, as is common for many of the official seal impressions. The impression reads, לסמך / צפניהו. It also contains vertical "grain lines" that appear to continue under the dividing lines and the strokes of the letters. These grain lines cause Deutsch and Heltzer to suggest that a wooden seal made this impression, and that the grain lines are wood grains.[131]

Several factors raise questions about Deutsch and Heltzer's conclusion. Although they point to several examples of wooden seals from classical archaeology and from the Hellenistic period, there are no other examples of such a phenomenon on known northwest Semitic seals and seal impressions. It seems odd that if such a practice were indeed common, no other examples of grain lines would be known in the corpus. Further, the grain lines seem too consistently vertical to originate from a piece of wood. One would expect a more circular pattern from wood grain.

Finally, a corrected error that occurs in the upper register of the seal impression is the most damaging factor to a theory that this impression was made from a wooden seal. As stated above, although the upper register reads לסמך, Deutsch and Heltzer fail to report that the third letter (a *mem*) was initially written as a *kaph* (𐤊), then corrected by the addition of three vertically slanting bars to form the head of a *mem*. The two bars closest to the downward shaft of the letter are inscribed at a nearly perpendicular angle over the bars that formed the head of the initial *kaph*, but the added bars do not prevent the identification of the earlier letter. If this seal had been constructed of wood, one would expect that the engraver would have simply made another seal instead of trying to salvage the present one. Thus, it seems that this correction would indicate that the seal responsible for the impression was constructed from some sort of semiprecious material rather than wood. All these factors strongly indicate that the seal responsible for this impression was not made from wood, but rather from some semiprecious material, and that the grain lines which are nearly perfectly vertical, represent a particular type of stylizing on the part of the engraver.

---

[131]Deutsch and Heltzer, *New Epigraphic Evidence*, 45.

Other factors also support the view that at least some of the seals responsible for the official seal impressions were made from semiprecious material. First, other impressions show signs of mistakes that indicate that the engraver felt it was necessary to correct rather than construct a new seal. The seal responsible for the לשוכ/י שבנ/א impression is a good example. The engraver obviously ran out of room in the first register, so the last letter in the name שוכ/י is found as the initial letter of the second register, as is common on many other seals. The larger problem occurs when the second name cannot be fitted in the second register. When this happened, the engraver had to squeeze the final letter (an *aleph*) below the second register in a manner that partially covers the *shin* in the second register. The fact that the first and second registers are separated by a single dividing line, whereas there is no dividing line between the second and third registers, confirms that the placement of this *aleph* in the lowest register was not initially intended. The existence of a second seal (לשכי / שבנא) with the complete name שבנא found on the second register further supports this conclusion. One questions why an engraver would attempt to correct a seal made of an inexpensive material rather than simply engrave a new seal. On the other hand, if the medium were some sort of semiprecious material, this correction would seem reasonable. Moreover, at least three additional seals that were used to form the official seal impressions show signs of errors that were corrected instead of fashioning new seals, thus providing corroboration for this conclusion: a) תנחם / לאחא, b) מנחם / ויהבנה, and c) לנחם / עבדי}י{.

Another clue from the official seal impressions that suggests that the seals were made of some sort of semiprecious material is that numerous impressions show signs of frames from a ring or pendant. Since the corpus of northwest Semitic seals contains many examples of semiprecious stones held in ring frames or in pendants with frame, the existence of these framing marks would indicate that the seal was made of such a material. One particularly clear example is found on one of the impressions cited above for a correction (לשוכ/י שבנ/א from Lachish). This impression, now stored at Cambridge University (D/X / J.15 / 6019), is found on a jar handle fragment with an impression deeply stamped to a total depth of 2-3 mm. On each side of this deep impression are two small indentations in the jar handle that indicate that the seal was connected at this point to a seal ring or pendant.[132]

---

[132]Cf. the recent publication by Lemaire of a semiprecious seal housed in a pendant with a frame. The publication contains a nice photograph of the pendant that would make indentations in a seal impressions (A. Lemaire, "Royal Signature—Name of Israel's Last King Surfaces in a Private Collection," *BAR* 21:6 [1995], esp. photograph on the cover).

Although most of the official seal impressions were not impressed deeply enough to reveal whether they were held by frames, there are a few additional examples. Several impressions of למנחם / יובנה, particularly the impression from Lachish stored at Cambridge University (H.17 / 47B:6), have dual prick marks on both sides of the oval impression. Likewise, יהוחל / שחר, a seal impression from Lachish (bucket no. 10612) contains prick marks on the left side of the impression where the seal was stamped deeply. An impression of לנבד / עבדי from Lachish, stored in the Rockefeller Museum (I.A.A. no. 33.2112) shows signs of a rectangular frame on the right side of the impression where it was stamped deeply. An impression of הושו / צפן (I.A.A. no. 33.2114) is stamped deeply on the right side and also contains these prick marks. These examples indicate that some of the seals responsible for making the official seal impressions were held in frames, possibly attached to rings or pendants.

On the other hand, not all of the seals seem to have been held in frames, because some of the impressions are stamped deeply but do not contain signs of the frames. One clear example is מנחם / ויהבנה from Beth Shemesh (I.A.A. no. I.8652) which is stamped very deeply on the right side but contains no signs of a prick mark, a chain, or a frame. The seals that were not held in frames on rings could possibly have been the type shaped like short triangular rods.

Also important for understanding the fabric of the seals is the fact that many of the impressions are concave, indicating that the seal was convex on the side with the inscription. This phenomenon is well known on other northwest Semitic seals, although not all gems contained writing on the convex side. However, the fact that some of the impressions are concave suggests that they were stamped by seals inscribed on semiprecious gems with convex side. Several examples among the official seal impressions are particularly clear. All of the impressions of לסמך / ב ן / צפניהו with the four-winged uraeus have concave impressions. These impressions are also particularly helpful because they contain a detailed iconographic representation of a four-winged uraeus that would have been very difficult to incise in a wooden seal without the wood grain showing. This fact, combined with the concave impressions, suggests that this detailed seal was inscribed on a semiprecious gem.

As one might expect, not all of the seals contained a convex surface with an inscription. There are seals with inscriptions on flat as well as convex surfaces among the corpus of northwest Semitic seals. Other official seal impressions that are particularly concave and thus indicate a convex seal are the following: a) לעבד/י, b) אחמלך / משלם, and c) לשבנ/א. שחר.

In summary, several factors point to the conclusion that at least some of the seals were made from semiprecious material. The corrected errors on some impressions suggest that the seals were made from a material that the engraver would prefer not to throw away. The fact that some of the impressions appear to have frames such as were common on seal rings, while some lack such frames, points to the use of a semiprecious gem for at least some of the seals. There are many parallels of seals made of gems framed in rings and seals made of gems that were used alone as stamps. Finally, the fact that many of the impressions were concave confirms the view that at least some of the seals were made from gems.

d. Multiple Seals Belonging to the Same Individual

Building on the conclusion that at least some of the seals were probably made of semiprecious material, one notes in the list of officials and seals in Appendix II that many owners of seals with private names owned multiple seals. This suggests a royal official who could afford multiple seals. It is impossible to tell how many seals one person may have owned, but we do know that at least twelve of the individuals whose names appear on these seal impressions owned two or more. One, שבנא (בן) נרא, owned at least five seals. Table 6 is a list individuals with at least two seals:

TABLE 6: INDIVIDUALS WHO OWNED AT LEAST 2 "OFFICIAL" SEALS

name of individual	minimum number of seals owned
נרא (בן) שבנא	5
צפן (בן) עזריהו	4
יהוחיל (בן) שחר	3
מנחם (בן) יובנה	3
נחם (בן) עבדי	3
אחזיהו (בן) תנחם	2
הושע (בן) צפן	2
חשי (בן) אלשמע	2
נחם (בן) הצליהו	2
סמך (בן) צפניהו	2
שבניהו (בן) עזריהו	2
שוכי (בן) שבנא	2

Once again, it seems unlikely that so many potters would have either the need or the resources to own so many separate seals. A signle seal would have sufficed for a potter whose purpose was to identify his or her work and demand payment. However, multiple seals do not seem extraordinary for royal officials. An official could use separate seals for a particular shipment, or a particular region, or might even distribute seals to functionaries.

A typological parallel to the existence of multiple seals owned by one person provides an even stronger means of corroborating that the owners of these stamps were officials, not private individuals or potters. In the corpus of bullae published by Avigad, there are numerous officials who owned more than one seal. Some contain titles and thus cast no doubt on their status as official. For example, אדניהו אשר על הבית owned at least two seals with the same orthographic spelling of his name and title.[133] Another group of bullae from Avigad's corpus belong to אלעז בן אחאב; these come from two different seals but lack the title identifying this person as an official. The typological parallel with the multiple seals owned by the official אדניהו אשר על הבית is especially strong since both sets of bullae were found in a related context. This suggests that the person without the title (אלעז בן אחאב) should also be viewed as an official. Cross, however, has questioned whether seal owners without titles were officials or simply prominent individuals or landowners.[134]

An explicit typological parallel for a royal official owning multiple seals but not having an extant title is found at Arad, where three actual seals (not bullae) belonging to the official אלישב were found in the same room, in a clear stratigraphic context of Stratum VII (destruction date 609 BCE). All three were found in Locus 779 of Square L8 at a level of 75.45 m. Two of the seals read לאלישב בן אשיהו (I.A.A. 67-1184 and 67-663); the third is written defectively and reads לאלשב >בב< אשיהו (I.A.A. 67-984).[135] It is clear from the many ostraca from Arad Stratum VII that אלישב was the commander of the city who was responsible for the distribution of the goods and resources from the city. Thus, Aharoni concludes that "it is clear that these 'private seals,' containing only the name of their bearer, were not at all private, but belonged to an official who had a great deal of authority....Thus it is clear that the lack of a title or emblem on a Hebrew seal does not prove that it was a private seal."[136]

Aharoni also explains the relevance of this find for interpreting the seal impressions containing PNN on *lmlk* jar handles. He states that the simple fact that the majority of these impressions lack titles or emblems should not hinder the interpretation that they belonged to royal officials.[137] Building on Aharoni's observations, one sees that the above new data

---

[133] Avigad, *Hebrew Bullae*, 21.

[134] Cross, "Judean Stamps," 20-27.

[135] Aharoni, *Arad Inscriptions*, 119-120, 185.

[136] Aharoni, *Arad Inscriptions*, 120.

[137] Aharoni, *Arad Inscriptions*, 120.

have shown that there is also a typological parallel between the owners of the impressions with PNN found on the *lmlk* jar handles, because many of them owned multiple seals. From the evidence available from northwest Semitic seals, it seems that individuals who used multiple seals were often officials.

e. A Conservative Estimate of the Number of Engravers Used

The number of engravers used to make these seals is another factor to consider in distinguishing the owners of these seal impressions. The paleographic discussion presented in Chapter 1 provides the basis for a conservative estimate of the minimum number of engravers used to create the official seal impressions discovered to date. This estimate presupposes that each engraver would be fairly consistent in the way he or she engraved the letters. It is assumed that each letter would not always look exactly the same, but that there would not be radical variations in forms.

The two letters used to make this estimate are *waw* and *ṣade*. An examination of Hebrew seals shows that these two letters involve a larger number of strokes that may exhibit more variation from engraver to engraver than most other letters. For example, the letter *pe* is a fairly simple letter to engrave and only involves two strokes—a horizontal bar connected to a downward vertical shaft. The letter *samek* involves more strokes—at least three horizontal bars, a vertical shaft, and sometimes a stroke connecting the lowest horizontal bar to the vertical shaft; however, the letter is formed in such a way that it is difficult to vary radically the relationship of the horizontal bars and the vertical shaft. On the other hand, the letters *ṣade* and *waw* are more stylized and allow for the particular habits of individual engravers to be seen.

The earlier examples of the letter *waw* on seals are formed by a semicircular head connected to a nonsloping vertical shaft (Ⴣ). During the 8th century this letter develops through the addition of a sloping bar that intersects at the meeting place of the semicircular head and the vertical shaft (Ⴣ). As this development occurs, several variations are seen. The semicircular head no longer remains a pure semicircle, but rather slopes to one side or the other and many instances of this letter contain curves in the head that have sharp edges and evolve into shapes that do not look like a semicircle at all (Ⴣ). Likewise, the vertical shaft often slopes to one side or the other in the late 8th century (Ⴣ). These changes indicate that engravers during the late 8th century were permitted to form a *waw* in many different ways as long as there was a head that resembled the older semicircle, an intersecting bar, and a vertical shaft. There is even one example[138] that contains only the semicircular head and the vertical shaft without the intersecting bar (ᛉ).

An examination of the examples of the letter *waw* from all of the official seal impressions reveals at least eight types, suggesting multiple engravers.[139] First, is the form with the opening of the head pointing to the top left and with curves formed without sharp edges (ᚤ). Second, is the form with the opening of the head pointing to the top left, but the curves contain sharp edges (ᚤ). Third, is the form with the opening of the head pointing to the top right and with curves formed without sharp edges (ᚤ). Fourth, is the form with the opening of the head pointing to the top right, but the curves contain sharp edges (Y). Fifth, is the form where the head opens directly above the vertical shaft without sloping to one side or the other (Y). Sixth, is the form where the head opens directly above the vertical shaft, but the intersecting bar is unique in that it is formed as a completely separate stroke from the semicircular head (ᚤ). Seventh, is a letter where the head is formed by two distinct strokes (ᚷ). Finally, is an archaic form that does not contain the intersecting bar (ᛉ).

Turning to the letter *ṣade*, one sees that there is even more variation. Table 7 illustrates this variation well:

---

[138]Cf. Chapter 1.

[139]It is important not to preclude the possibility that one engraver could utilize different forms on different seals or even on the same seal (cf. Cross, "Seal of *Miqnêyaw*," 59, figs. 1-3, for an example of a seal with two forms of the letter *qoph* on the same seal). Although some variation is to be expected, the presence of seven different forms indicates multiple engravers.

TABLE 7: VARIATION OF THE LETTER ṢADE

impressions with ṣade	example of ṣade
הושע / צפן	⟨shape⟩
הושע / צפן	⟨shape⟩ (letter not clear)
לנחם / הצליהו	⟨shape⟩
לנחם / הצליהו	⟨shape⟩
לסמך / ב ן / צפניהו	⟨shape⟩
לסמך / צפניהו	⟨shape⟩
לצדק / סמך	⟨shape⟩
לצפן / אבמעץ	⟨shape⟩
לצפן / אבמעץ	⟨shape⟩
צפן ע/זריהו	⟨shape⟩
צפן. / עזר.	⟨shape⟩
לצפן / עזר	⟨shape⟩
לצפן / עזריהו	⟨shape⟩

Once again the variant forms suggest multiple engravers.[140]

Summing up these data, multiple engravers made the 54 official seals known so far. Letters that exhibit pronounced variation that suggests mulitiple engravers are *ṣade* and *waw*. Other letters also support the conclusion, particularly *aleph*, *he*, and *mem* as listed in a separate study by the present author.[141]

The large number of engravers employed in making these seals provides further evidence that the seals did not belong to potters. Just as one would not expect a potter to own multiple seals made from semiprecious stones, it seems equally unlikely that a potter would have needed to employ multiple engravers. Indeed, as we have seen, if a potter used such stamps at all, it would have been to signify the completion of a job or fulfillment of a quota. In such a case, one would expect the potter to purchase or obtain a seal from one engraver, not more. Nor would variation and style have been important.

---

[140]Once again, the possibility for of variation in letters by the same engraver must be considered. For instance, note that the official seal impression, לצפן. א/במעץ, has two slightly different forms for the two occurences of the letter *ṣade* (⟨shape⟩ and ⟨shape⟩).

[141]Vaughn, "Palaeographic Dating," 43-64.

The paleographic data show that different engravers made the seals. Whatever the function of these seals, it was not an isolated one. This observation does not prove that the seals' owners were not potters, but it does corroborate other indicators that the owners were indeed officials. It also provides further evidence for viewing the proliferation of the *lmlk* jars as a larger phenomenon than previously recognized.

f. Titles on the Impressions with PNN on Royal Jar Handles

Several titles and emblems corroborate the typological parallel and suggest that this group of impressions belonged to officials. One seal contains an emblem of a four-winged uraeus (לסמך / ב ן / צפניהו). The emblem is stylized and of the type that one would expect on the seal of an important person. It is also typical of other Judean glyptics.[142] The owner, סמך (בן) צפניהו had another seal that produced an impression on a *lmlk* jar (לסמך / צפניהו). This second seal also contained stylized "grain" marks; thus, it appears that this individual owned at least two seals like was the case with אלישב of Arad, and that both of them were stylized.

Another seal with an emblem of the four-winged uraeus contains an inscription that provides an explicit identification of the owner as an official in the king's court. The collection in the Hecht Museum contains an impression that contains the inscription לשבניהו / בן המלך and an emblem of a four-winged uraeus.[143] The impression is blurred, but a faint four-winged uraeus is visible above the inscription with two registers. The first register contains a *lamed* preposition and the PN of the owner (לשבניהו), while the lower register contains the title בן המלך. Avigad noted that the impression was found "on a fragment of jar handle with bright brown ware," but he did not specify that it was a *lmlk* jar handle.[144] However, I examined the handle in March 1994 and concluded that it was identical in type to the hundreds of other *lmlk* jar handles I have examined.[145] Barkay also examined this jar handle and reached the same conclusion. In a separate report he states:

---

[142]Cf. B. Sass, "The Pre-exilic Hebrew Seals: Iconism vs. Aniconism," *Studies in the Iconography of Northwest Semitic Inscribed Seals*. *Proceedings of a Symposium Held in Fribourg on April 17-20, 1991* (ed. B. Sass and C. Uehlinger; OBO 125; Fribourg: University Press; Göttingen: Vandenhoeck & Ruprecht, 1993) 213, 244.

[143]N. Avigad, "Titles and Symbols on Hebrew Seals," *EI* 15 (1981) 304-305, pl. מ:2.

[144]Avigad, "Titles and Symbols," 304.

[145]I thank O. Rimon, curator of the Hecht Museum at the University of Haifa both for granting permission to examine this handle and for assisting me in my visit to the museum.

This seal impression . . . probably belongs to the general phenomenon called "private" seal impressions, which appear together with the "למלך," or royal seal impressions from the late eighth century (Ussishkin, "Royal Judean Storage Jars," 1-13). A seal impression on the jar handle found at Tell Goded (Tell ej-Judeideh) in the Shephelah may be a second example of the one mentioned above (Bliss and Macalister, *Excavations in Palestine*, p. 56:25). Although it is broken and missing the inscription, the emblem of the winged scarob was preserved.[146]

This identification is important because it provides an example of an impression with a PN on a *lmlk* jar belonging to an official.

It has been debated whether the term בן המלך refers to a generic official without royal blood or to an actual son or relative of the king. C. Clermont-Ganneau first suggested more than 100 years ago that in some cases the title בן המלך might be used for a functionary or minor official of the king rather than for a relative.[147] His arguments have been represented and advanced by de Vaux,[148] Yeivin,[149] and Brin.[150] The major arguments against interpreting the title בן המלך literally as a relative of the king stem from four biblical passages that contain this title but where the relationship to the king is ambiguous (1 Kgs 22:26, Jer 36:26, Jer 38:6, and 2 Chr 28:7). Only Brin[151] has included arguments from other ancient Near Eastern texts, but all of these examples were refuted by Rainey.[152]

A. Lemaire has addressed each of these four biblical passages. In the first case, 1 Kgs 22:26 (= 2 Chr 18:25), he shows that the phrase יואש בן המלך, which follows the title שר העיר, does not necessarily mean anything regarding the royal status of the official יואש. Moreover, 2 Chr 21:2-3 reports that Jehosaphat put his children over the cities of Judah while saving the kingdom for his firstborn, Jeroboam. It seems likely that, in addition to giving some children responsibilities outside Jerusalem, others likely would have been given responsibilities in Jerusalem.[153]

---

[146]G. Barkay, "A Bulla of Ishmael, the King's Son," *BASOR* 290-291 (1993) 111.

[147]C. Clermont-Ganneau, *Recueil d'archéologie orientale I* (Paris, 1888) 36.

[148]R. de Vaux, *Ancient Israel: Its Life and Institutions* (London: Darton, Longman & Todd, 1961) 119-120.

[149]S. Yeivin, "Son of the King," In *Encyclopedia Biblica II* (Jerusalem: Bialik Institute, 1954) 160.

[150]G. Brin, "The Title בן (ה)מלך and Its Parallels," *AION* 29 (1969) 433-466.

[151]Brin, "The Title בן (ה)מלך," 433-466.

[152]A. F. Rainey, "The Prince and the Pauper," *UF* 7 (1975) 427-32.

[153]A. Lemaire, "Note Sur le Titre *BN HMLK* Dans L'Ancien Israël," *Semitica*

The royal status of the next two figures from biblical examples in Jeremiah is called into question because they are both described as part of the royal guard. Jer 36:26 states the following:

ויצוה המלך את־ירחמאל בן־המלך ואת שריהו בן־עזריאל ואת־ שלמיהו בן־עבדאל ...

And the king commanded Jerahmeel the son of the king, and Seraiah the son of Azriel, and Shelemiah the son of Abdeel ...

Brin and others argue that if ירחמאל were the real son of the king, the word בנו "his son" would have been used instead of בן המלך.[154] However, Lemaire correctly points out that ירחמאל could very well have been Jehoiakim's uncle (the son of another king) or another member of the royal family. Moreover, if ירחמאל were not part of the royal family, one would expect the patronym to be given as was done with the other two people named.

A similar case is found in Jer 38:6, where the royal lineage of מלכיהו בן המלך should not be doubted simply because he plays a role in the royal guard.[155] Lemaire's final example (2 Chr 28:7) actually supports the interpretation of a literal son of the king, because the death of מעשיהו בן המלך after Ahaz the king has been killed is just what one would expect since the king's son would be seen as a threat.[156]

In light of all these examples, it seems most probable that the title בן המלך was used for a literal son—or at least a relative—of the king. Often in the biblical corpus, one finds that this relative functions as an official in the kingdom, carrying out different roles. Such an interpretation accords well with the understanding of שבניהו בן המלך as one of the royal officials whose PNN occur on the *lmlk* jars. Since we know of two additional seals belonging to שבניהו (בן) עזריהו from the official seal impressions on *lmlk* jar handles, it is possible that the impression of לשבניהו / בן המלך was

---

29 (1979) 60-61; Rainey, "Prince and the Pauper," 428.

[154]Brin, "The Title בן (ה)מלך," 435.

[155]Lemaire, "Le Titre *BN HMLK*," 61-62; cf. Rainey, "Prince and the Pauper," 428. Recently a malachite seal of unknown provenance with an inscription containing this same PN and title (למלכיהו בן המלך) was published in an auction catalog of antiquities (NFA Classical Auctions, Inc., *Egyptian, Near Eastern Greek & Roman Antiquities: New York, December 11, 1991* [New York: NFA Classical Auctions, 1991] no. 50). If this seal were authentic and belonged to the same individual who threw Jeremiah and Baruch into the pit, it might support an interpretation that מלכיהו was a relative of the king, because one would expect an official of royal blood to own a seal on a semiprecious stone. However, this seal is from the antiquities market, and it may be a forgery.

[156]Lemaire, "Le Titre *BN HMLK*," 62-63.

owned by this same official, who might have been the son of King Uzziah/ Azariah.

The only other title found to date in the corpus of the official seal impressions is that of נער in the impression לאליקם / נער יוכן. When the impression was believed to have belonged to a servant of King Jehoiachin, this title was taken to be the equivalent of עבד as used to convey the title of a servant of the king.[157] However, the renewed excavations at Lachish have shown that this chronological identification (see discussion above in Chapter 2) was in error by about 100 years. Thus, Avigad and others have asked if the title נער in this seal could have been used by a royal official. Avigad doubts that a servant of a private individual could also be considered a servant of a king, and he asserts that if someone were the servant of the king, that person would never be labeled as the servant of someone else. Avigad goes so far as to conclude that the title עבד is reserved on seals for a royal official, while the title נער on seals is used solely for private officials not in royal service.[158] If Avigad's interpretation is correct, such a stance would have negative ramifications for the interpretation of the PNN found on *lmlk* jar handles as belonging to officials. Thus, it is important to look more closely at the title נער in the Hebrew Bible and in the extrabiblical Hebrew corpus.

Two thorough studies of the noun נער completed independently in 1976 are instructive. In one study, J. Macdonald[159] focuses on the status of the נער in the Hebrew Bible, especially in military contexts. The other study is H.-P. Stähli's dissertation, completed in 1976 but not published until a few years later.[160] Stähli presents an extensive etymological development of the noun נער as well as a treatment of the social status of the נער in the Hebrew Bible. These studies focus on different issues surrounding the noun נער in the Hebrew Bible, and both should be evaluated.[161]

---

[157]Cf. W. F. Albright, "The Seal of Eliakim and the Latest Pre-exilic History of Judah, with Some Observations on Ezekial," *JBL* 51 (1932) 77-106.

[158]Avigad, "Titles and Symbols," 303.

[159]J. Macdonald, "The Status and Role of the Naᶜar in Israelite Society," *JNES* 35, no. 1976 (1976) 147-70.

[160]H-P. Stähli, *Knabe, Jüngling, Knecht: Untersuchung Zum Begriff נער Im Alten Testament* (BBET; Frankfurt am Main and Bern: Peter Lang, 1978).

[161]Stähli does mention Macdonald's work in his bibliography, but states in his Forward that "die seit dem Frürhjahr 1976 erschienene Literatur konnte dabei nur in Anmerkungen berücksichtigt werden" (Stähli, *Knabe, Jüngling, Knecht*, 7). I am grateful to my colleagues, G. Bilkes and M. T. Davis, for sharing their independent works on the noun נער and their views of Macdonald and Stähli.

Stähli begins his study with an etymological treatment of the noun נער. He concludes that the previous etymologies for the noun from נער I "to cry" or from נער II "to shake" are unfounded, and that the noun נער does not seem to develop from a known verbal root of נ-ע-ר. He states that נער is a particularly primitive noun and its etymological origin from Canaanite is uncertain.[162] He thus posits that the noun נער in the Hebrew Bible and in Ugaritic come from the verbal נער III and concludes that the meaning of the noun must be determined by its usage in each context.[163]

Having established that the meaning of the noun must be based solely on context, Stähli presents a comprehensive survey of its occurrences in the Hebrew Bible and texts from related dialects. He finds that the underlying meaning conveys the idea of a person having the status of a minor or one "under age." Within this general concept of meaning, the noun first of all can designate someone who lives in dependence on the *pater familias*.[164] In this case, the person (including a female—נערה) is someone who is not married but may be any age from a child to an older person. Such individuals cease to be considered a נער or נערה when they marry.[165]

A second type of use for the noun describes individuals who live in a relationship of dependence (*Abhängigkeitsverhältnis*) to someone else, not necessarily family. People in this category can be adults and include slaves, servants, functionaries, sacral servants, officials, and military professionals.[166]

For the purposes of the present study, it is the second category—the individual in a relationship of dependence—that has the most relevance for the use of the title נער in the seal impression לאליקם / נער יוכן. It seems clear that whoever used this seal on jars that contained royal impressions was some sort of functionary or official. The question remains, however, if Avigad is correct assuming that because אליקם is in a relationship of dependence to יוכן (a person who is clearly not the king), that אליקם cannot be a royal official. At this point it is helpful to turn to Macdonald's study of the noun, which that focuses on the status of the נער.

---

[162]Stähli, *Knabe, Jüngling, Knecht*, 275.

[163]Stähli, *Knabe, Jüngling, Knecht*, 37.

[164]For the function of the *pater familias* over the houshould and how a נער could be seen as in a relationship of dependence to the household, cf. L. E. Stager, "The Archaeology of the Family in Ancient Israel," *BASOR* 260 (1985) 20. I thank N. Fox for calling this reference to my attention.

[165]Stähli, *Knabe, Jüngling, Knecht*, 77-135, 275-276.

[166]Stähli, *Knabe, Jüngling, Knecht*, 135-217, 276.

One of Macdonald's first observations is that in the Hebrew Bible the term נער is always used in reference to a person of noble birth or high status. He concludes that "the *neᶜarim* are never mere slaves or menial servants. It is probable that in Israelite society, as in the society of Ugarit centuries before, there were distinctive classes or guilds of *neᶜarim*."[167] In evaluating this initial conclusion, one notes that a little more caution is needed before such a sweeping generalization can be made. It is true that in the Hebrew Bible, a נער often refers to a person of high rank, but it is difficult to conclude that this was necessarily so. One need only think of Abraham's נערים in Genesis chapter 22 who seem to function merely as servants to carry the stores and take care of the livestock. These servants may have had a high status, and they may have come from "noble" stock, but it also seems just as likely that they were merely slaves or servants who carried out Abraham's orders. Nonetheless, whether or not Macdonald's general claim of a noble birth can be substantiated in every case, it is clear that the term is often used in that manner in the Hebrew Bible and in the Ugaritic texts. Several examples of such high-status נערים are helpful in gaining a better grasp of the meaning conveyed in the seal לאליקם / נער יוכן.

The נער of Boaz (Ruth 2:5) serves as a functionary or official in charge of the reapers and also plays the role of a functionary in carrying out the harvest. From the context of the story, it seems that this man has some power of his own as well. However, other נערים are mentioned later in the passage (Ruth 2:15); they are addressed directly by Boaz and seem to be equivalent to harvesters (קוצרים). In Ruth 2, it seems that there are two types of נערים—one who is in a relationship of dependence with Boaz and serves as a functionary or official, and others, also in a dependency relationship with Boaz, who seem to be mere servants.[168] It is possible that the latter group could have also been officials and in charge of other קוצרים,[169] but the context of the passage suggests that the more probable interpretation is that they were merely servants.

Another helpful parallel is the עבד and נער of Saul. In response to Avigad's suggestion that on Hebrew seals the title נער is reserved for servants of individuals, while the term עבד is reserved for servants of the king, note that Ziba is called the עבד of David and Saul (cf. 2 Sam 9:2) and the נער of Saul (cf. 2 Sam 9:9; 19:18). Although Avigad could be correct in asserting that this term was used differently on Hebrew seals than in the

---

[167]Macdonald, "Status and Role," 150.

[168]Cf. Stähli, *Knabe, Jüngling, Knecht*, 179-180; Macdonald, "Status and Role," 155.

[169]So Macdonald, "Status and Role," 155.

Hebrew Bible, such a distinction seems unlikely, especially since other extrabiblical Hebrew texts use the term עבד for a servant of a high official other than the king.[170]

Another point that is relevant to the discussion of the meaning conveyed by the seal of לאליקם / נער יוכן is that in the latter citation of Ziba as a נער (2 Sam 19:18) he is identified as a נער בית שאול. This designation of the house of Saul is particularly clear in demonstrating the relationship between Ziba and Saul that Stähli describes as an *Abhängigkeitsverhältnis* (relationship of dependence). Moreover, this relationship and identification as a נער continues even after Saul's death and after Ziba has begun to receive commands from David in 2 Samuel 9.

Ziba's life as a נער of Saul and Saul's family does not prevent him from being or becoming wealthy. In 2 Sam 19:18, he is described as having fifteen sons and twenty servants of his own. Obviously, someone with so many sons and personal servants was both wealthy and powerful in his own right. This distinction is also important with regard to אליקם נער יוכן, as it shows that the relationship of אליקם to יוכן would not prohibit him from having a position of status himself. The question that still remains, however, is whether the נער relationship of אליקם to יוכן prohibits the former from being a royal official.

At this point, it is helpful to look at Amnon and Absalom, the sons of David, and their נערים. Both Absalom and Amnon are described as having their personal נערים who serve as functionaries. In 2 Sam 13:17, Absalom instructs his נער to throw his sister, whom he has just raped, out of the house. Just a few verses later, in 2 Sam 13:28, Absalom instructs his נערים to kill his brother Amnon. In each case, it seems reasonable to assume that the respective נערים, who were royal servants, would have been referred to as a נער אמנון and a נער אבשלום instead of a נער דוד. Similarly, it seems reasonable to conclude that אליקם could very well have been the functionary of one of Hezekiah's children or a high official of the king.

A final example makes explicit the possibility that a person could be the נער of a high official of the king and be considered a servant of the king (עבד המלך) as well. 2 Samuel 2 contains the description of a battle between David's general Joab and Abner, the general from the house of Saul. Both generals decide in 2 Sam 2:14 to send their נערים into a contest to the death instead of having a larger battle. The נערים who go into combat are designated שנים עשר לבנימן ולאיש בשת בן שאול and שנים עשר מעבדי דוד (2 Sam 2:15). In each case, the text states explicitly that the נערים of the respective generals are also considered servants of their kings, and

---

[170]Cf. Lachish Letter IV.

in the case of Joab's נערים, the term עבד is even used.[171] Therefore, turning to the seal נער יוכן / לאליקם, one sees that there is no problem with understanding אליקם as both a נער of יוכן and as a servant of the king, regardless of whether or not יוכן was part of the royal family.

We can now turn to another extrabiblical attestation of the PN אליקם and the noun נער to clarify some previous scholarly conclusions that have failed to consider the above uses of the title נער in the Hebrew Bible. Perhaps the most prominent example cited with relevance to the status of נער יוכן אליקם is a Hebrew seal of unknown provenance that contains the same PN אליקם plus the title עבד המלך. The seal (לאליקם / עבד המלך) was published by P. Boudreuil and F. Israel, who argued that the seal with the title עבד showed that אליקם was promoted from the status of נער to עבד המלך, probably after the death of Hezekiah.[172] There are several problems with this analysis. First, the above examples show that there is no reason that אליקם could not have had both titles—עבד המלך and נער יוכ—at one point in time. Further, when comparing the letters from both seals with the paleographic analysis presented above, none of the letters are found to be diagnostic, so it is impossible to date conclusively the עבד seal by paleographic means. Finally, since the provenance is unknown, the עבד seal could be a forgery. The seal appears authentic, but one should still avoid placing too much weight on a seal without proof that it is genuine. In light of these factors, if the עבד seal is authentic, it could very well be taken as explicit evidence of אליקם as the נער יוכן who is also an עבד המלך.

Avigad rightly pointed out that all of the other occurrences of the noun נער in the extrabiblical Hebrew contain the use of the title in a relationship to an individual who is not known to have been related to a king. The relevant examples are as follows:

---

[171]Macdonald, "Status and Role," 164.

[172]P. Bordreuil and F. Israel. "À Propos de la Carrière D'Elyaqim Du Page Au Majordome (?)," *Semitica* 41/42 (1991/2) 81-87.

1. Arad Ostracon no. 110, line 1: שמריה משלם נער אלנתן[ן].[173]
2. Arad Ostracon no. 110, line 2: מכי . נער . גדליה . קן[...].[174]
3. Unprovenanced Hebrew seal: לבניה/ו נער חגי.[175]
4. Unprovenanced Hebrew seal: למכיהו נער שפט.[176]
5. Unprovenanced Hebrew seal: לנתביהו נער מתן.[177]
6. Unprovenanced Hebrew seal: לאדנמלך / נער פרעש.[178]
7. Unprovenanced Phoenician seal: לעבדא נ/ער פרעש.[179]
8. Unprovenanced Phoenician seal: לבטש / נער ברכאל.[180]

The large number of these seals made from semiprecious stones provides additional support to the interpretation of נער as the title of a person who was an important official or individual, but the fact that none of these PNN found on these seals or the ostracon can be linked with a royal figure really says little about the possibility that אליקם / נער יוכן was an official in the royal court. Since the term is used both for private individuals of importance (such as the נער of Boaz) and for נערים in the royal court, one would expect the occurrences outside the Hebrew Bible to reflect this same realm of possibilities.

    In summary, one of the handles was stamped by a person holding the title בן המלך, showing that this person was a part of the royal family. This fact alone provides strong evidence that these are the stamps of royal officials and almost rules out the possibility that one of them belonged to a potter. The second stamp discussed, לאליקם / נער יוכן, belongs to a functionary who is labeled as the נער of יוכן. Drawing on the arguments presented above that the official seal impressions are to be associated with the royal stamped jars, and that this particular seal impression is likely from the same jar as known *lmlk* impressions from Tell Beit Mirsim,[181] one may assume that the title נער refers to a functionary in the royal

---

[173]A. F. Rainey, "Three Additional Texts," *Arad Inscriptions* (ed. Y. Aharoni; Jerusalem: Israel Exploration Society, 1981) 122-123.

[174]Rainey, "Three Additional Texts," 122-123.

[175]N. Avigad, "New Light on Naᶜar Seals," *Magnalia Dei, The Might Acts of God: Essays on the Bible and Archaeology in Memory of G. E. Wright* (eds. F. M. Cross, W. E. Lemke, and P. D. Miller; Garden City, NY: Doubleday, 1976) 296-297.

[176]Avigad, "New Light," 295-296.

[177]Avigad, "Titles and Symbols," 303.

[178]Deutsch and Heltzer, *Forty New Ancient West Semitic Inscriptions*, 52-53.

[179]N. Avigad, "Seals and Sealings," *IEJ* 14 (1964) 192-193, pl. 44:B.

[180]M. F. Martin, "Six Palestinian Seals," *Rivista degli studi orientali* 39 (1964) 207-208, no. 2, pl. I:2.

[181]Ussishkin, "Royal Judean Storage Jars," 6-12.

court. Contrary to Avigad's position,[182] examples of officials and functionaries from the Hebrew Bible show that this does not mean that אליקם could not have been considered an עבד המלך at the same time. The second seal originating from the antiquities market, לאליקם / עבד המלך, does not preclude אליקם from being both the נער of יוכן and an עבד המלך at the same time.

Summary

Previous proposals presented arguments for interpreting the owners of these seals with PNN whose impressions were found on *lmlk* jars as being either potters or royal officials. The various data in this section pointed towards viewing these individuals as royal officials. First, it was noted that since royal impressions were found on the same jar, the owners of the seals were somehow involved in royal service. The owners could have been either royal potters who had their own trademark in the form of seals containing their names, or the owners could have been royal officials. However, the presence of the royal stamps probably precluded ownership by a private merchant. Next, it was noted that care was often taken to insure that the impressions with PNN could be deciphered. In some cases, this concern was seen through the phenomenon of double stamping. In others, soft clay was added to a leather-hard handle to insure that the impressions with the PN could be read. These instances seemed to suggest an official who was concerned that the name be readable. Next, data were presented that suggested that the seals themselves were made of a hard substance and that some were encased in rings. Typological parallels were presented for other seals made from semiprecious stones encased in rings, so the data pointed to officials who owned and used such seals. An argument was presented for the use of multiple seals that belonged to the same individual. Typological parallels from Arad showed that other officials owned and used multiple seals, so the presence of as many as five seals belonging to the same person suggested a vocation of a royal official rather than a potter. A similar argument was presented with a conservative estimate of the number of engravers used to make these seals. Multiple engravers were used, and one person (צפן [בן] עזריהו) actually owned seals made by at least four different engravers. Such a scenario seemed more likely for a royal official than for a potter making a royal jar. Finally, the various titles found on the official seal impressions showed that the owners of these seals were part of the royal court and not potters. Most convincing in this regard was one seal impression that contained the title, בן המלך "son of the king."

---

[182]Avigad, "Titles and Symbols," 303.

2. Evidence for Non-Military Uses of the *lmlk* Jars

a. Introduction and History of Discussion

As alluded to above in the review of the history of scholarship on the theories for the uses of the *lmlk* jars (cf. Chapter III.A.3), the predominant view (first suggested by Naʾaman) is that these jars were used as part of Hezekiah's siege preparation for Sennacherib's campaign against Judah. Naʾaman begins by noting that the Assyrian sources describe Sennacherib's campaign as focusing on the Shephelah and Jerusalem. According to Naʾaman, this is where the vast majority of the *lmlk* stamps have been found, and he concludes that the sites with larger numbers of the stamps represent sites that were besieged and, in most cases, destroyed by the Assyrians. Thus he asks, "Could the *lmlk* stamps on jars have been connected in some manner with Hezekiah's preparations in anticipation of the Assyrian campaign against Judah, prior to 701 B.C.[E.]?"[183]

Although Naʾaman's 1979 article did not answer this question completely in the affirmative, he developed this hypothesis in a later report after the dating of the *lmlk* stamps had been secured by the renewed excavations at Lachish. He stated that because Hezekiah did not have much time to prepare for Sennacherib's attack, the king chose "several strategically located towns along the main approach and supply lines to his capital Jerusalem and the Judean hill country and fortified them against the expected Assyrian advance from the west, storing in them the necessary supplies for a siege." He continued that "some of the commodities sent to the fortified cities were stored within the *lmlk* jars, which can now be understood to have been connected with Hezekiah's preparation for war."[184] Further, Naʾaman suggested that siege preparation was the sole purpose of these *lmlk* jars. He said, "The king and his officials, while organizing and controlling the preparation for war, distributed stamped jars of high quality among the towns of Judah. The jars were filled and loaded in these places and then transported to the fortified cities of Judah in accordance with the order of priorities established by the king."[185]

Naʾaman's proposal of siege preparation as the sole use of the *lmlk* jars has been generally accepted among scholars. In publishing a more general account of the findings from Lachish regarding the redating of Level III, Ussishkin uses that theory as a starting point.[186] Even though

---

[183]Naʾaman, "Sennacherib's Campaign," 75.

[184]N. Naʾaman, "Hezekiah's Fortified Cities and the LMLK Stamps," *BASOR* 261 (1986) 12.

[185]Naʾaman, "Hezekiah's Fortified Cities," 17.

[186]Ussishkin, *The Conquest of Lachish*, 47.

Garfinkel challenges Naʾaman's views on reassigning the *Sitz im Leben* of 2 Chr 11:5-10 (the list of Rehoboam's fortified cities), he, too, concedes that the *lmlk* jars were probably used by Hezekiah in preparation for siege by Sennacherib.[187] Halpern takes Naʾaman's proposal a step further and argues that the *lmlk* jars are not only used for siege preparation, but "the exiguous numbers of jars and fragments so far recovered suggest rather that their use was restricted to the professional soldiery."[188] In his 1993 dissertation on the kingdom of Hezekiah, P. K. Hooker reexamines the entire subject as follows:

> Naʾaman is almost surely correct in his argument that the royal storage jars upon which the *lmlk* stamps were fixed were a part of some royal system for supplying the most sensitive areas in advance of Sennacherib's invasion. The concentration of seals at Lachish, the site of the most important military engagement between Assyrian and Judean forces points strongly in that direction. Even stronger is the fact that the highest concentrations of *lmlk* seals of all types and place-names are found in precisely those locations which lay in Sennacherib's path and which Hezekiah fortified in preparation for war. . . The most reasonable explanation for the seals then seems to be that they marked stores of provisions set aside to supply troops or garrisons in places most likely to be attacked by Sennacherib.[189]

Most recently, in an as-yet unpublished article, Barkay summarizes scholarly opinion with this assessment: "Most scholars agree that the jars were somehow related to Hezekiah's military preparations for revolt against the Assyrians."[190]

Despite what has become a scholarly consensus that understands the sole function of the *lmlk* jars as supplying goods to towns that faced imminent siege, a reevaluation of the evidence shows that it is necessary to redefine "siege preparation." As noted above, scholars tend to understand siege preparation via the *lmlk* jars in a limited sense, referring to the final preparations and shipments of goods once an attack is imminent. In fact, scholars tend to assume that if a *lmlk* impression is found at a particular location, that site must have been attacked by Sennacherib. However, several factors suggest that Hezekiah's use of the *lmlk* jars in

---

[187]Garfinkel, "Reply to Nadav Naʾaman," 69.

[188]Halpern, "Jerusalem and the Lineages," 23.

[189]Hooker, *Kingdom of Hezekiah*, 287-288.

[190]Barkay, "Judah in Israel," unpublished essay.

preparation for siege was not limited to the final days or weeks before Sennacherib's invasion. First, there is much evidence that the storage jar type on which the *lmlk* stamps are found is not unique to the late 8th century. This indicates that the function of the *lmlk* jars is not unique to the period of Sennacherib's campaign. Second, a glaring problem is that many sites where *lmlk* jar handles have been found were not fortified during the late 8th century. Finally, other sites that were fortified and do contain *lmlk* stamps were not besieged or destroyed by Sennacherib.

b. Typological Overview of the *lmlk* Jars
     One of the interesting things about Naᵓaman's theory that the *lmlk* jars were used solely for siege preparation is that it intimates that the *lmlk* jars were developed only for that purpose. He says that during the preparation for war, Hezekiah had "jars of high quality" distributed throughout the kingdom.[191] One assumes from this comment that these jars were at the very least of a specialized type and may even have been developed specifically for the task. Actually, the opposite is true. The jars are of a standard quality and far from unique. The prototype of this jar type arises in the late ninth century, and various forms develop until at least the early 6th century BCE. All the various forms serve domestic and public storage functions. Although this fact is not necessarily fatal to Naᵓaman's theory, a thorough overview of the various forms of this jar type and of its domestic and public usages is informative for concluding that the jars with the royal stamps were indeed used for purposes other than siege preparation in the final period before Sennacherib's campaign. In fact, the extensive use of this jar type in both domestic and public structures raises questions for subsequent developments of Naᵓaman's theory, such as the one in which Halpern asserts that the *lmlk* jars were used only by professional soldiers.[192]
     Typological studies of pottery from Gezer, Lachish, and Arad show that storage jars similar to the *lmlk*-stamped jars did not arise out of a vacuum in the late 8th century. In earlier levels at all three sites, there are storage jars related to the *lmlk* type but without royal—or any other—stamps. To date, no storage jars similar to the fully developed *lmlk* jars have been found in Lachish Level IV (10th to 9th century BCE),[193] but but Gitin has noted a prototype form from Lachish Level IV.[194] At Gezer, storage jars of the *lmlk* type but without royal stamps (Gezer Type

---

[191]Naᵓaman, "Hezekiah's Fortified Cities," 17.
[192]Halpern, "Jerusalem and the Lineages," 23-24.
[193]Zimhoni, "Two Ceramic Assemblages," 15.
[194]Gitin, *Gezer III*:123; cf. Aharoni, *Lachish V*, pl. 44:10

4A = Lachish Type 484 = Zimhoni's Group IIIA) were discovered *in situ* in Stratum VIA, which has a destruction date of about 733 BCE.[195] In addition to these four-handled storage jars of *lmlk* type, there are related two-handled jars that correspond to Zimhoni's Group IIIC jars.[196] Since Gezer Stratum VIA was established around 840 BCE, these finds mean that at Gezer there is a *terminus post quem* of about 840 BCE for these related *lmlk* type jars without royal impressions. Gitin stresses this point by stating, "It is worth emphasizing that not one sherd that could be associated with any part of these forms was found either in the make-up of the floors or in the fills sealed below the floors of Stratum VIA, i.e., before ca. 840 B.C."[197]

Further evidence for the use of unstamped storage jars of the *lmlk* type is found at Arad where several were found in Strata X and IX.[198] As discussed above in relation to settlement at Arad during the late 8th century,[199] it is debated how early Stratum X begins at Arad. The excavators hold that Stratum X begins at least by the first half of the 9th century,[200] but other scholars have questioned this dating because the pottery in Strata X-VIII is homogenous. These critics date the beginning of Stratum X to the 8th century.[201] Without resolving this debate, it is possible for the purposes of the present study simply to note that it is clear that the unstamped *lmlk* type jars came into use at least by the first half of the 8th century BCE at Arad, while none of the stamped jar handles are found before Stratum VIII—the end of the 8th century.[202]

Similarly, this pottery form did not die out immediately after Hezekiah's reign. Although both the stamped and unstamped *lmlk* type jars were most widely used during the late 8th century,[203] variant forms developed during the 7th century. There were several varieties. One type (Lachish Group IIA) was almost identical to the *lmlk* type jar, but it

---

[195]Gitin, *Gezer III*, 48, pls. 15:11,12,14,15, and 16:1,2. The destruction date of 733 BCE is based on a relief of Tiglath Pileser III from Nimrud that mentions the siege of a city called *Gazru* (cf. ANEP no. 369). It is commonly accepted that this *Gazru* is biblical Gezer.

[196]Zimhoni, "Two Ceramic Assemblages," 23-25.

[197]Gitin, *Gezer III*, 122.

[198]Herzog et al., "Arad," figs. 13:1, 19:1; cf. Gitin, *Gezer III*, 123.

[199]Cf. Chapter 2.

[200]Herzog et al., "Arad," 12.

[201]Zimhoni, "Pottery of Tel ʿEton," 89-90; A. Mazar and Netzer, "Arad," 89; Ussishkin, "Judaean Shrine at Arad," 149.

[202]M. Aharoni, "Weights and Royal Seals," 126.

[203]Cf. Gitin, *Gezer III*, 123.

can be distinguished by a plain, rounded rim and a coarser, more porous ware.[204] Another type (Lachish Group IIB) was composed of similar clay; it had four handles but had a plain rim and was somewhat smaller than the *lmlk*type jars. Often these jars were stamped with a rosette seal impression.[205] There was also a variant form (Gezer Type 4B = Lachish Group IIC) that was thinner than the *lmlk*type jars and had two handles instead of four.[206]

The evidence from Gezer shows that a prototype of the *lmlk* jar originated sometime during the 9th century, and the examples from Arad date at least to the first half of the 8th century. Both the unstamped and stamped *lmlk*type jars are found most frequently during the latter part of the 8th century, while variant forms continue well into the 7th. It is clear that this jar type, with which the *lmlk* seal impressions are associated, is not unique and not a phenomenon known only in the late 8th century. Even though Zimhoni follows Naᵓaman's theory that the jars were used for siege preparation, she rightly acknowledges that "apparently these storage jars were not specifically made in preparation for the revolt, but rather production was simply continued, and those jars intended for official use were stamped."[207]

This is an important distinction because the theory of siege preparation as described by Naᵓaman seems to imply a unique function for these jars within a time frame limited to the final weeks before Sennacherib's campaign.[208] However, it is clear that whatever the purpose of the stamped *lmlk* jars, similar unstamped jars were used for the same commodities[209] both before the stamping of *lmlk* jars and after. Moreover, many unstamped jars were used contemporaneously with the *lmlk* jars. As Zimhoni rightly observes, if the jars were used for siege preparation, this use must be consistent with earlier and later usages. The question that still remains is whether the stamping of the jars occurred solely at the time Sennacherib's campaign was imminent and was done solely to prepare for siege in the final weeks preceding the campaign, or whether the stamping occurred earlier in Hezekiah's reign as part of his general economic buildup and increase of civil strength. If the latter scenario is

---

[204]Zimhoni, "Two Ceramic Assemblages," 30-31.

[205]Zimhoni, "Two Ceramic Assemblages," 30-33.

[206]Cf. Gitin, *Gezer III*, 122-124; Zimhoni, "Two Ceramic Assemblages," 34-35.

[207]Zimhoni, "Two Ceramic Assemblages," 18.

[208]Naᵓaman, "Hezekiah's Fortified Cities," 17.

[209]Cf. the summary to this section, below, for a discussion of the commodities of the *lmlk* jars.

found to be true, then it is necessary to redefine "siege preparation" as including Hezekiah's general economic buildup that began at least several years before the expected response from Sennacherib materialized.

c. Unfortified Sites with *lmlk* Impressions

The evidence presented in Chapter 2 shows that Judah experienced its highest degree of economic buildup and civil strength under Hezekiah's reign, and the archaeological survey data suggest that this buildup was a gradual one that reached an apex in the years following the death of Sargon II in 705 BCE. This fact alone suggests that the stamping of the royal jars in Hezekiah's kingdom could have been part of a general program of economic buildup that was broader than mere preparation in the final days or weeks before a particular siege. This suggestion is supported by the fact that many sites where *lmlk* impressions have been discovered show little or no sign of fortifications, contrary to Naʾaman's theory the royal jars were sent out only to sites where siege was imminent.[210] This point is even more important in the analysis of later developments of Naʾaman's theory, because other scholars have suggested that if *lmlk* impressions are found at a particular site, then it must be concluded that this site experienced imminent danger of being attacked by Sennacherib.[211] The discovery of *lmlk* stamps at the following unfortified locations suggests that Naʾaman's interpretation is too simplistic and does not take into account Hezekiah's efforts for economic buildup throughout his reign.

α. Tell ej-Judeideh (Tel Goded)

Tell ej-Judeideh (probably biblical Moresheth-Gath) is the most significant settlement in the Shephelah that yielded many discoveries of both *lmlk* and official seal impressions in an unfortified Iron II site. Bliss, the co-excavator of the site, states that the wall associated with the city did not arise until the Roman period. He says:

> As to the date of this wall. . . it represents the latest construction on the Tell after most of the debris now found had accumulated. This debris contains some of the earliest types of pre-Israelite pottery. The pottery found in connection with the gates and their flanking towers, however, is Roman or Byzantine.[212]

---

[210]Naʾaman, "Hezekiah's Fortified Cities," 17.

[211]Halpern, "Jerusalem and the Lineages," 23-24; Hooker, *Kingdom of Hezekiah,* 287-289.

[212]F. J. Bliss, "First Report on Excavations at Tell Ej-Judeideh," *PEFQS* (1900) 93.

Bliss reiterates this conclusion following more investigation in a later excavation report:

> At two different points an examination was conducted to ascertain whether a Jewish [Israelite] or pre-Israelite [Canaanite] wall was to be found underlying the later wall, which rests on debris, or whether such a wall existed in a line outside or inside that later wall, but in each case the negative was proved.[213]

Inasmuch as thirty-nine *lmlk* impressions and fifteen official seal impressions were reported from Bliss and Macalister's excavations from the turn of the century,[214] this single site could be fatal to a theory interpreting the *lmlk* jars as used solely for siege preparation in the final days or weeks before Sennacherib's campaign. However, Bliss's evaluation of the fortifications cannot be confirmed definitively. It is possible that some Iron Age walls might have been missed by Bliss and Macalister, and it is difficult (but not impossible) to imagine the many Iron Age finds and buildings they discovered without any defensive walls. In the most recent reassessment of Bliss and Macalister's excavations, Gibson provides the following overview:

> Attempts were made by the excavators to ascertain whether the [Hellenistic] city wall was built over an earlier fortification system, but the results of their investigation were negative in the three shafts which they sunk to bedrock next to the wall. For the moment, it remains an open question whether the Early Bronze Age and Iron Age settlements at the site were fortified.[215]

In light of this uncertainty, it seems prudent to take Tell ej-Judeideh as evidence that is most suggestive that the *lmlk* jars were used for purposes other than siege preparations in just prior to Sennacherib's invasion. On the other hand, the fact that the excavations undertaken did not employ modern archaeological techniques necessitates that this site not be relied upon for conclusive evidence.

---

[213]Bliss, "Second Report at Tell Ej-Judeideh," *PEFQS* (1900) 200.

[214]As was the case with Beth Shemesh, this high ratio of official seal impressions to *lmlk* impressions suggests that the excavators might not have reported all of the *lmlk* impressions. Since Macalister did not keep an accurate count at Gezer, it is likely that he did not keep an accurate count at Tell ej-Judeideh either.

[215]S. Gibson, "The Tell Ej-Judeideh (Tel Goded) Excavations: A Reappraisal Based on Archival Records in the Palestine Exploration Fund," *Tel Aviv* 21 (1994) 213.

β. Beth Zur

The site was excavated extensively in 1931 and again in 1957. The first season revealed eleven *lmlk* impressions after excavating most of the center of the tell (more than two acres) to bedrock.[216] As described in depth above (Chapter 2), no signs of fortifications from the Iron Age II were found during either season of excavations. With Beth Zur, such a negative verdict regarding fortification can be considered more conclusive than with Tell ej-Judeideh, because the 1957 campaign to Beth Zur was devoted almost completely to determining if any Iron Age fortifications existed there. Further, the extensive nature of the earlier digs made it most probable that the negative verdict for Iron Age fortifications could be relied upon. The site seemed to have been destroyed by Sennacherib and there were signs (though not extensive) of resettlement in the 7th century. The absence of signs of fortifications from the Iron II would explain why only limited destruction debris was found because without fortifications the site would probably have been abandoned before Sennacherib reached Beth Zur.[217]

In summary, one finds at Beth Zur a prime example of a site with a significant number of *lmlk* impressions (12), but these jars clearly were used for something other than siege preparation since Beth Zur was not fortified during the Iron Age. At the same time, the significance of these twelve impressions should be put into perspective; with more than 1700 *lmlk* impressions known to date, twelve impressions represent only a small fraction of the total. However, these impressions do suggest that at least one small shipment was sent to an unfortified site during Hezekiah's reign. This knowledge, combined with the fact that very few unfortified Iron Age sites have been excavated, gives their presence more significance. In addition, the presence of a significant unfortified settlement at Beth Zur also supports the interpretation of Tell ej-Judeideh as unfortified, even though this inference cannot be proven.

γ. Khirbet El-Burj

This site is just a few kilometers northwest of Jerusalem in Ramot, a modern suburb of the city. It has been excavated by R. De Groot, and twenty-three *lmlk* impression have been discovered. Although the details of De Groot's excavations are unpublished, there is evidence of extensive Iron Age II settlement from the survey of the Benjamin Hill Country by Finkelstein and Magen. This survey reports that of 212 sherds collected, roughly 74% came from the Iron Age II. According to the survey, the

---

[216]Sellers and Albright, "Beth-Zur," 8.

[217]Funk, "History of Beth-Zur," 8; Funk, "Beth-Zur," 261.

settlement consisted of a tel with an area of about 30 dunams, but no signs of fortifications were reported.[218] Even though de Groot's excavations are not published, S. Wolff, one of his colleagues at el-Burj and an official with the I.A.A., reports that no Iron Age fortifications were found there.[219] Thus, el-Burj provides further evidence for the use of *lmlk* jars for purposes other than siege preparation.

δ. Agricultural Sites Around Jerusalem

At several agricultural sites around Jerusalem *lmlk* stamps have been discovered, along with other ceramic finds from the late 8th century. Since these sites did not have a military function in preparing for the expected siege of Sennacherib during the final days or weeks before the campaign materialized, a study of them is helpful to the questions asked in this chapter.

The site with the most *lmlk* impressions to date is Mevasseret Yerushalayim, which lies about 7 km west of modern Jerusalem. A rural agricultural site with Iron Age II terrace farming was discovered there. G. Edelstein and M. Kislev report four layers dating from four periods—Early Arab, Byzantine, Roman, and Iron Age II. The Iron Age II settlement dates to the late 8th century, as evidenced by numerous ceramic finds and a four-winged *lmlk* Hebron handle. The terraces also date to the late 8th century.[220] As noted below (Appendix I), N. Zori has found four additional *lmlk* handles at the site.[221]

Khirbet Er-Ras was another important agricultural site near Jerusalem. Er-Ras is the modern name given to Givat Malḥa, and the farming site was located at the base of the hill in the Rephaim Valley. The excavators, Edelstein and E. Eisenberg, reported a farm with an area of about 7 dunams, a four-room house, and a rock-cut winepress. They stated that "the finds consisted mainly of Iron II store jars and two *lamelekh* stamped handles."[222] Another *lmlk* impression (I.A.A. no. 77-1) was located at Er-Ras by Barkay and S. Gibson during a survey of the region in 1977.[223] Edelstein shows that the rock-cut winepress was related to the terracing compound and was used during the Iron Age I.[224]

---

[218]Finkelstein and Magen, *Hill Country of Benjamin*, 231-233, site no. 311.

[219]S. Wolff, personal communication.

[220]G. Edelstein and M. Kislev, "Mavasseret Yerushalayim: The Ancient Settlement and Its Agricultural Terraces," *BA* 44 (1981) 53-54.

[221]G. Barkay, personal communication.

[222]G. Edelstein and E. Eisenberg, "Emeq Refraim," *ESI* 3 (1984) 52.

[223]G. Barkay, personal communication.

[224]G. Edelstein, "The Terraced Farm at Er-Ras, Jerusalem," forthcoming.

A third site, ʿEin Yaʿel, lies directly accross the Rephaim Valley from Er-Ras, and Edelstein states that one *lmlk* and one official seal impression were found there.[225] Although the excavated architecture from ʿEin Yaʿel dates to the Roman period, Edelstein reports that the *lmlk* and official seal impressions join other Iron Age sherds to suggest that remains of an Iron Age farm corresponding to the one at Er-Ras probably lies underneath the Roman layer.[226]

Still, excavations at another agricultual site, Beit Ṣafâfâ, south of modern Jerusalem, produced another *lmlk* stamp. The excavator, N. Feig, reports that this *lmlk* handle was found in a clear stratigraphic context with body fragments from a *lmlk* type jar. The main agricultural feature at Beit Ṣafâfâ is a large wine vat with a capacity of 20,000 liters. Feig states that there are no signs of destruction and that the site seems to have been in use from the late 8th through the 7th century.[227]

ε. Agricultural Sites in the Shephelah

Dagan also discovered five agricultural sites in the Shephelah with pottery from the late 8th century, including at least one *lmlk* impression. The identification of these five sites is important because there can be no doubt that agricultural settlements were not fortified. Almost as important, these sites can be taken as suggesting that there probably are a large number of unidentified agricultural sites with *lmlk* impressions in addition to those around Jerusalem. These are probably smaller settlements, and unfortunately, with the current state of research, the major investigations and the systematic excavations required to reveal large amounts of any pottery evidence—including *lmlk* stamped jars—have been concentrated on the larger, mostly fortified, tels.

At agricultural site no. 62 from Dagan's survey (site no. 15105 12350, located at grid point 15-12/13/12), two, two-winged, *lmlk* impressions were discovered. One read נשמה and the GN on the other was unidentifiable. The impressions were found with remains of several late 8th-century buildings. The unfortified site was approximately 8 km directly east of Tel Azekah in the northeast part of the Shephelah; it had a built-up area of 2 dunams.[228]

Dagan's survey at Agricultural site no. 66 (site no. 13415 12260 located at grid point 13-12/42/3) yielded one *lmlk* impression. The site had remains of foundations of several buildings and isolated sections of

---

[225]G. Edelstein, "A Roman Villa at ʿEin Yaʿel," *Qad* 26 (1993) 116.

[226]G. Edelstein, personal communication.

[227]N. Feig, personal communication.

[228]Dagan, "Shephelah," 112.

two walls. The built-up area during the Iron II period was about 3 dunams. It is located approximately 2 km southwest of Tell eṣ-Ṣâfi (Philistine Gath) on the northeast edge of the Shephelah. It, too, was unfortified.[229]

One two-winged *lmlk* impression was discovered at Khirbet Jannaba et Tahta (el Gharbiya). This site corresponds to site no. 101 from Dagan's survey and was defined as a site with remains of residential settlements (site no. 14495 12145 located at grid point 14-12/41/1). It had a built-up area of about 30 dunams. Remains of building foundations and walls were located, and farming implements were also found on the surface, indicating that this might have been an agricultural site. The site does not appear to be fortified. It is located in the north central Shephelah about 3 km south of Tel Azekah and 4 km west of Tel Sokoh.[230]

At agricultural site no. 199 from Dagan's survey (site no. 14442 10393 located at grid point 14-10/43/7), one *lmlk* impression was discovered. This unfortified settlement, a few kilometers north of Tel ʿEton, had a built-up area of about 3 dunams. Remains of about ten buildings were discovered, along with signs of farming activity.[231]

At site no. 187 from Dagan's survey, one *lmlk* impression was discovered. This site was defined as a site with remains of residential settlements, and the impression was found together with remains of a few buildings with a built-up area of 2 dunams. On the slopes surrounding the site were signs of agricultural terracing. The site was located just a few kilometers north of Tel ʿEton, and it, too, was unfortified.[232]

d. Sites with *lmlk* Impressions—Not Destroyed by Sennacherib

As we have seen, part of Naʾaman's theory suggested that the *lmlk* jars were sent only to fortresses where the threat of siege was imminent.[233] Moreover, we have seen that this interpretation influenced other scholars as well. Halpern assumed that sites with large concentrations of *lmlk* stamps were attacked by Sennacherib.[234] As recently as 1993, Hooker stated, "The most reasonable explanation for the seals then seems to be that they marked stores of provisions set aside to supply troops and garrisons in places most likely to be attacked by Sennacherib."[235] A.

[229]Dagan, "Shephelah," 114.

[230]Dagan, "Shephelah," 131-132.

[231]Dagan, "Shephelah," 196.

[232]Dagan, "Shephelah," 189.

[233]Naʾaman, "Hezekiah's Fortified Cities," 17.

[234]Halpern, "Jerusalem and the Lineages," 23-24, 34-36.

[235]Hooker, *Kingdom of Hezekiah*, 288.

Mazar even used the presence of unstratified *lmlk* handles to argue that General Stratum VI at Gezer was destroyed by Sennacherib in 701 BCE instead of by Tiglath Pileser III in about 733 BCE as the excavators reported.[236]

If Naʾman's theory were indeed valid, one would expect to find that all sites with *lmlk* jars were besieged and destroyed. But Hooker rightly observes that a limited number of sites may have received smaller shipments of *lmlk* jars before Sennacherib's siege route was certain. In general, if this last-minute supply theory were true, sites with large numbers of *lmlk* jars would have been besieged and destroyed. However, evidence points to exactly the opposite. At least three significant sites with large numbers of *lmlk* jars exhibit no signs of siege or destruction during Sennacherib's 701 BCE campaign. The presence of *lmlk* impressions at those sites suggests that Hezekiah's use of the *lmlk* jars was more generalized than during the final period before a particular siege.

α. Gezer

As noted a few paragraphs above, A. Mazar[237] draws on the presence of unstratified *lmlk* impressions to suggest redating the 8th-century destruction layer (General Stratum VI) to 701 BCE during Sennacherib's campaign instead of during the campaign of Tiglath Pileser III in 733 BCE as reported by the excavators.[238] However, as the above discussion emphasizes, caution must be exercised at interpreting the *lmlk* jars too simplistically as a means of proving destruction by Sennacherib. To judge between Mazar's suggestion and the dating of the excavators, it is first necessary to review the archaeological strata affected by this interpretation, as well as the relevant Assyrian inscriptional evidence.

The question of whether Gezer was destroyed in 733 or 701 BCE involves the dating of the end of Gezer General Strata VI and V. At Gezer, the various archaeological areas of the sites are called Fields, and each of them has its own numbering system for strata. To make sense out of the chronological picture for the entire site, a different set of stratum numbers is used to refer to the general stratigraphy, and all of the individual fields are then transposed to this system. Thus, Gezer General Stratum V

---

[236] A. Mazar, "Northern Shephelah," 259-260.

[237] A. Mazar, "Northern Shephelah," 259-260.

[238] Cf. W. G. Dever, H. D. Lance, and G. E. Wright, *Gezer I:˙ Preliminary Report of the 1964-66 Seasons* (Jerusalem: Hebrew Union College, 1970) 6; W. G. Dever and D. P. Cole, "Gezer: The 1968-70 Seasons, Field II," *Gezer II: Report of the 1967-70 Seasons in Fields I and II* (ed. W. G. Dever; Jerusalem: Hebrew Union College/ Nelson Glueck School of Biblical Archaeology, 1974), 69-73; Gitin, *Gezer III*, 17.

is assigned a destruction date of about 597-586 BCE and corresponds to Local Stratum 3 from Field III (Solomonic Gate Area) and to Local Stratum 4 from Field II. On the other hand, Gezer General Stratum VI was assigned a destruction date of 733 BCE and corresponds to Local Stratum 4 from Field III and Local Stratum 5A-B from Field II. A similar method is used to relate the layers from all ten fields at Gezer to a general stratigraphical sequence.[239]

When each of the local strata that correspond to General Strata VI and V is examined, the pottery shows that General Stratum VI has a destruction date sometime during the last half of the 8th century; General Stratum V has a destruction date at the beginning of the 6th century.[240] The important question for the current study is whether General Stratum VI should be dated to 733 BCE or to 701 BCE. Unfortunately, both General Strata VI and V experience a lifetime of over 100 years without destruction layers in between, so it is impossible to separate the pottery to determine conclusively which campaign brought about their destruction.

The situation is further complicated by the fact that the destruction evidence is not as universal in General Stratum VI as it is in General Stratum V. In Field II, two phases were discovered for General Stratum VI. Local Stratum 5B in Field II seems to be the earlier phase corresponding to the late 9th and mid-8th centuries, but no destruction has been detected. W. Dever and D. Cole note, "There was possible evidence of a [Local] Str. 5B destruction only in two areas, and both layers are probably best understood simply as the accumulation of domestic refuse."[241] Dever and Cole continue, "[Local] Str. 5A ended with a disturbance more serious than that of Str. 5B, but still hardly a major destruction."[242] However, the destruction evidence was widespread in other fields containing strata corresponding to General Stratum VI. In Field VII, Gitin states, "[Local] Stratum VIA [= General Stratum VI][243] came to a violent end. . . . Meters-deep mud brick destruction debris, including burnt wood beams as well

---

[239]For an overview of all the strata from Gezer, cf. J. D. Seger *Gezer V: Field I Caves* (ed. J. D. Seger and H. D. Lance; Jerusalem: Hebrew Union College/Nelson Glueck School of Biblical Archaeology, 1988) 6-7.

[240]Gitin, *Gezer III*, 17.

[241]Dever and Cole, "Field II," 69.

[242]Dever and Cole, "Field II," 70.

[243]The use of Roman numerals for the local strata in *Gezer III* is unique to this volume of the site's publications. In all other volumes, local strata (including those published in *Gezer III*) are listed with Arabic numerals. The method adopted in the present study is to use Arabic numerals for local strata except when direct quotes from *Gezer III* are involved.

as mud brick roof tiling covered most of the rooms in [Local] Stratum VIA [= General Stratum VI]."[244] Likewise, there is significant destruction debris found in Local Stratum 4 (= General Stratum VI) of the Solomonic Gate in Field III.[245] In light of all these factors, it seems that "the destruction [of General Stratum VI] may have been confined to the city gate and other crucial areas."[246]

In summary, it appears clear that a destruction, possibly limited, took place at Gezer in the last half of the 8th century, but it is not possible to point to stratigraphic destruction features to attribute it conclusively to either 734/3 BCE or 701 BCE. The definitive key to the puzzle was found in an Assyrian relief from a palace of Esarhaddon at Nimrud. Part of the palace was constructed using reliefs that had previously belonged to Tiglath Pileser III, and several of them described his campaigns against Palestine. The identification of these reliefs with Tiglath Pileser III was certain because they flank annals describing the monarch's campaigns.[247] Several contain depictions of the Assyrian army besieging a city from Palestine. Above one of the depictions, the following label identifying the city was found: URU Ga-az-ru (URU Gazru).[248] The Akkadian spelling of *Gazru* is exactly what one would expect for the Hebrew Gezer. This epigraphic evidence together with the fact that the northern kingdom of Israel was allied in a coalition against Tiglath Pileser III, makes it certain that the Assyrian relief from Nimrud describes the siege of Gezer by Tiglath Pileser III in 734/3 BCE during one of several campaigns that the Assyrian ruler conducted against Israel and the Coastal Plain city-state of Gaza. Since no other destruction layer corresponding to the last half of the 8th century was found at Gezer, it seems that the city did *not* fall to Sennacherib in 701 BCE.

In light of these data, the count of at least 37 *lmlk* stamps from Gezer[249] points to a Judean presence there during the last quarter of the 8th century, but certainly not before 734/3 when the site was controlled by the northern kingdom of Israel. None of the *lmlk* stamps were found in General Stratum VI, but all of them came from fills in layers above that

---

[244]Gitin, *Gezer III*, 30.

[245]Cf. Dever and Cole, "Field II," 73.

[246]Dever and Cole, "Field II," 73.

[247]H. Tadmor, *The Inscriptions of Tiglath-Pileser III King of Assyria: Critical Edition, with Introductions, Translations and Commentary* (Jerusalem: Israel Academy of Sciences and Humanities, 1994) 11.

[248]Cf. *ANEP*, no. 369; Tadmor, *Tiglath-Pileser III*, 210-211, Misc. II,3, fig. 11.

[249]Cf. Gitin, *Gezer III*:17 n. 16.

stratum. Thus, the archaeological data suggest that the Judeans established a presence at Gezer during the last quarter of the 8th century when the Assyrian influence would have been diverted towards suppressing a rebellion in Babylon by Marduk-apla-iddina. Further, the fact that Gezer was not destroyed by Sennacherib shows that the shipment of *lmlk* jars was not limited solely to siege preparation during the period shortly before Sennacherib's attack. Conversely, the evidence suggests that they functioned in a more general way as part of Hezekiah's overall effort to strengthen the Judean presence on the western borders of his kingdom. This strengthening of Hezekiah's border can also be seen as preparation for siege, but it probably occurred several years before the expected response from Sennacherib materialized.

β. Mizpah (Tell en-Naṣbeh)

The detailed discussion in Chapter 2 draws on the reexaminaton of the stratigraphy of Tell en-Naṣbeh in Zorn's 1993 dissertation and shows that the town was not destroyed during the Iron Age II. Although it is not necessary to reiterate all of the arguments, an additional piece of evidence from Zorn's dissertation concerning the existence of, or lack of, large public buildings is relevant to the discussion here of proposals for a sole-siege-preparation function of the *lmlk* jars during the period immediately before Sennacherib's attack.

Zorn begins with the observation that since more than two-thirds of the site was completely excavated, Tell en-Naṣbeh presents the researcher with a unique opportunity to draw fairly accurate conclusions about town planning. One striking feature is that "extensive areas of the Stratum 3 town were uncovered, but nowhere are there remains of any large public buildings, let alone one that might be characterized as a barracks.'[250] Zorn draws the logical conclusion that a full-time, professional military unit was not responsible for the defense of Tell en-Naṣbeh, but rather for the most part "it seems that the inhabitants were responsible for the defense of their town.'[251] Building on Zorn's observations, one notes that while we cannot preclude the assignment of professional soldiers to fortresses like Tell en-Naṣbeh in times of need, it is clear that the town was not designed to support a cadre of military professionals.

Considering that Tell en-Naṣbeh was not destroyed in 701 BCE and that the ruins did not reveal buildings to house professional soldiers, we have important data for analyzing the theories regarding the use of the *lmlk* jars for siege preparation. Naʾaman, Hooker, and Halpern all

---

[250]Zorn, *Tell En*-Naṣbeh: *A Re-evaluation,* 338.

[251]Zorn, *Tell En*-Naṣbeh: *A Re-evaluation,* 338.

develop interpretations about how the *lmlk* jars were used solely at sites where siege was imminent. Halpern narrows the function further by stating that the jars only provided supplies to professional soldiers. At Tell en-Naṣbeh, however, eighty-six *lmlk* impressions were found, but the site was presumably not besieged, nor were there public buildings to house the professional military.[252] Once again, if the *lmlk* jars were used for siege preparation, this preparation must be understood within a more generalized time frame than the final weeks before Sennacherib's campaign. Conversely, the presence of large numbers of *lmlk* impressions at Tell en-Naṣbeh points to a strong government infrastructure that was established at least several years before Sennacherib's campaign.

γ. Gibeon (Tell el-Jib)

Gibeon also did not experience destruction during the late 8th century.[253] The site was treated extensively above (Chapter 2), so it is sufficient here to state that the excavations at Gibeon produced a significant number of *lmlk* impressions (95), but the site does not seem to have been besieged by Sennacherib.

δ. Gibea (Tell el-Fûl)

Gibea, another site north of Jerusalem, shows signs of 8th-century occupation and it, too, does not seem to have been destroyed by Sennacherib. Unfortunately, the argument is not as clear with Gibea as with the previous examples because the excavators published the findings before Ussishkin's work from Lachish that showed that many layers dated by parallels to Lachish Level III actually correspond to the late 8th century. The excavators held that Period III at Gibea began in the middle of the 7th century and did not end until it was destroyed during

---

[252]This same dearth of large adminstrative or public buildings is also found at other sites where *lmlk* impressions have been discovered, Tell Beit Mirsim and Beth Shemesh. Those towns, along with Tell en-Naṣbeh, are referred to a "provincal" towns (cf. Z. Herzog, "Settlement and Fortification Planning in the Iron Age," in *The Agriculture of Ancient Israel From the Prehistoric to the Persian Periods* [A. Kempinski and R. Reich, eds.; Jerusalem: Israel Exploration Society, 1992] 261-263; cf. also A. Mazar, *Archaeology of the Land of the Bible—10,000-586 B.C.E.* [ABRL; New York: Doubleday, 1990] 464-465). Herzog ("Settlement and Fortification Planning," 264) says, "By contrast with the administrative cities, the provincial towns have no or few public structures. Most of the city's area is occupied by private dwellings which are not planned but rather emerged within the city according to the agglutinative principle." I am grateful to J. W. Hardin for discussing Iron Age town planning with me and for sharing these references.

[253]Pritchard, *Where the Sun Stood Still*, 161.

Nebuchadnezzar's invasion in the early 6th century. To support this dating, they point to predominant parallels with pottery from Lachish Level II, Ramat Raḥel VA, and Ein Gedi V.[254] Indeed, these parallels suggest 7th-century occupation, but there are also ceramic parallels from the late 8th century. Further, since the site does not contain destruction debris from the late 8th century, it is not surprising that the predominant pottery finds are later. Indeed, N. Lapp concludes that Gibea, Gibeon, and Mizpah "have similar occupational histories and are in the same geographical area."[255]

Summary

The lack of fortification in cities where *lmlk* impressions are found, as well as the existence of similar seal impressions at other fortified sites that were not attacked by Sennacherib, raise questions concerning the popular theory associating the *lmlk* seal impressions solely with siege preparation during the final weeks before Sennacherib's campaign. When these facts are combined with the fact that the *lmlk* jars as a ceramic type do not appear out of a vacuum, but rather are part of a development seen in store jars from the Iron II period, it becomes clear that the *lmlk*type jars were not invented and produced solely for siege preparation on the eve of Sennacherib's attack. It is reasonable to assume that not only would the same commodities have been stored in both unstamped and stamped jars, but that both the stamped and unstamped jars would have also had similar functions. The question remains, however, why some jars were stamped with a royal seal and others were not.

The inscription of *lmlk* (= [belonging] to the king) points to some sort of royal commodity that was traded or deployed to government employees throughout Hezekiah's kingdom. The jars' steep mouth makes it certain that they were used for storing some sort of liquid, so it seems that the jars played a general role of distributing and storing liquid commodities, probably wine and/or olive oil, in Hezekiah's economic buildup.

If Hezekiah did in fact control large amounts of oil and wine, then one would expect that those commodities—and the jars that held them—would pass through major cities like Jerusalem, Ramat Rahel, Lachish, and Gibeon as the royal goods were deployed to government officials or troops or traded on the market. Such a scenario would explain the large number of *lmlk* impressions in fortified cities. This understanding

---

[254]N. L. Lapp, "Tell El-Fûl," *NEAEHL* (ed. E. Stern; New York: Macmillan; Jerusalem: Israel Exploration Society, 1993), 448.

[255]N. L. Lapp, "Tell El-Fûl," 448.

of the *lmlk* seal impressions would also explain why large numbers of the impressions were found in cities that were not fortified. Further, understanding the *lmlk*impressed jars as a reflection of some sort of normal royal trade fits well with the typological information of those jars. Given the existence of Gezer Type 4A and Type 4B jars from the late 9th to the late 7th century, one would expect the function of these jars to be similar throughout this time period. Understanding the *lmlk* seal-impressed Type 4A jars as being used for the same sort of trade functions as associated with all of these jars over this 200 year time span also fits the typological data. However, understanding *lmlk*-impressed jars as having a function separate from the other jars—namely, siege preparation alone as opposed to normal trade—raises questions.

The association of the *lmlk* jars with normal trade seems especially likely at Lachish where the largest number of the seal impressions to date have been found. An active trade life is suggested at Lachish by the discovery of numerous weights. These weights vary in size and shape (round, oval, rectangular, and square), and contain different numerical markings, indicating that they were used to assure equity in the trading of commodities.[256] Ussishkin's renewed excavations at Lachish confirm these early findings of weights in Level III. He says that by the time of Level III, the city had become densely populated with many of the houses crowded together. Further, the destruction debris of Level III contained signs of trade such as "grinding stones, pestles, many clay 'loom weights' and arrowheads."[257]

Of course, Lachish does not stand alone as a fortified city that would likely have *lmlk* jars within its gates apart from siege preparation in the final period before an expected attack. Trade in wine (or oil), and the jars that contain it, is easy to envision in Gibeon because that city was a large wine production center. Pritchard labels two areas discovered in Gibeon during this period[258] as "industrial."[259] It seems that one was used for the production of olive oil, wine, or wheat, but unfortunately it is not

---

[256]D. Diringer, "Early Hebrew Weights Found at Lachish," *PEQ* (1942) 82-103, pls. XII-XIII.

[257]Ussishkin, "Lachish (1973-1977)," 52-53.

[258]Pritchard, (*Winery, Defenses, and Soundings*, 39) dates these two areas to 7th century, relying heavily on a wrong dating for the *lmlk* seal impressions. The close parallels that Pritchard notes between the pottery and other utensils from these areas and the pottery from Beit Mirsim, Tell Qasile, and Tell en-Naṣbeh (all sites now believed to have experienced destruction in 701 BCE) confirms the late 8th-century date for this material from Gibeon.

[259]Pritchard, *Winery, Defenses, and Soundings*, 39.

possible to identify with certainty which commodity was produced.[260] However, a second industrial area was located where the production had to be either olive oil or wine because the storage vats in this area did not leak and stored commodities at a constant temperature of 65 degrees F. This area also contained a wine or olive oil press, numerous jar fragments, stoppers, a fermenting tank, and cellars for storage of either wine or oil.[261]

In his final analysis, Pritchard concludes that wine, not olive oil, was the major commodity. He states that the facilities with the capacity to hold in excess of 1500 U.S. gallons of liquid "appear too large for the amount of oil which would normally be produced in a village the size of Gibeon."[262] He theorizes that wine, with its much higher rate of consumption, seems to be the more likely product. In addition, the constant temperature assured by these storage facilities was needed for wine production but not for olive oil. Finally, from his study of the facilities at Gibeon, he concludes that they are "better suited for getting the juice from the grapes than they are for extracting the oil from olives."[263]

In light of industrial activity associated with Gibeon, the occurrence of ninety-five *lmlk* seal impressions on the handles of jars that could have held wine does not seem out of the ordinary for trade, apart from siege preparation in the final weeks before a campaign. Pritchard writes:

> Further evidence that Gibeon was a thriving commercial city at the end of the Judaean kingdom has been supplied by the finding of a great number of stamp-seal impressions on jar handles. A total of 95 [plus the 12 cited below in Appendix I] stamped jar handles have been found. Eighty-three [plus the 12 cited below in Appendix I] of them bear the royal stamp; among them are represented the familiar place names of Hebron, Socoh, Ziph, and mmst. Obviously trade was carried on with the important centers of commerce in Judah. Among the private seal impressions one belonging to *tnhm ngb* was impressed by the same stamp which produced an impression on a jar handle found at Beth-Shemesh.

---

[260]Pritchard, *Where the Sun Stood Still*, 86.

[261]Pritchard, *Where the Sun Stood Still*, 90-98; cf. also J. B. Pritchard, "Industry and Trade at Biblical Gibeon," *BA* 23 (1960) 23-28.

[262]Pritchard, *Winery, Defenses, and Soundings*, 25; cf. also Pritchard, *Where the Sun Stood Still*, figs. 42-53.

[263]Pritchard, *Winery, Defenses, and Soundings*, 25.

Beth-Shemesh also contains signs that it was a thriving industrial center during the reign of Hezekiah, which would explain why so many *lmlk* and official seal impressions are located there although it was not fortified during the late 8th century. Beth Shemesh had copper smelting and iron forging for larger tools. Several installations were originally published as dyeing vats, but more recent research has shown that they were actually facilities for oil extraction.[264] These installations are relatively scarce in comparison to those at Tell Beit Mirsim. The large number of presses found throughout Stratum II suggests that the most common industries in Beth Shemesh were wine and olive oil production. In fact, the excavators state that the site was probably one of the largest establishments in the area for making wine or olive oil by the time of Stratum IIc.[265] Other objects found there confirm this picture. Items found *in situ* in loci with *lmlk* seal impressions, include various types of pottery, stone weights, and lamps.[266] Grant and Wright conclude that "more pottery was preserved in the ruins of Stratum II than in any other stratum, and undoubtedly the occupation between the 10th and 8th centuries was the most intensive, and perhaps prosperous, in the city's history."[267]

Grant and Wright state that olive oil production was probable in the rectangular presses with hollow interiors. Perhaps the flat presses similar to those found at Gibeon were also used for pressing olives, but since "the pulp of olives needs to be pressed to extract the oil, it is more probable that these flat stones [of the presses at Beth-Shemesh] were for mashing grapes from which the juice runs quickly and freely."[268] This interpretation is further confirmed by new evidence from Tel Miqne (Ekron), where a major olive oil production site has been discovered. The olive oil presses at Tel Miqne typically have a hollow rectangular crushing basin in which the olives were smashed by a crushing stone that was pressed into the basin by a pressbeam.[269] This system is markedly different from the flat presses found at Gibeon and Beth-Shemesh, where the crushing stone was rolled back and forth over a flat slab of rock with the juice running through a niche and into a catch basin.

---

[264]Cf. A. Mazar, *Archaeology*, 489-491.

[265]Grant and Wright, *Ain Shems V*, 76-77, pls. XVIII:2-4; XIX:1-3; XX:1-2.

[266]Grant and Wright, *Ain Shems V*, 67-68.

[267]Grant and Wright, *Ain Shems V*, 134.

[268]Grant and Wright, *Ain Shems V*, 76.

[269]D. Eitam, "Tel Miqne (Ekron)—Survey of Oil Presses—1985," *ESI* 5 (1985) 72-73.

In light of the evidence from Gibeon and Beth Shemesh, it seems probable that the *lmlk* seal impressions should be associated with jars for some sort of royal trade or distribution of wine. These data fit well with the Cross's observation that the presence of GNN on the *lmlk* stamps suggests that the jars held wine. Cross notes that on all other known jar stamps where a GN is present the commodity in question is wine. He says, "Wines are known by their district. It is the key to their taste and quality. But it matters little where grains are grown or where oil is pressed."[270] If this is the case, it explains the correlation Na²aman correctly notes between many military sites from Hezekiah's kingdom and the sites where *lmlk* seal impressions have been discovered. Royal troops would quite probably require wine as part of their provisions in times of peace and of war. Therefore, it is reasonable that sites where there were significant fortifications had a large number of these *lmlk* sealimpressed jars within their gates when they were destroyed by Sennacherib in 701 BCE. The presence of the royal storage jars does not necessarily mean that the jars themselves related to siege preparations in the final period before Sennacherib arrived at the city.

Such a scenario also explains why some *lmlk*type jars were stamped with a royal seal while others were not stamped at all. Both stamped and unstamped jars were used for the storage of wine (or possibly oil). The stamped jars were used for royal commodities. They were found throughout Judah, and their wide distribution provides further evidence for Hezekiah's economic development. This more general economic development is the key to understanding Hezekiah's preparation for a possible siege. The *lmlk* jars point towards a strong royal administration that would have been able to supply troops in various locations while preparing for a siege. Thus, while the *lmlk* jars may be seen as part of Hezekiah's overall preparation for siege, it is a mistake to limit this preparation to the final weeks or months before Sennacherib's campaign. As soon as Hezekiah made the decision to withhold tribute, he must have known that a military response was inevitable from the Assyrian ruler. Thus, the preparation for siege began from the very moment Hezekiah began strengthening his governmental infrastructure. Once Sennacherib's expected military response became imminent, royal jars would have likely been sent to sites facing imminent attack, but other stamped jars would have remained at other places in the kingdom.

---

[270]F. M. Cross, Jr., "Judean Stamps," *EI* 9 (1969) 21. As noted above, Rainey ("Royal Vineyards") develops Cross's observation and posits that the GNN represent four royal wine centers in the Judean Hill Country from which royal distribution of wine took place.

A modern analogy of the recent conflict in Bosnia illustrates this point well.[271] The United States has sent a strong military presence to Bosnia. Much of this presence both in terms of troops and equipment is positioned at key strategic locations facing imminent threat of attack; however, the United States was able to quickly mobilize its resources because both troops and equipment were stockpiled in nearby countries that were not under imminent threat of attack. A similar situation must have been the case in Judah under Hezekiah's reign. Once the expected campaign of Sennacherib materialized, Hezekiah responded by mobilizing available resources to meet the Assyrian threat. However, the stockpiling of these resources must have occurred much earlier for these goods to be available during any siege. In other words, Hezekiah had to establish a strong infrastructure at least several years before Sennacherib attacked so as to have any hope of mobilizing enough resources to stop the Assyrian onslaught.

It is precisely this type of scenario that the evidence from the *lmlk* jars suggests. The detailed analysis presented above in Chapter 2 shows that Hezekiah had great economic buildup and civil strength. This buildup had to have taken place over a number of years, and the *lmlk* jar phenomenon should be understood in this context of buildup occuring over an extended period of time.

This situation also has ramifications for an interpretation of various sections of 2 Chronicles 29-32. These chapters detail the shipment of goods to Judean storage centers at times other than the period before an imminent siege. By doing so, these descriptions are an important part of the Chronicler's overall depiction of Hezekiah's economic buildup and great civil strength. In other words, these chapters describe Hezekiah has having established a solid infrastructure that could be utilized during a military crisis, and the factors cited above suggest that the establishment of this infrastructure did not occur in the final months before Sennacherib's campaign.

3. Distribution of the *lmlk* Jars as a Kingdomwide Phenomenon

a. Introduction

Building on the conclusion that the impressions with PNN on *lmlk* jar handles belong to Hezekian officials, one may learn something about the administrative order of Hezekiah's kingdom by studying the distribution of impressions belonging to the same official. Y. Garfinkel

---

[271]I am thankful to R. E. Whitaker for sharing this analogy with me.

attempted in the 1980s to make sense of the distribution patterns,[272] but more recent data have raised questions about some of his presuppositions. Thus, it is instructive to review Garfinkel's findings briefly and to define some parameters for this type of investigation that can avoid his methodological errors.

b. Garfinkel's Proposals

Garfinkel began his work by analyzing all the published official seal impressions according to their distribution. With these data, he attempted to analyze the administrative makeup of Hezekiah's kingdom in terms of individual officials or adminstrators and in terms of adminstrative centers at different locations. In one article[273] he focused on the sites where official seal impressions had been found. In a second article[274] he focused on the administrative role played by the officials whose seal impressions appear on the *lmlk* jars.

In his study focusing on the officials themselves, Garfinkel concluded that the adminstrative hierarchy of Hezekiah's kingdom had three layers—kingdomwide, regional, and local. He arrived at the list of kingdomwide officials by adding the total distance between sites where impressions of a particular official were found. If this distance was greater than a day's journey, the official was considered to be a "kingdomwide" official. For example, Garfinkel reported that impressions belonging to נחם (בן) עבדי were found at three locations (Lachish, Tell ej-Judeideh, and Naḥal Arugot), and the total distance between the sites was 49 km. Garfinkel postulated that a reasonable day's journey was 24 km, so he concluded that this official was a kingdomwide administrator.[275] Similarly, officials whose impressions were found at sites within a day's journey he classified as regional officials, while those whose impressions were found at only one site he labeled local officials.[276]

Garfinkel used a similar method of measuring distances between sites to arrive at a list of administrative centers during Hezekiah's reign. Instead of adding the total distance between sites with impressions belonging to the same official, for each location he added the total distance among all sites containing an impression found at the first site. For

---

[272]Y. Garfinkel, "The Distribution of the 'Identical Seal Impressions' and the Settlement Pattern in Judah on the Eve of Sennacherib's Campaign," *Cathedra* 32 (1984) 35-53 (Hebrew); Garfinkel, "Hierarchic Pattern."

[273]Garfinkel, "Settlement Pattern."

[274]Garfinkel, "Hierarchic Pattern."

[275]Garfinkel, "Hierarchic Pattern," 108-110, Table 1.

[276]Garfinkel, "Hierarchic Pattern," 110-111, Tables 2-3.

example, with the data available to him, Garfinkel reported that in the case of Lachish, seven officials were known to have impressions both there and at six other sites. He added the total distances between Lachish and each of the additional sites, and this number (221 km) gave him a relative indicator of the administrative importance of Lachish. In determining the hierarchy of a site, Garfinkel also incorporated the number of officials at one site with parallel impressions at a second site.[277] After combining all of these indicators, he found that three sites served as the adminstrative centers during Hezekiah's kingdom—Jerusalem, Lachish, and Beth Shemesh. Further, he held that Jerusalem ranked first, Lachish was second, and the site located in the middle (Beth Shemesh) was the center between the two. Using similar techniques, he proposed a hierarchy for all the other sites in Judah where official seal impressions had been found.[278]

In analyzing Garfinkel's attempts to make sense out of the distribution of these official seal impressions, one should immediately ask what effect new discoveries of official seal impressions would have on the conclusions. He realized that this was a limitation and stated that one of the biggest methodological problems for his system was that some sites had been extensively excavated, others excavated very little, and at other sites impressions were discovered on the surface without any excavations. In response, he pointed to sites like Gezer and Tell en-Naṣbeh, where extensive excavation had yielded only a limited number of impressions with parallels elsewhere in Judah. On the other hand, Garfinkel stated that at sites like Tell ej-Judeideh and Tell eṣ-Ṣâfi, where the excavations were more limited, large numbers of impressions with parallels elsewhere were discovered. Thus, he concluded that his figures had a solid basis for general conclusions even if future finds might alter the analysis in particular cases.[279]

Although Garfinkel recognized the negative effect that additional data might have on his conclusions, he was incorrect in stating that these data would not change the general picture in addition to particular details. His error can be seen especially well in the system he posited for the hierarchy of officials. Because his study showed that no official had impressions at more than three sites, he concluded that they were kingdomwide officials, headquartered at one of the three sites. Further, these officials would send goods in *lmlk* jars to the other two sites. Even without new finds, this part of Garfinkel's system rested on a thin

---

[277]Garfinkel, "Settlement Pattern," 38-45.

[278]Garfinkel, "Settlement Pattern," 45-48.

[279]Garfinkel, "Settlement Pattern," 38-39.

foundation. For example, to posit that no official had impressions at more than three sites, he had to combine the impressions from Ramat Raḥel with those from Jerusalem as being from the same general vicinity.[280] Since the two sites are clearly separate both in terms of distance and function, this is a questionable connection.

Apart from this questionable presupposition, the new finds reported in Appendix II necessitate reevaluating Garfinkel's picture. The most dramatic evidence is found from impressions belonging to מנחם (בן) יובנה. With the evidence available at the time of his study and by combining Jerusalem with Ramat Raḥel, Garfinkel reported that this official had impressions at only three sites.[281] In fact, impressions of this official were actually discovered in eight sites, counting Ramat Raḥel as separate from Jerusalem: Ramat Raḥel, Jerusalem, Tel Sokoh, Gibeon, Tell ej-Judeideh, Lachish, Adullam, and Beth Shemesh. In addition, eight impressions of unknown provenance were located in private collections. Some of these impressions were attached to large jar fragments with fresh breaks—indicating that they came from illicit digs—and thus they point towards even more sites with impressions of this same official.[282]

Another example, which is even more damaging for Garfinkel's system, is found with the official שלם (בן) אחא. Garfinkel reports that this person was a regional official, for whom only four impressions had been found at two different sites, Tell ej-Judeideh and Khirbet Rabûd.[283] The research presented in Appendix II, however, shows fifteen known impressions of this individual from at least six sites: Tell ej-Judeideh, Khirbet Rabûd, Lachish, Ramat Raḥel, Beth Shemesh, and Arad. Once again, the existence of seven additional identical impressions of unknown provenance suggests that the actual number of sites with impressions belonging to this official is even higher.

Other finds presented in Appendix II further refute Garfinkel's conclusions both generally and regarding specific officials. For example, at least eleven of the twenty examples Garfinkel gave for local officials[284] would have to be bumped up to kingdomwide officials with these new data. Enumerating each example is not necessary here. Rather, in building on Garfinkel's valid attempt to make sense of the distribution of official impressions currently known, one must *not* adopt a model that will radically change with additional finds. A much more comprehensive

---

[280]Garfinkel, "Hierarchic Pattern."

[281]Garfinkel, "Hierarchic Pattern," 111.

[282]Barkay, "Group of Stamped Handles."

[283]Garfinkel, "Hierarchic Pattern," 111.

[284]Garfinkel, "Hierarchic Pattern," 111.

model could be developed if more complete data were available, but the research presented in Appendix II has shown that the picture is still very limited.

c. Official Seal Impressions as Pointers to a Kingdomwide Political Organization

A criterion for establishing the connection in the distribution of the *lmlk* jars between towns would be very helpful. Unfortunately, such a criterion cannot be derived directly from studying the distribution patterns of the official seal impressions. Garfinkel attempted such a comparision by positing a relationship between towns where impressions of the same official were found. For instance, he argued that if impressions of official "A" were found in Lachish, Jerusalem, and Beth Shemesh, then those towns were connected by the trade of material in *lmlk* jars administered by the this one official. However, when impressions of official "A" are found in many more than three sites, his system begins to break down. As noted above, impressions of מנחם (בן) יובנה were found at eight sites. Following a criterion similar to Garfinkel's would lead to the conclusion that Ramat Raḥel, Jerusalem, Tel Sokoh, Tell ej-Judeideh, Lachish, Adullam, and Beth Shemesh were all interconnected through the distribution of the *lmlk* jars.

Such a conclusion is called into question because most of the *lmlk* and official seal impressions were stamped before firing—at the place of production rather than at the destination. It is impossible to be certain if the distribution of the jars took place from the point of production or if the jars were subsequently sent to another location where they were filled and distributed; however, it seems probable that the jars would have been distributed from one site, whether that site was the point of production or another location. In light of this situation, the official mentioned above, מנחם (בן) יובנה, would have likely distributed all of the jars from only one site, so the presence of his impressions at eight sites says nothing about the interconnection of the sites. Therefore, it seems that there is no certain way to establish the interconnection between sites simply by looking at the distribution of the official seal impressions. One can safely state that at least these eight sites received shipments that were administered by the official מנחם (בן) יובנה, but the sites did not necessarily trade with each other.

Garfinkel's criterion for determining if an official was part of a kingdomwide political organization does hold up against the new data presented in Appendix II; the problem comes from his attempt to use the same criterion to establish the negative conclusion that an official did not have kingdomwide adminstrative duties. It seems reasonable to conclude that if impressions of one official are found at sites that are more than a day's journey apart, then the official was part of a political organization that functioned over a kingdomwide area. The positive conclusion can be supported with the known data, but the possibility of new data surfacing mitigates against assuming that simply because impressions of a particular official have not yet been found over a wide area, they will not be discovered in the future. The latter has actually happened with Garfinkel's list. Based on data presented here (Appendix II) one must reclassify eleven of the officials that he lists as "local"[285] to "kingdomwide."

Using Garfinkel's criterion of establishing a conservative number of officials who served within Hezekiah's political organization over a kingdomwide area, we can produce a considerable listing of such officials. The following is an alphabetic listing of officials with impressions found at sites more than a day's journey apart. No attempt has been made to establish the exact distance as the accuracy of this figure would necessarily be dependent on better knowledge of ancient roads than is presently available.

TABLE 8: ALPHABETIC LISTING OF KINGDOMWIDE OFFICIALS

name of official	list of sites	unprovenanced impressions
1. אחזיהו (בן) תנחם	Beth Shemesh Lachish Tell en-Naṣbeh + unknown	5
2. אליקם נער יוכן	Beth Shemesh Ramat Raḥel Tell Beit Mirsim.	
3. הושע (בן) צפן	Gezer Kh. ʿAbbad (Tel Sokoh) Lachish Tell ej-Judeideh + unknown	4
4. יהוחיל (בן) שחר	Jerusalem Kh. ʿAbbad (Tel Sokoh) Lachish Ramat Raḥel + unknown	2
5. כרמי (בן) יפיהו	Jerusalem Lachish	

---

[285]Garfinkel, "Hierarchic Pattern," 111.

TABLE 8 (CONTINUED)

name of official	list of sites	unprovenanced impressions
6. מנחם (בן) יובנה	Adullam Beth Shemesh Gibeon Jerusalem Kh. ʿAbbad (Tel Sokoh) Lachish Ramat Raḥel Tell ej-Judeideh + unknown	8
7. משלם (בן) אלנתן	Gibeon Lachish + unknown	2
8. נחם (בן) הצליהו	Gibeon Jerusalem Lachish + unknown	5
9. נחם (בן) עבדי	Lachish Naḥal Arugot Tell ej-Judeideh + unknown	12
10. נרא (בן) שבנא	Beth Shemesh En Gedi Jerusalem Lachish Ramat Raḥel + unknown	4
11. סמך (בן) צפניהו	Jerusalem Lachish Tell ej-Judeideh + unknown	2
12. צפן (בן) אבמעץ	Azekah Jerusalem Tel Batash (Timnah) Tell eṣ-Ṣâfi (Philistine Gath)	
13. צפן (בן) עזריהו	Beth Shemesh Gibeon Lachish Ramat Raḥel + unknown	
14. שבנא (בן) שחר	Lachish Ramat Raḥel Tell en-Naṣbeh	

TABLE 8 (CONTINUED)

name of official	list of sites	unprovenanced impressions
15. שלם (בן) אחא	Arad	7
	Beth Shemesh	
	Jerusalem	
	Kh. Rabûd	
	Kh. Qeila	
	Lachish	
	Ramat Raḥel	
	Tell ej-Judeideh	
	+ unknown	
16. תנחם (בן) מגן	Gibeon	3
	Lachish	
	Ramat Raḥel	
	Tel Tekoa	
	Tell Erani	
	+ unknown	
17. תנחם (בן) נגב[286]	Beth Shemesh	1
	Gibeon	
	Jerusalem	
	Ramat Raḥel	
	+ unknown	

This list is important because only eleven officials are left with impressions from controlled excavations or surveys. Of these, four officials are known only from Beth Shemesh and two only from Lachish. Both Beth Shemesh and Lachish have been excavated extensively, so it is not surprising that unique seal impressions are found at these sites. It is further highly probable that parallels to these impressions will be found elsewhere.[287] On the other hand, their absence in the present corpus should not be taken as proof that these officials did not serve in a widespread political organization like the others. Indeed, many of the officials that Garfinkel

---

[286]Rainey ("Historical Geography of the Negeb," 88) has shown that the meaning of "dry" for the verbal root נגב is a late development. The original meaning is likely "south" or "foreign." Thus, the appearance of נגב as a PN is unique; however, it should not be assumed that נגב in this instance is a GN because it conveys the meaning of "dry."

[287]As recently as October 18, 1995, I received photographs of official seal impressions from Kenyon's excavation in Jerusalem that confirmed that another one of Garfinkel's "local" officials was in fact an official with kingdomwide administrative duties. The photograph is of the impression כרמי / יפיהו, and it was considered "unreadable" to the excavators. Doubtless other impressions exist from Gezer, Jerusalem, and other sites that will change this picture even more when they are deciphered and published.

attributed to only one site were shown subsequently to have impressions all over Judah. Since very little of the Judean Hill country has been excavated extensively, it is quite likely that many more official seal impressions will be discovered at sites like Adullam and Tel Sokoh, which are presently known only from surveys.

In light of all these data, it seems that most, if not all, of the officials with impressions on *lmlk* jars were part of a program that encompassed Hezekiah's national and international political reforms. The kingdomwide role played by these officials is especially apparent in the Judean Hills and the Shephelah.[288] Whatever role they played in Hezekiah's kingdom seems to have been part of a larger program that involved the entire kingdom rather than only some sections. These data also contribute to the conclusion that Hezekiah's kingdom had a highly developed infrastructure and political organization. However, with the present data, a hierarchy of officials such as Garfinkel attempted to describe cannot be singled out.

D. Summary of *lmlk* Conclusions

This chapter shows that the phenomenon of the *lmlk* jars and the associated official seal impressions is limited to the reign of Hezekiah. Further, the phenomenon of the *lmlk* jars is much larger than previously recognized and points to a more significant distribution of goods than previously realized. Another aspect to this phenomenon is that the vast majority of these impressions are known from a relatively small number of sites. These points can be identified in Table 9 (following) which summarizes the corpora of *lmlk* and official seal impressions presented in Appendixes I and II:

---

[288]In general, there is a dearth of *lmlk* jars and official impressions in the Negeb; however, as noted (above), Rainey ("Wine From the Royal Vineyards," 57-62) has shown that the small numbers in the Negeb are due to a separate system of taxation and supply of government posts for this area on the outskirts of the Judean kingdom.

TABLE 9: SUMMARY OF NUMBERS OF ROYAL IMPRESSIONS BY SITE

site	lmlk	official	site	lmlk	official
Lachish	407	76	Bethlehem	1	
Jerusalem	275+	15	Beth-Horon	1	
Ramat Rahel	160	17	En Gedi	1	3
Gibeon	95	7	Estaol	1	
Tell en-Nasbeh	86	5	Kefar-Ata	1	
Beth Shemesh	48+	13	Kh. el-ᶜAbhar	1	
Tell ej-Judeideh	39	17	Kh. Dorban	1	
Gezer	37+	2	Horvat Maon	1	
Kh. El-Burj	24	1	Kh. Qumran	1	
Mareshah	19	6	Kh. Rabûd	1	2
Azekah	18	3	Horvat Shilhah	1	
Tell ᶜErani	15	1	Tell ᶜIra	1	
Gibea	14		Tell ash-Shuqf	1	
Kh. ᶜAbbad (Tel Sokoh)	13+	3	Qh. el-Qom	1	
Beth Zur	12		Ein Yael	1	1
Arad	10	1	Nes Harim	1	
Tel Batash	11	2	Hir. Jaresh	1	
Tell eṣ-Ṣâfi	6	4	Adullam	1	1
Mavasserit	5		Hir. Zawiyeh	1	
Hebron	5		Givat Haphurit South	1	
Tell Beit Mirsim	4	2	Beit Ṣafâfâ	1	
Aroer	3		Dagan site no. 62	2	
Ekron	3		Dagan site no. 66	1	
Hir. Marah el-Jumma	3 or 4		Kh. Jannaba et Tahta	1	
Er Ras	3		Dagan unamed site	1	
Jericho	2		ag. site (14-10/43/7)	1	
Beersheba	2		Tel ᶜEton	1	
Anatot	2		Gedor	1	
Kh. Qeila	2	1	Beithar	1	
Kh. es-Samrah	2		Hor. Shovav	--	1
Tel Halif	2		Nahal Zimra	--	1
Tel Jezreel	2		Tel Tekoa	--	1
Ashdod	1		unknown provenance	355	82
Bethel	1				

TOTAL: **1716** **268**

With the large number of *lmlk* and official seal impressions presented here, the role that a site with only thirty or forty impressions played in the overall distribution scheme of the royal jars is called into question. These observations have bearing on the evaluation of the economic buildup and civil power of Hezekiah compared with Josiah. The PNN found on the related official seal impressions are the names of officials who carried out the distribution of royal commodities during the late 8th century. This distribution was also a kingdomwide phenomenon, and not regional as previous interpreters have argued. Because the majority of the impressions are known from a small number of sites, this distribution probably took place from a few storage centers throughout the Judean kingdom. Next, a study of the distribution of the *lmlk* and official seal impressions shows that these jars were not used primarily for siege preparation solely on the eve of Sennacherib's campaign. Rather, Hezekiah's siege preparation probably began several years before Sennacherib's invasion, and that preparation included economic buildup and a strong infrastructure. It is seen that the *lmlk* jars also were primarily stored in a few major centers throughout the Judean kingdom. Finally, the contents of the *lmlk* jars are narrowed to two options: wine and olive oil. Several indicators suggests that wine is more probable than olive oil, but this conclusion is not certain. Whatever the contents, the additional data suggest that the contents were used in everyday life by individuals outside the royal court.

All of these conclusions fit the description of Hezekiah's ecomomic buildup by establishing storehouses through the Judean kingdom (2 Chr 32:27-29). In general, these additional data corroborate the account of Hezekiah as prosperous as detailed in 2 Chronicles 29-32, and they suggest that the infrastructure of Hezekiah's kingdom was as well developed, and probably even more developed, than Josiah's adminstrative infrastructure.

FOUR

CONCLUSIONS: SIGNIFICANCE OF THIS STUDY

This monograph advances the present state of research in two areas: the historical reconstruction of the kingdom of Hezekiah and the integration of historical data and historical categories into an interpretation of Chronicles. With regard to the first category, several small advances in the historical understanding of Hezekiah's kingdom were made. Hezekiah is seen to have undertaken major economic buildup of his kingdom and to have had a generally prosperous reign. The *lmlk* jars are seen to be an indicator of that build-up. They point toward a general establishment of a strong kingdom not limited to a brief or short-term siege function. The monograph argues instead that Hezekiah's siege preparation involved a general economic buildup that took place over several years rather than only during the final weeks or months preceding Sennacherib's invasion.

The relevance of this study to an interpretation of the Chronicler's account of Hezekiah—the second category—warrants some elaboration. At present, one group of commentators tends to highlight the need for studying the Chronicler's theological message apart from historical questions, while another group argues that the Chronicler had a historical source apart from the Deuteronomistic History. Japhet, in the conclusion to her landmark article on the use of Chronicles for reconstructing Israelite history, highlights the studies of Welten, North, and Klein as representative of the school that is skeptical about the historical reliability of Chronicles separate from Kings and about the role of historiography in interpreting Chronicles.[1]

Welten challenges the historical validity of any material of a political nature from Chronicles not found in Kings except for four very brief passages. He especially challenges the historical reliability of sections in Chronicles that contain war reports, descriptions of military techniques, and reports about buildings and fortifications. Welten argues that such passages reveal the setting of the late post-exilic period and do not contain a description of events from pre-exilic Judah or Israel.[2]

North and Klein develop different arguments for how a theological or ideological interpretation of scripture by the Chronicler could account for passages in Chronicles not found in Kings. Both thus suggest that the

---

[1] Japhet, "Historical Reliability," 98-99.
[2] Welten, Geschichte, 195-196.

Chronicler's ideology, and not historiographic concerns, account for passages not found in Kings.[3] North states:

> No single use of extra-biblical sources by the Chronicler has ever been proved. From this further follows not the fact but the undeniable possibility that any information communicated to us only by the Chronicler may be due in every case to his own legitimate inference or paraphrase from the canonical Scripture.[4]

Welten also views the Chronicler as a theologian who interpreted earlier scripture as opposed to someone who wrote history from both biblical and other sources. He states:

> With the books of Chronicles the historiography of Israel enters an entirely new stage; no more are traditions being collected and reworked; no more are earlier works being re-edited. The Chronicler writes history from beginning to end, anew and independently.[5]

The net result of Welten's views, as Japhet rightly states, is that "he excludes Chronicles from the very definition of historiography."[6]

In light of this history of debate, it is necessary to have an idea of how historically suspect material might be identified. At the risk of generalizing the discussion, the following may be offered as typical of the criteria used to identify historically suspect material that may have been invented by the Chronicler. An aspect of the Chronicler's account is held to be factually suspect if a) it is *not* found in Kings,[7] b) is consistent

---

[3]North, "Does Archaeology Prove," esp. 392; Klein, "Abijah's Campaign," esp. 211, 216-217.

[4]North, "Does Archaeology Prove," 392.

[5]Welten, Geschichte, 205. The English translation given here Japhet's ("Historical Reliability, 98-99).

[6]Japhet, "Historical Reliability," 99.

[7]This criterion does not mean that Kings is presupposed to be more reliable than Chronicles; rather, it merely points out that material could not be the invention of the Chronicler if it is already found in Kings. In other words, the material from Chronicles not found in Kings makes up the block of material that the Chronicler may or may not have invented apart from a historical source or historical remembrance.

with the ideological or theological agenda of the Chronicler,[8] and c) is *not* verifiable with extrabiblical, historical data.[9]

As stated in the preceding chapters, the sections in Chronicles without parallels in Kings (the first criterion listed above) are the key passages for the debate of the usefulness of historical questions in interpreting Chronicles.[10] Many scholars who affirm the role of historical questions in interpreting Chronicles concentrate on specifying verses that may originate in a source other than Kings. On the other hand, many scholars who emphasize the theological character of Chronicles (cf. Welten, North, and Klein) hold that locating a theoretical source other than earlier scripture is impossible. This monograph thus brackets the identification of verses that comprise a source separate from Kings (or other parts of scripture that the Chronicler might have used), and investigates the role historical categories can play in interpreting passages found in Chronicles but not in Kings.

The monograph chooses 2 Chronicles 29-32 (the Chronicler's account of Hezekiah) as an excellent place to test the relationship of extrabiblical historical data to an interpretation of Chronicles, because about 70% of this section has no parallel in Kings (note that the first criterion for historically suspect material is something that is *not* paralleled in Kings). Four major sections from 2 Chronicles 29-32 are unparalleled in Kings: a) 29:3-36, which details the purification and restoration of the temple; b) 30:1-27, which describes the re-establishment of the Passover; c) 31:2-19, which specifies how the clergy will maintain the temple; and d) 32:27-30, which lists in some detail Hezekiah's economic buildup and his mighty acts.

One recognizes that extrabiblical, archaeological, and historical data can corroborate only one of these four sections—the detailed list of Hezekiah's economic buildup and mighty acts found in 2 Chr 32:27-30. It is not possible with the present data to find material remains that have

---

[8]This criterion assumes that the Chronicler would not invent material apart from a historical source if the invented material contradicted the major theological agenda of the Chronicler. Thus, it is possible that material that supports the Chronicler's agenda was invented specifically to provide that support.

[9]Just because material may be consistent with extrabiblical, historical data, it does not necessarily follow that the material is authentic or factually reliable. However, factual consistencies do raise varying degrees of probability that the material is indeed reliable and not the mere invention of the Chronicler.

[10]The work of S. McKenzie (*The Chronicler's Use of the Deuteronomistic History* [Atlanta: Scholars Press, 1985] 36-41) is particularly helpful in discussing how the Chronicler both omits material from parallel passages in Samuel-Kings and adds material not found in Samuel-Kings for ideological reasons.

bearing on the rearrangement of the political structure of either the temple or Hezekiah's kingdom. Nevertheless, archaeological data can be of assistance in evaluating the statements concerning Hezekiah's economic[11] buildup and his great civil and administrative power.

To summarize the historical conclusions presented in this monograph, archaeological data reveal that Hezekiah undertook a general program of economic buildup, and that the economic buildup and infrastructure of Hezekiah's reign rivaled that of Josiah. A thorough reinvestigation of the *lmlk* jars further reveals that Hezekiah established storehouses throughout the kingdom of Judah as part of this economic buildup. Thus, these historical data substantiate the description of Hezekiah found in 2 Chr 32:27-30.

Looking at this conclusion in terms of the criteria outlined above, one observes that the historical data are relevant for the third criterion—the material in Chronicles that is *not* found in Kings is verifiable with, or at least consistent with, historical data. The very fact the material in these verses is indeed consistent with historical evidence from the pre-exilic period raises several challenges for studies such as Welten's that place the setting for such lists of accomplishments in the late Persian period; yet, the question must be asked whether this consistency proves that these verses are historically reliable. If one could show that these verses were inconsistent with the Chronicler's ideological agenda but still substantiated by historical data, then the case with regards to their historical reliability would be much more certain.

That did not happen. The opposite scenario proved to be the case. These verses are not only consistent with the Chronicler's ideological agenda, but the language seems to have been invented by the Chronicler to make an ideological point, not a historical one. Anticipating the final conclusion in this monograph, one sees that these verses are still historically consistent in spite of their adherence to the Chronicler's overall ideological agenda. To understand this conclusion, it is instructive to take a focused look at 2 Chr 32:27-30:[12]

---

[11]I define "economy" to refer to the distribution of scarce goods and resources.

[12]This is precisely the type of list challenged by Welten, *Geschichte*, 195-196.

27. ויהי ליחזקיהו עשר וכבוד הרבה מאד ואצרות עשה־לו
לכסף ולזהב ולאבן יקרה ולבשמים ולמגנים ולכל לכלי חמדה
28. ומסכנות לתבואת דגן ותירוש ויצהר וארות לכל בהמה ובהמה ועדרים לאורות
29. וערים עשה לו ומקנה צאן ובקר לרב כי נתן־לו אלהים רכוש רב מאד
30. והוא יחזקיהו סתם את־מוצא מימי גיחון העליון ויישרם למטה־מערבה לעיר דויד
ויצלח יחזקיהו בכל מעשהו

And Hezekiah had very great riches and honor. He made for himself treasuries for gold and silver, precious stones, spices, shields, and all kind of valuable vessels; (28) storehouses for the production of grain, wine and oil; and stalls for all kinds of cattle and sheepfolds. (29) He made cities for himself and flocks and herds in abundance, for God gave him very great property. (30) And this same Hezekiah stopped up the gushing of water from the upper Gihon, and directed them down to the west, to the City of David. Hezekiah succeeded in all his activity.

Chapter 2 corroborates the first three verses of this section (2 Chr 32:27-29) by detailing Hezekiah's economic buildup and great wealth. Chapter 3 presents a thorough reinvestigation of the *lmlk* jar phenomenon and shows that these jars functioned in Hezekiah's general economic buildup and that large numbers were stored at central locations. Thus, the data available from the *lmlk* jars fits well the description in 2 Chr 32:28 of Hezekiah's economic buildup by means of establishing storehouses throughout the Judean kingdom.

This correlation between the events described in 2 Chr 32:27-29 and the extrabiblical historical data that are available do not specifically necessitate the conclusion that these verses from Chronicles originate from a written source other than Kings. The correlation between these verses and what one is able to reconstruct of the historical events from Hezekiah's reign could very well be due to a historical remembrance or oral tradition from which the Chronicler drew. In fact, even if he utilized an additional written historical source other than Kings, it is entirely possible that the Chronicler reinterpreted and rewrote this section detailing Hezekiah's economic buildup and mighty deeds. In light of this situation, the monograph brackets the question of whether these verses comprise part of a separate source; however, even while doing that, one must address the consistency of 2 Chr 29:27-29 with the extrabiblical data.

The reference in verse 30 comprises the final datum in this section from Chronicles detailing the economic buildup and mighty acts of Hezekiah. As was noted in Chapter 1 of this study, the paleography of the Siloam Tunnel inscription does not necessitate dating the tunnel to the reign of Hezekiah. Further, since there is no firm stratigraphy associated with the Siloam Tunnel, it is impossible with the present data to link its founding securely with Hezekiah solely on the basis of archaeological and extrabiblical data.[13] On the other hand, Ussishkin utilized the remains of the Assyrian siege camp just north of the modern Damascus Gate, along with other general archaeological remains in Jerusalem, to show how 2 Chr 32:30 makes sense of all the known extrabiblical data.[14] In the end, however, ascription of the Siloam Tunnel to Hezekiah's reign is a result of biblical references and is not based solely on archaeological data.

Given this situation, the substantiation of the three verses preceding 2 Chr 32:30 strengthens the case for viewing verse 30 as at least an authentic remembrance. It seems reasonable to conclude that the Chronicler was utilizing a memory of Hezekiah's greatness and economic accomplishments in these four verses. Even though the modern interpreter cannot corroborate 32:30 in the same way that is possible for 32:27-29, it is reasonable to posit that the reference to the establishing of the Siloam Tunnel by Hezekiah is an additional datum that the Chronicler's community would have recognized as authentic.

Although these verses might be corroborated by the extrabiblical data presented in this monograph, the conclusion does not mean that one should view the Chronicler as a historian whose primary concern is the recording of factual events in the past. The Chronicler has a particular message to present, and he reinterprets the past in order to present that message. Thus, one must also look for other, ideological reasons for the presence of 2 Chr 32:27-30 in the Chronicler's work. As noted in the introduction, Ackroyd is certainly correct in his assessment that "However good his [the Chronicler's] sources, it is the way he uses them which ultimately counts."[15] A brief look at how the Chronicler uses 2 Chr 32:27-30 is thus important to understanding any possible role historiography (the writing of history) plays in the Chronicler's ideological message.

Indeed, a study of the key words and phrases in 2 Chr 32:27-30 reveals that the words and phrases chosen by the Chronicler have the effect of linking Hezekiah to Solomon, specifically to the economic and military buildup of Solomon. However, this conclusion could also detract from the correlation between the account in 2 Chr 32:27-30 and the extrabiblical data that are known for Hezekiah. It could be argued, with Welten, that the stock words and phrases in 2 Chr 32:27-30 are like other descriptions of a political nature that present an ideological message and

---

[13]Cf. North, "Does Archaeology Prove," 377; D. Ussishkin, "The Water Systems of Jerusalem During Hezekiah's Reign," *Cathedra* 70 (1994) 11 (Hebrew).

[14]Ussishkin, "Water Systems of Jerusalem," esp. 6, 9, 16.

[15]Ackroyd, "History and Theology," 506.

reveal more of a post-exilic than a pre-exilic setting. With this question in mind, it is instructive to review some of the key words and phrases in 2 Chr 32:27-30.

עשר and כבוד ("Riches and Honor")

The word pair עשר and כבוד ("riches and honor") occurs multiple times in the historical books of the Hebrew Bible to describe the gifts that God bestows upon a faithful king. Although it occurs only once in the Deuteronomistic History and only describes one Judean monarch (Solomon), it appears seven time in Chronicles, describing four separate kings: David, Jehosaphat, and Hezekiah in addition to Solomon. Thus, it is instructive to examine the use of the word pair in Kings and then to evaluate how this theme is developed to apply to additional monarchs in Chronicles.

In 1 Kings 3, God offers in a dream to grant Solomon any wish he desires. Instead of choosing personal gain, Solomon requests the ability to be a just ruler for the benefit of his people. The request pleases God, and in 1 Kgs 3:12 Solomon is granted a לב חכם ונבון אשר כמוך לא־היה לפניך ואחריך לא־יקום כמוך "wise and discerning mind so that no one like you has arisen before you, and none like you shall arise after you." Moreover, God is so pleased with this request that the reward is expanded (1 Kgs 3:13): "I give you also that which you did not ask, both riches and honor (גם-עשר גם-כבוד), so that no other king will compare with you all your days."

One notices that the gift of לב חכם ונבון "wise and discerning mind" results in the incomparability of Solomon. As a result of these gifts, the author claims that no king has been like Solomon in the past, and no king will arise like Solomon in the future. However, a different sort of incomparability is presented for the gifts of עשר and כבוד. These gifts only result in the incomparability of Solomon during his lifetime-- "all your days." This apparent contradiction has been explained well by Gary Knoppers who points out that the Deuteronomistic Historian holds that while Solomon is incomparable in terms of his wisdom, Hezekiah is a king without parallel because of his incomparable trust. Josiah, too, could be described as a king without parallel because of his incomparable reforms.[16] Thus, the Deuteronomistic Historian does not state explicitly that the riches and honor (עשר and כבוד) of Solomon make him incomparable from all other Judean kings, but the reader does notice that the words are not used in Kings to describe any other Judean Monarch.

---

[16]G. N. Knoppers, "'There was None Like Him': Incomparability in the Books of Kings," *CBQ* 54 (1992) 411-431, esp. pp. 413, 417, 425, 430-431.

In fact, in Kings the three words wisdom (חכם or חכמה), riches (עשר), and honor (כבוד) are used to describe no Judean or Israelite king except Solomon.

The situation is different in Chronicles. In the Chronicler's version of the same scene, God's assurance of Solomon's incomparability (2 Chr 1:12) includes past, present, and future for all of the attributes found in the Kings passage. 2 Chr 1:12 states:

החכמה והמדע נתון לך ועשר ונכסים וכבוד אתן־לך אשר לא היה כן למלכים
אשר לפניך ואחריך לא יהיה־כן

> Wisdom and knowledge are given to you. I will also give you riches, possessions, and honor such that none of the kings who were before had thus, and none after you will have the like.

Solomon here is explicitly described as the paradigmatic king for all time in terms of honor, riches, *and* wisdom. This being the case, another king could be described as having great riches, honor, *or* wisdom (but not all three) and not compromise the claim made in 2 Chr 1:12.

Such a scenario is precisely what one finds in Chronicles. Whereas in Kings no monarch besides Solomon is described as possessing wisdom (חכם or חכמה), riches (עשר), and honor (כבוד), in Chronicles the designation of riches and honor (עשר and כבוד) is also used to describe David, Jehosaphat, and Hezekiah. In the case of David, the monarch acknowledges in 1 Chr 29:12 that God is the only source of riches and honor (עשר and כבוד). Then, later in the same chapter following David's death, the author describes David's life as being full of riches and honor (עשר and כבוד). Similarly, two summary statements (2 Chr 17:5 and 2 Chr 18:1) describe Jehosaphat as having riches and honor (עשר and כבוד) in abundance. Finally, 2 Chr 32:27 summarizes Hezekiah's life by stating that he had "very great wealth and honor" (עשר וכבוד הרבה מאד). In summary, one finds that Chronicles presents Solomon as the paradigm for wisdom (חכם or חכמה), riches (עשר), and honor (כבוד), but other monarchs can be described as possessing at least two of these attributes, riches (עשר), and honor (כבוד), even if not on the scale of Solomon. One also finds a similar scenario in the next phrase in 2 Chr 32:27-30—"treasuries" (אצרות) and the items found in them.

Establishment of "Treasuries" (אצרות)

Whereas Chronicles describes both Solomon and Hezekiah as adding to the treasuries (אצרות), Kings mentions only Solomon as doing so. In 1 Kgs 7:51, Solomon is described as bringing all of the items that had been dedicated to God by David his father into the "treasuries (אצרות) of the house of the Lord." Moreover, in 1 Kgs 7:51 the list of items brought by Solomon into these treasuries is similar to the list of items found in the treasuries (אצרות) of Hezekiah—את־הכסף ואת־הזהב ואת־הכלים "the silver and gold and the vessels." In all the other verses in Kings where the treasuries are mentioned, the reference is to a particular Judean king removing items to pay tribute to a foreign ruler. 1 Kgs 14:26 states that Shishak took the treasury of Rehoboam, and he also took the gold shields (מגני הזהב) that had been placed there by Solomon. Similarly, 1 Kgs 15:18 states that Asa gave tribute to Ben-hadad of Syria from the treasuries, and 2 Kgs 12:18 states that Jehoash of Judah used the treasuries to give tribute to Hazael of Syria. Similar descriptions of removing items from the treasuries to pay tribute are found for Ahaziah of Judah (1 Kgs 14:14), Ahaz (1 Kgs 16:8), Hezekiah (2 Kgs 18:15),[17] and Jehoiachin (2 Kgs 24:13). In every case, an abundance of silver and gold (כסף וזהב), shields (מגן), and vessels (כלים) was evidence of great military and political strength; being forced to remove them in order to pay tribute was a consequence of military and political weakness.

Two final items found in the treasuries (אצרות) that Hezekiah made for himself are precious stones (אבן יקרה) and spices (בשמים). These items are associated with both Solomon and Hezekiah. In Kings, the term "precious stone(s)" (אבנים יקרות) is associated only with Solomon. The phrase "precious stones" (אבנים יקרות) is used in 1 Kgs 5:17 and 1 Kgs 7:9-11 to refer to items that Solomon gathers to lay the foundation of the temple. Later, in 1 Kgs 10:2, 10-11, the phrase is used to describe part of the gifts sent to Solomon by the Queen of Sheba and by Hiram.

Similarly, the term "spices" (בשמים) is used exclusively in Kings to describe items belonging both to Solomon and Hezekiah; however, even here, Solomon is given a higher status with regard to this rare commodity. Although both rulers are described as having stores of spices (cf. 1 Kgs 10:2, 10, 25; 2 Kgs 20:13), 1 Kgs 10:10 makes it clear that Solomon's accumulation was never exceeded by another monarch. 1 Kgs 10:10 states that "never again did spices such as these which the Queen of Sheba gave to Solomon come in abundance" (לא־בא כבשם ההוא עוד לרב אשר־נתנה מלכת־שבא למלך שלמה).

The situation is similar in Chronicles although King David is also included in the description of precious stones (אבן יקרה). Just as David dedicated the silver, gold, and vessels that would be used in the treasuries of the house of God by Solomon, 1 Chr 29:2 states that he also provided

---

[17]Hezekiah is also described in 2 Kgs 20:13, 15 as showing the goods in his treasuries (אצרות) to envoys from Babylon. The wealth of those goods is taken as a sign of his military and political strength, but the narrative of 2 Kings 20 does not end on a positive note. Once the prophet Isaiah heard about Hezekiah sharing the secrets of the realm with Babylon, he prophesies that the goods will be taken away to Babylon as booty in the future.

the precious stones (אבן יקרה) for Solomon's building of the temple. In addition, 1 Chr 20:2 describes David as having precious stones (אבן יקרה) in his crown. Other than these references, no kings except Solomon and Hezekiah are described by the Chronicler as possessing precious stones (אבן יקרה).

In summary, one again sees that in the description of Hezekiah's establishment of treasuries in 2 Chr 32:27, the Chronicler changes minor details found in Kings to portray Hezekiah as following in the steps of Solomon, who was considered as the paradigmatic king in terms of wealth and honor. The establishment of the treasuries and the items contained within them point to Hezekiah's great political and military strength and portray him as a second Solomon.

Establishment of Storehouses (מסכנות)

2 Chr 32:28 states that Hezekiah also made storehouses (מסכנות) for himself. Just as in the previous examples, this act links Hezekiah to Solomon. The word occurs only one time in Kings to refer to storage cities built by Solomon as part of his military buildup. 1 Kgs 9:19 mentions the establishment of storage cities (ערי מסכנות) in conjunction with Solomon's establishment of cities for his chariotry and his other military building endeavors.

Once again, a phrase used in Kings strictly to describe Solomon is used in Chronicles to describe multiple Judean kings. Here, the term storehouses (מסכנות) refers to Jehosaphat and Hezekiah in addition to Solomon. 2 Chr 8:4, 6 describes the military function of the establishment of storage cities by Solomon and parallel the passage in Kings. In a summary statement describing Jehosaphat's reign, 2 Chr 17:12 states that the monarch built "fortresses and supply cities" (בירניות וערי מסכנות). Finally, one finds the passage under discussion in this section, 2 Chr 32:28, where a summary statement of Hezekiah also attributes the establishment of storehouses (מסכנות) to that monarch.

Establishment of Livestock Stalls (ארות)

The continuation of 2 Chr 32:28 specifies that Hezekiah also erected livestock stalls for himself. Once again, this act links Hezekiah to Solomon's paradigmatic military preparations. The word "livestock stalls" (ארות) is rare in the Hebrew Bible; it only occurs four times, and it only refers to livestock stalls constructed by Solomon and Hezekiah. The word occurs once in Kings to describe the horse stables erected by Solomon as part of his military buildup (2 Kgs 5:6), andit is also found in the parallel passage, 2 Chr 9:25, which describes Solomon's stables. The Chronicler adds two additional references in 2 Chr 32:28 that are not paralleled in Kings.

These latter two occurrences refer to livestock stalls constructed by Hezekiah as part of his economic buildup. Thus, the use of "livestock stalls" (ארות) provides yet another example of the Chronicler's adaptation of a word or phrase that is specific to Solomon's economic and military buildup in Kings, and once again, that word applies to Hezekiah.

Given that these verses are heavily ideological and present Hezekiah as a second Solomon, one must ask what relationship extrabiblical, historical data have in the interpretation of an ideological text. In a recent article Knoppers addresses this issue:

> Recourse to archaeology and epigraphy does not deny the role of the Chronicler as either a theologian or an expositor. Nor does it exclude the application of other criteria, such as comparative biblical analysis and verisimilitude. Rather this approach seeks to determine, inasmuch as possible, the degree to which the Chronicler's account of a particular reform, coheres with information gleaned from ancient Near Eastern epigraphy and archaeology.[18]

In keeping with Knoppers' conclusions, one notices that there is indeed a high degree of congruence between the known, extrabiblical data and the Chronicler's ideological portrayal of Hezekiah. Thus, it is important to investigate the possibility that the Chronicler couples this ideological description with a historical remembrance that Hezekiah was a great king. If this is indeed the case, one must also ask why the Chronicler would want to present Hezekiah as a great king. The answer lies in the Chronicler's desire to support the post-exilic priesthood and Jerusalem Temple.

It is well known that one of the Chronicler's main goals is to support the post-exilic priesthood by showing the continuity of the post-exilic temple and priesthood with Israel's history. In doing so, the Chronicler provides a rationale for the existence of both the post-exilic priesthood and the Jerusalem Temple during the Persian period.[19] Recognizing this goal, it is not surprising that three of the four sections

---

[18]G. N. Knoppers, "History and Historiography: The Royal Reforms," in *The Chronicler as Historian*, eds. M. P. Graham, K. G. Hoglund, and S. L. McKenzie (Sheffield: JSOT Press, 1997) 186. I am grateful to Knoppers for providing a pre-print of this article before it was published when the present monograph was in the final stages of revision. Knoppers' study and this monograph draw similar conclusions regarding the use of historical data to interpret Chronicles even though they were reached independent of each other and use different types of data as support.

[19]Cf., among others, Klein, "Abijah's Campaign," 211.

from the Chronicler's account of Hezekiah directly support the Levites and the royal establishment and maintenance of the Temple. 2 Chr 29:3-36 relates how Hezekiah purified and restored the First Temple—a task that was certainly a concern to the Second Temple community. 2 Chr 30:1-27 relates how Hezekiah insured that the Passover was observed. Finally, 2 Chr 31:2-19 addresses another concern of the post-exilic priestly group and details how the Levites maintain the Temple and are supported by contributions from both the king and all of the people of the kingdom.

Although these sections as they are now found in Chronicles are most likely the ideological creation of the Chronicler and use language specific to the Chronicler,[20] one verse, 2 Chr 31:5, uses language that is nearly identical to that found in 2 Chr 32:28. 2 Chr 31:5 relates that the people of Israel supported the Temple by contributing their first fruits from the field ("wheat, wine, oil, honey, and all the produce of the field"—דגן תירוש ויצהר ודבש וכל תבואת שדה). The reference in 2 Chr 32:28 to the storehouses of the king that is corroborated by the extrabiblical material contains nearly this same list of produce ("storehouses for the produce of wheat, wine, and oil"—מסכנות לתבואת דגן ותירוש ויצה). Thus, the same goods donated by the Judean populace in 2 Chr 31:6 make up the commodities found in the royal storehouses described in 2 Chr 32:28.

From a literary standpoint, the reader observes that the description of Hezekiah's economic buildup and mighty deeds in 2 Chr 32:27-30 lends credence to the official sanction and support of the Levites and the Temple outlined in the three previous chapters. 2 Chr 32:27-30 show that the same king who supported the Levites and the Jerusalem Temple was prosperous. The implication is that Hezekiah's faithfulness in giving this support resulted in his prosperity and his mighty deeds as outlined in 2 Chr 32:27-30. The point is emphasized by the fact that the same goods donated by the people of Israel for the support of the Temple (cf. 2 Chr 31:6) make up the agricultural goods found in Hezekiah's storehouses.

Therefore, the interpreter of the Chronicler's account of Hezekiah recognizes that by using this historically accurate tradition (or source) in 2 Chr 32:27-30, the Chronicler lends credence to his ideological effort to support the post-exilic Levites and the Temple.[21] It is as if he is saying to the post-exilic community, "Remember the famous king Hezekiah who

---

[20]Cf. Japhet, *I and II Chronicles*, 914-915, 935, 960-961. Japhet also states that it is possible that these sections draw on an authentic memory, but there are no extrabiblical data to support such an interpretation.

[21]This statement does not mean to imply that the book of Chronicles should be reduced to an ideological piece that only supports the post-exilic needs. Rather, it is clear that the writer of Chronicles has an investment in presenting a positive case for the post-exilic priestly establishment.

was faithful to God in maintaining the Temple and the Levites. He was prosperous and famous because he supported God through these actions."

As Rosenbaum has shown, the Josianic redaction of the Deuteronomistic History had a different agenda and did not have the need to emphasize the prosperity and mighty deeds of Hezekiah. Assuming that at least a major redaction of the Deuteronomistic History took place during the reign of Josiah, one understands the need for Dtr to stress the status of Josiah as opposed to his famous ancestor, Hezekiah.[22] The data presented in Chapter 2 of this study substantiate Rosenbaum's position and show that Hezekiah did indeed rival, if not exceed, the status of Josiah. This scenario also explains why the Chronicler would have found it beneficial to include this historically accurate tradition describing the prosperity of Hezekiah, whereas Dtr would have tended not to emphasize it, even if he had been aware of it.[23]

These conclusions suggest that although the Chronicler presented an ideologically laden message to the post-exilic community, historical data were used in its service. Indeed, 2 Chr 32:27-30 probably developed from a historical source or historical memory of facts not recorded in Kings, and the Chronicler used this reference to Hezekiah's economic buildup and mighty acts to authenticate his ideological message.

---

[22]Even if one does not accept a Josianic redaction, the conclusions presented here are valid if a later post-exilic redactor had a preference for Josiah. Whenever the Deuteronomistic History was written, it seems clear that its author has a bias towards Josiah.

[23]This conclusion would also be valid if the first edition of Kings and the Deuteronomistic History end with Hezekiah's reign. Cf. I. W. Provan, *Hezekiah and the Books of Kings: A Contribution to the Debate About the Composition of the Deuteronomistic History* (Berlin: Walter de Gruyter, 1988) 133-155, 172-173.

APPENDICES

lmlk Jars: New Data on an Old Phenomenon

The first *lmlk* impressions were found by C. W. Warren in Jerusalem in 1869. Just a few years later, an abundance of impressions came to light between 1898-1900 with the excavations of F. J. Bliss and R. A. S. Macalister.[1] Since that time, more than 1000 of these royal seal impressions from sites all over Judah have been listed in various corpora,[2] making them the topic of much discussion.

The *lmlk* jar phenomenon has often been used in historical studies of Hezekiah; however, new data call into question many previously accepted conclusions. The issue revolves around the question of what the jars were actually used for and how their use played a role in the kingdom of Hezekiah. These issues are addressed in depth in Chapter III; Appendices I and II focus on presenting new data on the *lmlk* and official impressions that will provide more clues towards an answer to these questions.

---

[1]Cf. Bliss and Macalister, *Excavations in Palestine.*

[2]Cf. Y. Garfinkel, "2 Chr 11:5-10 Fortied Cities List and the *lmlk*—Reply to Nadav Naʾaman," *BASOR* 271 (1988) 70.

APPENDIX I
A New Corpus of The *lmlk* Impressions[1]

Garfinkel's corpus of *lmlk* impressions lists 1198 occurrences.[2] The corpus presented here lists 1716 *lmlk* impressions (cf. summary listing on p. 166) and supplements Garfinkel's lists in three ways: a) by including impressions from controlled excavations subsequent to his corpus, b) by including impressions from controlled excavations that for various reasons were not reported accurately in the publications of each respective excavation, and c) by including impressions found in private and public collections originating from noncontrolled (or illicit) excavations. This last category was much more extensive than might have been suspected (more than 350 examples), and its value for this study is, of course, much less than that of those from provenanced finds. However, these additional impressions from "chance finds" provide important data that show that phenomenon of the *lmlk* impressions is much larger than previously acknowledged.

In general, the impressions are listed according to site, then by collection for the unprovenanced finds. The extent of details provided in the following listing depends on whether or not the impressions were previously accounted for in Garfinkel's corpus. In some places, particularly Jerusalem, details are provided for sites where Garfinkel simply cites "oral communication" and lists an estimate. For impressions not compiled in previous studies accessible in a European language, adequate information is given so that the listing may be verified. In other cases, the published reports are ambiguous, so a justification of the number reported here is given when warranted.

1. Lachish: 407[3]
2. Jerusalem: approximately 286

In Garfinkel's listing of the *lmlk* impressions from Jerusalem, he records "250+" and cites "personal communication from G. Barkay."[4] Most of the details for this figure are contained in Barkay's unpublished Hebrew

---

[1] I am indebted to G. Barkay for his collaboration in compiling this listing of *lmlk* impressions. Many of the impressions were first listed in Barkay's own dissertation, and many others came to light as a result of our joint research.

[2] Garfinkel, "Reply to Nadav Naʾaman," 70.

[3] G. Barkay and A. G. Vaughn, *"LMLK* and Officials Seal Impressions From Tel Lachish," *Tel Aviv* 23 (1996) 61-64, 73.

[4] Garfinkel, "Reply to Nadav Naʾaman," 70.

dissertation.[5] Unless otherwise noted, the discussion of the *lmlk* handles from Jerusalem summarizes the data presented in Barkay's dissertation. In the following list, Barkay's general presentation format of recording the impressions by date of discovery is maintained.

  A. C. W. Warren Excavations: 8+ (3 with concentric circles).[6]

  B. Clermont-Ganneau Excavations: 1[7]

  C. Parker Excavations (published by Vincent): 6[8]

  D. R. Weill Excavations: 1[9]

---

[5]Barkay, "Northern and Western Jerusalem." Under the guidelines of the Department of Archaeology of Tel Aviv University the dissertation is not circulated, but a copy is held in the library of that department. The dissertation was examined on several occassions. In addition, Barkay and I have collaborated over a period of more than 5 years on a complete corpus of official and lmlk seal impressions, so the figures given in Barkay's dissertation have been supplemented by this collaboration.

[6]These were the first recorded discoveries of the *lmlk* impressions in Israel. They were found southeast of the Temple Mount. These impressions were never completely published. It seems likely that more impressions were discovered but not reported (cf. C. W. Warren, "Phoenician Inscription on Jar Handles," *PEFQS* [1869] 372; Charles W. Wilson and C. W. Warren, *The Recovery of Jerusalem: A Narrative of Exploration and Discovery in the City and the Holy Land* [New York: D. Appleton & Company, 1871] 152, 473-474; C. W. Warren, *Underground Jerusalem: An Account of Some of the Principal Difficulties Encountered in its Exploration and the Results Obtained* [London: Richard Bentley and Son, 1876] 71, 142, 422-423; C. W. Warren and C. R. Conder, *The Survey of Western Palestine. Jerusalem* [London: Palestine Exploration Fund, 1884] 155-156. These *lmlk* impressions were found at about 24 ft. below the surface on top of the bedrock at the level of the foundation of walls of the Temple Mount. Barkay rightly concludes (contra Vincent, *Jérusalem*, 582) that these impressions suggest that the walls date from the Iron Age II, not earlier (Barkay, "Northern and Western Jerusalem," 427).

[7]Clermont-Ganneau, "Inscribed Jar-Handles of Palestine," *PEFQS* (1900) 251-253.

[8]The excavations took place between 1909 and 1911 on the eastern slope of the City of David. All 6 impressions come from a fill or mixed context (Vincent 1911:30, pls. 13-14; A drawing of a complete handle with a MIIc impression is found in L. H. Vincent, "Les Récentes Fouilles d'Ophel," *RB* 9 (1912) 548-551.

[9]This impression was discovered in a fill south of the City of David (R. Weill, *La Cité de David: Compte rendu des fouilles exécutées, à Jérusalem, sur le site de la ville primitive. Campagne de 1913-1914* [Paris: Librairie Paul Geuthner, 1920] 138-139).

E. C. A. Macalister and J. J. Duncan Excavations: 8+ (3 with cc) + 6 cc.[10]

F. Crowfoot and Fitzgerald Excavations: 1[11]

G. C. N. Jones Excavations: 1[12]

H. Kenyon's Excavations: 107 (18 with cc) + 16 cc.[13]

I. U. Lux Excavations: 3[14]

---

[10]These excavations were conducted in the eastern part of the City of David. The exact number of impressions found is unknown because the excavators failed to publish a complete list. A general book on the holy land by Duncan refers to at least 8 *lmlk* impressions (3 with concentric circles) (J. G. Duncan, *Digging up Biblical History. Recent Archaeology in Palestine and Its Bearing on the Old Testament Historical Narratives. Vol. II* [London: Macmillan, 1931] 139, 145).

[11]This impression was found during the 1927-1928 excavations in the northwestern part of the City of David. No details were given in the report (J. W. Crowfoot and G. M. Fitzgerald, *Excavations in the Tyropoen Valley, Jerusalem, 1927* [London: Palestine Exploration Fund, 1929] 67).

[12]This impression was discovered in the citadel area in the western part of Jerusalem in Level A, the lowest level, lying on bedrock (C. N. Jones, "The Citadel, Jerusalem, [A Summary of Work Since 1934]" *QDAP* 14 [1950] 130, pl. 57).

[13]These handles will be published in full by A. Lemaire. Lemaire gave a list to Barkay, and I in turn drew on this information from Barkay's dissertation. These impressions were discovered during Kenyon's excavations from 1961 to 1967 in the City of David and the Christian and Armenian Quarters of the Old City of Jerusalem. Kenyon's meticulous methods of examining every sherd that was dug doubtless resulted in the collection of the most handles with *lmlk* impressions. This fact also explains why some other more extensive digs have failed to produce as many impressions. Despite the meticulous methodology that resulted in the collection of such a large number of impressions, no mention of these impressions was made in Kenyon's publications. There is only a brief mention by Lang in a review of Welten's work on the *lmlk* stamps (B. Lang, Review of *Die Königs-Stempel. Ein Beitrag zur Militärpolik Judas unter Hiskia und Josia,* by Peter Welten, *RB* 79 [1972] 441). Barkay, thanks to a list provided by Lemaire, has given the details for 107 *lmlk* impressions and 16 handles with concentric circles. Most of these come from within the City of David. 6 were found in a fill resting upon the base of Wall NA (Locus 957.7, Square 26), and prove that this wall of Kenyon's excavations in the City of David dates from the time of Hezekiah. The impressions found in the Armenian and Christian Quarters, provide additional evidence that these areas, too, were builtup and occupied as early as the time of Hezekiah (Barkay, "Northern and Western Jerusalem," 429-431).

[14]These impressions were found by 1970-1971 in the excavations at the Church of the Redeemer in the Christian Quarter of the Old City of Jerusalem, in a fill with an abundance of other pottery fragments dating from the Iron Age II

J. S. Ben-Arieh and E. Netzer Excavations of Third Wall: 1[15]

K. M. Broshi Excavations along the Western Wall of the Old City: 19 (4 with cc) + 10 cc.[16]

L. B. Mazar Excavations: 22 (1 with cc) + 12 cc.[17]

M. D. Bahat and M. Broshi Excavations in Armenian Garden: 10 (2 with cc) + 2 cc.[18]

(U. Lux, "Vorläufiger Bericht über die Ausgrabung unter der Erlöserkirche im Muriston in der Altstadt von Jerusalem in den Jahren 1970 und 1971," *ZDPV* 88 [1972] 191).

[15]The "Third Wall" is located north of the Old City of Jerusalem. The impression was found in a Byzantine-era water cistern that contained a fill of material from the Iron Age II. It should be assumed that this fill material came from a nearby area that was cleared in the Byzantine period, and thus provides more support for viewing Jerusalem as having been expanded to the north during the reign of Hezekiah (Barkay, "Northern and Western Jerusalem," 431-432).

[16]In these excavations, very few loci were found with clear Iron II deposits *in situ*; however, many areas contained fills with Iron II material, including these *lmlk* impressions. Much of the excavating was done with mechanical digging tools, which may explain the the chance discoveries of *lmlk* impressions in the dumps of this dig (several collectors of antiquities in Jerusalem claim to have impressions originating from these dumps, and the use of mechanical tools in the excavation process would explain why at least a few impressions would escape discovery). The preliminary reports of this excavation make no mention of the *lmlk* impressions found. (Barkay, "Northern and Western Jerusalem," 432; cf. preliminary report in M. Broshi, "Recent Excavations along the Walls of Jerusalem," *Qad* 9 [1976] 75-78).

[17]All of these handles, except 1 *lmlk* impression (cf. Barkay, "Northern and Western Jerusalem," 445), were published by Nadelman in the excavation report of E. Mazar and B. Mazar (Y. Nadelman, "Hebrew Inscriptions, Seal Impressions, and Markings of the Iron Age II," *Excavations in the South of the Temple Mount: The Ophel of Biblical Jerusalem* [ed. E. Mazar and B. Mazar; Qedem Monographs 29; Jerusalem: Keterpress Enterprises, 1989] 134, pls. 143-169). The excavations took place in the area southwest of the Temple Mount (the Ophel). The context of these finds is similar to those found in Warren's excavations (above). Most of the *lmlk* impressions were found in a fill resting on the bedrock, suggesting the establishment of this area at least during the late 8th century (Barkay, "Northern and Western Jerusalem," 433). These conclusions drawn from fill areas is supported by 2 *lmlk* handles found in a stratified context from the late 8th century in Room 23043. This room preserved stratified remains of a floor from the Iron II period (E. Mazar and B. Mazar, *Excavations in the South of the Temple Mount: The Ophel of Biblical Jerusalem* [Qedem Monographs 29; Jerusalem: Keterpress Enterprises, 1989] 22).

[18]These impressions were discovered in the excavations dating from 1970-1971 in the garden of the Armenian Monastery at the western edge of the

N. Shiloh's City of David Excavations: 22+ (5 with cc) + 15 cc.[19]
O. Avigad's Excavations: 44 (7 with cc) + 8 cc.[20]
P. D. Davis and A. Kloner Excavations: 1[21]
Q. S. Margalith and D. Chen, and B. Pixner Excavations: 1[22]
R. M. Broshi Excavations in the Armenian Garden: 1
S. M. Broshi Excavations at Caiaphas' House: 1
T. A. Meyer Excavations at Russian compound: 1
U. Excavations at David's Citadel: 1[23]
V: Shiloh's City of David Excavations (1982 season): 7[24]
W: Kiriat Menahem Excavation in West Jerusalem: 3[25]

3. Ramat Raḥel: 162[26]

Old City of Jerusalem. The *lmlk* impressions came from a fill that contained much pottery from the Iron II period (D. Bahat and M. Broshi, "Exacavations in the Armenian Garden," *Qad* 5 [1972] 103; Barkay, "Northern and Western Jerusalem," 435).

[19]The handles have not been completely published, but Shiloh made a preliminary list available to Barkay (cf. Y. Shiloh, "Jerusalem: the City of David, 1978," *IEJ* 28 [1976] 276; Y. Shiloh and M. Kaplan, "Digging in the City of David," *BAR* 5:4 (1979) 49; Barkay, "Northern and Western Jerusalem," 434).

[20]Avigad, *Discovering Jerusalem*, 43; cf. Barkay, "Northern and Western Jerusalem," 434-435.

[21]This impression was found near burial caves on the west slope of Mount Zion during 1975. The cave excavations were published without a reference to the *lmlk* impression (Barkay, "Northern and Western Jerusalem," 436; cf. the excavation report in D. Davis and A. Kloner, "A Burial Cave of the Late Israel Period on the Slopes of Mt. Zion," *Qad* 11 [1978] 16-19).

[22]This unpublished impression was found in the area surrounding the excavations of burial caves at the southwest corner of the Western Hill in Jerusalem near Mount Zion (cf. Barkay, "Northern and Western Jerusalem," 436).

[23]This impression is of the two-winged type, but the GN could not be deciphered. Reg. no. 1091, Locus 4032 (cf. Barkay, "Northern and Western Jerusalem," 439, n. 39).

[24]Barkay, "Northern and Western Jerusalem," 439, n. 39

[25]Barkay lists the following impressions: one two-winged *zyp*; one four-winged; one additional two-winged (Barkay, "Northern and Western Jerusalem," 439, n. 39).

[26]Aharoni published 147 *lmlk* seal impressions of various types (Y. Aharoni, "Excavations at Ramat Raḥel, 1954: Preliminary Report—II," *IEJ* 6 [1956] 144-145, pls. 25:2-3; Y. Aharoni, *Excavations at Ramat Raḥel, Seasons 1959 and 1960* [Rome: Centro di Studi Semitici, 1962] 19-20, 45-48, figs. 15:1-7, 31:4-9, pls. 7:1-6, 29:1-12, 30:1-4; Y. Aharoni, *Excavations At Ramat Raḥel, Seasons 1961 and 1962*

4. Gibeon: 95[27]
5. Tell en-Naṣbeh: 86[28]
6. Beth Shemesh: 48+[29]

[Rome: Centro Di Studi Semitico, 1964] 33-34, 61-63, pls. 38:1-12, 39:1-11). In the renewed excavations directed by Barkay in 1984, 12 more impressions were discovered (G. Barkay, personal communication). A. F. Rainey discovered an additional handle—now in a study collection at Tel Aviv University—on the surface during the 1970s (Rainey, personal communication). Finally, Barkay and I found 2 additional handles on the surface during the summer of 1997. These 2 handles were given find numbers according to Barkay's 1984 excavation and are together with his excavation materials.

[27]Pritchard originally published 83 *lmlk* impréssions (J. B. Pritchard, *Hebrew Inscriptions and Stamps From Gibeon* [Museum Monographs; Philadelphia: The University Museum, University of Pennsylvania, 1959] 18-26). I reviewed the Gibeon finds currently stored at the Museum of Archaeology and Anthropology of the University of Pennsylvania and found an additional 12 *lmlk* impressions (4 of which also contained incised concentric circles) and an additional 5 handles with only incisions of concentric circles. All of these handles were found in Pritchard's excavations at Gibeon, but for some reason were not reported in the various publications. 14 of the above *lmlk* handles contained incisions of concentric circles while 14 handles contained only the incisions of concentric circles without a *lmlk* impression (Pritchard, *Stamps From Gibeon*, 20-21. Pritchard actually recorded: 13 with both concentric circles and *lmlk* impressions and 15 with only *lmlk* impressions. However, a reexamination of the actual handles showed that 1 handle published as containing only incisions of concentric circles [field no. 120] also contained a *lmlk* stamp (Type ?II?).

The field numbers and Lemaire types for the *lmlk* impressions not published by Pritchard are as follows: 711/S.506 (?II? with concentric circles); 1128/S.515 (SIb); 1451/S518 (MIa? on a Pithos handle); 995/S.509 (MIIb); 3680/insc. 311 (HIIb); 685/S.480 (ZIIb with concentric circles); 3121/insc. 300 (?II?); 983/S.504 (?II? with concentric circles); 825/S.489 (?Ia with concentric circles); 927/S.496 (HIIb); el Jib 7/12/56 I.918 (?II? with incised cross mark); 120/S.36 (?II? with concentric circles; published as only with concentric circles).

The field numbers for the additional handles with incisions of concentric circles are as follows: 931/S.507; 987/S.508; 1059/S.518; 341/S.95 (*not a lmlk* jar handle but rather a smaller handle similar to those on cooking pots); el Jib 7656/III El 7/14/56. (In addition to these handles from the late 8th century, I located 2 additional impressions on jar handles that were not published by Pritchard: a handle with an impression of a roaring lion from the Persian Period [field no. 3502/insc. 308] and a rosette impression with eight petals [field no. 753/S.486]).

[28]McCown, *Tell En-Naṣbeh I*, 156-164.

[29]Details of my notes from the collection at the University Museum, University of Pennsylvania, will be published in A. G. Vaughn, "*LMLK* and Official Seal Impressions From Tel Beth Shemesh," the forthcoming preliminary excavation report of the renewed Beth Shemesh excavations, eds. Sh. Bunimovitz and Z.

7. Tell ej-Judeideh: 39[30]
8. Gezer: 37+[31]
9. Khirbet El-Burj (near Ramot suburb of Jerusalem): 24[32]
10. Azekah: 18[33]
11. Tel Mareshah: 19[34]
12. Tel ʿErani: 15[35]

Lederman.

[30]37 impressions were reported in F. J. Bliss, "Second Report on the Excavations at Tell ej-Judeideh," *PEFQS* (1900) 207. I examined an 2 others at Tel Aviv University that were found during Aharoni's surveys. The 2 impressions (types ?II? and ?I?) are now stored at the Insitute of Archaeology, Tel Aviv University, but no collection numbers were available.

[31]Gitin (S. Gitin, *Gezer III: A Ceramic Typology of the Late Iron II, Persian and Hellenistic Periods at Tell Gezer* [Annual of the Nelson Glueck School of Biblical Archaeology 3; Jerusalem: Hebrew Union College, 1990] 17 n. 16) summarizes the situation at Gezer as follows: "The number of *lmlk*-stamped handles from R.A.S. Macalister's (PEF) excavations has always been problematic, as Macalister did not publish an accurate record of his finds. H. D. Lance's documentation (Lance, "Royal Stamps," n. 70.) provides a minimum number of 31, but the number could be as high as 50." 6 impressions were found during the renewed excavations at Gezer, bringing the total to at least 37 (Gitin, *Gezer III*, 17 n. 16).

[32]This site was excavated by A. de Groot. D. Amit has been assigned responsibility for the publication of the *lmlk* handles and in a letter to me dated November 5, 1995 he reported 23 two-winged *lmlk* stamps (2 with concentric circles) and an additional 14 handles with incisions of concentric circles. Amit said, "Most [of the *lmlk* handles] were very worn, but from the shape of the handle and fabric we are confident that they are indeed *lmlk*s. All of the handles were two-winged. 2 also had concentric circles." In addition, a private collector from the Ramot suburb of Jerusalem found an additional MII? handle with concentric circles (G. Barkay, personal communication).

[33]1 stamp was reported in F. J. Bliss, "Second Report on the Excavations at Tell Zakarîya," *PEFQS* (1899) 103-105. Twelve stamps were reported in F. J. Bliss, "Third Report on the Excavations at Tell Zakarîya," *PEFQS* (1899) 184-186. 4 were reported in F. J. Bliss, "Fourth Report on the Excavations at Tell Zakarîya," *PEFQS* (1900) 12-13. 1 stamp now stored at the École Biblique was reported by Lang (Review, 441).

[34]A general reference to the *lmlk* handles is found in the the site report (F. J. Bliss, "Report on the Excavations at Tell Sandahannah," *PEFQS* [1900] 329-330). A list of 17 stamps is given by Bliss and Macalister (*Excavations in Palestine,* 107). A. Kloner reports 2 additional stamped handles from Cave 75 at Mareshah (A. Kloner, "Mareshah [Marisa]," *NEAEHL* [ed. E. Stern; New York: Macmillan; Jerusalem: Israel Exploration Society, 1993] 952).

[35]3 handles are reported in Shmuel Yeivin, "Tell Gath (Tell Sheikh

13. Gibeah: 14[36]
14. Beth Zur: 12[37]
15. Kh. ᶜAbbad: 13+[38]
16. Arad: 10[39]
17. Tell Batash: 11[40]
18. Tell eṣ-Ṣâfi: 6[41]
19. Mavasseret Zion: 5[42]
20. Hebron: 5[43]

---

el-ᶜAreini)," *IEJ* 9 (1959) 270. 10 additional handles are mentioned in Yeivin's preliminary report (S. Yeivin, *The First Preliminary Report on the Excavations of Tel "Gath" 1956-1958* [Jerusalem: The Gat Expedition, 1961] 9). Lang (Review, 441) reports a handle in the collection of Father G. Roux that was found at ᶜErani in January 1963. Finally, an additional handle was found at the tel by S. Wolff (G. Barkay, personal communication).

[36]N. L. Lapp, "Other Finds from the 1964 Campaign," *The Third Campaign at Tel El-Ful: The Excavations of 1964* (AASOR 45; Cambridge, MA: American Schools of Oriental Research, 1981) 111-112; W. F. Albright, "A New Campaign of Excavations at Gibeah of Saul." *BASOR* 52 (1933) 10. In addition, 1 impression was found on slopes of the tel by S. Gibson (G. Barkay, personal communication).

[37]O. R. Sellers and W. F. Albright, "The First Campaign of Excavation at Beth-Zur," *BASOR* 43 (1931) 8. An additional seal impression (type MIIa) was discovered in 1978 on the surface by A. Cohen Zohar (G. Barkay, personal communication).

[38]10+ found in Garfinkel ("Reply to Nadav Naᵓaman," 70). Barkay (personal communication) informs me of 3 additional impressions: 1 found in 1989 by D. Amit, 1 found by Y. Meshorer, and 1 now stored in the museum of Kefar Etzion.

[39]M. Aharoni, "Inscribed Weights and Royal Seals," *Arad Inscriptions,* (ed. Y. Aharoni; trans. J. Ben-Or; ed. and revised by A. F. Rainey; Jerusalem: Isreal Exploration Society, 1981) 126-127; R. Amiran, "Arad 1980," *Hadashot Arkhiologiot* 34 (1980) 74-75, (Hebrew).

[40]G. L. Kelm and A. Mazar, "Three Seasons of Excavations at Tel Batash--Biblical Timnah," *BASOR* 248 (1982) 29; G. L. Kelm and A. Mazar, *Timnah: A Biblical City in the Sorek Valley* (Winona Lake: Eisenbrauns, 1995) 133.

[41]2 impressions are reported in F. J. Bliss, "First Report of the Excavations at Tell eṣ-Ṣâfi." *PEFQS* 31 (1899) 193. In a later summary discussion of the royal stamps Bliss reports a total of 6 royal impressions from Tell eṣ-Ṣâfi (Bliss, "Second Report at Tell ej-Judeideh," 211-212).

[42]1 impression was found by Edelstein and Kislev (G. Edelstein and M. Kislev, "Mavasseret Yerushalayim: The Ancient Settlement and Its Agricultural Terraces," *BA* 44 [1981] 54). 4 impressions were found by N. Zori (G. Barkay, personal communication).

[43]All of the impressions are of the two-winged variety and 2 mention

21. Tell Beit Mirsim: 4^{44}
22. Aroer: 3^{45}
23. Ekron (Tel Miqne): 3^{46}
24. Hir. Marah el-Jumma: 3 or 4^{47}
25. Jericho: 2^{48}
26. Er Ras: 3^{49}
27. Ashdod: 1^{50}

---

the GN name Hebron. P. Hammond excavated the site on behalf of Princeton Theological Seminary between 1964 and 1966, but unfortunately none of the findings from those digs have been published. Therefore, while the site seems to have diminished in importance during the Iron II, we cannot be sure about the details of its occupation and defense system. Although Hammond did not report any *lmlk* impressions, the renewed excavations of Ofer did uncover 5, causing one to question if some were uncovered but not reported by Hammond's much more extensive excavations (A. Ofer, "Tell Rumeideh—1984," *ESI* 3 [1984] 95; A. Ofer, "Tell Rumeideh (Hebron)—1985," *ESI* 5 [1986] 93; A. Ofer, "Tell Rumeideh (Hebron)—1986," *ESI* 6 [1987-8] 93). Even though it cannot be known with certainty until Hammond's finds are published, it seems that the city was fortified during the Iron II period because there are indications in Area I3 (Southern City Wall) that the outer wall and tower from the Middle and Late Bronze Ages were reused throughout the Iron Age (A. Ofer, "Hebron," *NEAEHL* [New York: Macmillan; Jerusalem: Israel Exploration Society, 1993] 607-608).

[44]2 impressions are reported in Albright, *Tell Beit Mirsim I*, 78, pl. 40:3,4. 2 impressions are reported in Albright, *Tell Beit Mirsim III*, 74, pl. 29:8,10.

[45]Biran and Cohen, "Aroer," 22.

[46]T. Dothan and S. Gitin, "Tel Miqne, 1986," *IEJ* 37 (1987) 65; Gitin, personal communication.

[47]Barkay (personal communication) reports that Ofer found 3 or 4 impressions at site 105-16-12/41/3.

[48]1 impression was reported by E. Sellin and C. Watzinger, *Jericho: die Ergebnisse der Ausgrabungen* (WVDOG 22; Leipzig: Hinrichs, 1913) 158, pl. 42h. The other impression reported by J. R. Bartlett ("Iron Age and Hellenistic Stamped Jar Handles from Tell Es-Sultan," *Excavations at Jericho IV* [eds. K. M. Kenyon and T. M. Holland; London: British School of Archaeology in Jerusalem, 1982] 537-545).

[49]2 impressions were reported by Edelstein and Eisenberg (G. Edelstein and E. Eisenberg, "Emeq Refraim," *ESI* 3 [1984] 52). The third impression was reported by Barkay (personal communication). The impression was found by Barkay during a 1977 survey and is now stored at the I.A.A. (no. 77-1).

[50]This major Philistine city was probably destroyed by Sargon II during the late 8th century (Stratum VIII). The succeeding Stratum VII revealed 1 *lmlk* impression, an after-firing, incised inscription in Hebrew on a late 8th century pot (החפזה "the potter"), and several Hebrew weights (M. Dothan, "Ashdod," *NEAEHL* [ed. E. Stern; New York: Macmillan; Jerusalem: Israel Exploration

28. Beer-Sheba: 2^{51}
29. Anatot: 2^{52}
30. Khirbet Qeila: 2^{53}
31. Bethel: 1^{54}
32. Bethlehem: 1^{55}
33. Beth-Ḥoron (lower): 1^{56}
34. En Gedi: 1^{57}
35. Estaol: 1^{58}
36. Kefar-Ata: 1^{59}

Society, 1993] 100). These finds indicate connections between Judah and this coastal plain city after its destruction by Sargon and before the campaign of Sennacherib in 701 BCE.

[51]Naʾaman, "Sennacherib's Campaign," 75 n. 37.

[52]G. Barkay, personal communication.

[53]2 impressions are reported in E. Mader (Evaristus Mader, *Mambre; die Ergebnisse der Ausgrabungen Im Heiligen Bezirk Ramet El-Ḥalil in Sudpalästina, 1926-1938*, 2 vols, [Freiburg: E. Wewel, 1957] 206 n. 30). Dagan reports that Kh. Qeila is a large tel with a built-up area of about 55 dunams. Illicit excavations at the site have left remains of segments of walls, agricultural installations, and burial caves. There is also evidence of a residential community from the Iron II west of and outside the boundaries of the tel itself (Dagan, "Shephelah," 161). The site is about 11 km east of Tel Judeideh, and it controlled one of the access routes from this area of the Shephelah to Hebron. Since no systematic excavations have been conducted here, it is difficult to know if the site was fortified during the Iron II period. For the purposes of this study that note that at least part of the settlement was outside the tel boundaries, and that there are signs of agricultural activity.

[54]H. Eshel, "*lmlk* Stamp from Beth-El," *IEJ* 39 (1989) 60-62.

[55]R. P. B. Bagatti, "Bethléem," *RB* 62 (1965) 271. Note: Welten (*Die Königs Stempel*, 187) and others following his corpus incorrectly cite p. 72 of Bagatti's note.

[56]Naʾaman, "Sennacherib's Campaign," 75 n. 37.

[57]B. Mazar and Dunayevsky, "En-Gedi: Fourth and Fifth Seasons," 137.

[58]A. Kuschke, "Kleine Beiträge Zur Siedlungsgeschichte der Stamme Asser und Juda," *HTR* 64 (1971) 300.

[59]This find is a fragment of a jar handle with an MIIb impression, discovered on the surface at Tel Sharti (= Khirbet Sharta). Today Tel Sharti lies within the city limits of Kefar Ata. The site lies in the territory of northern Israel near modern Acre. Some Iron Age II pottery was discovered during the excavations, but the site does not seem to have been fortified during the late 8th century (A. Ovadiah, "Kefar Ata," *Hadashot Archaeologiot* 14 [1965] 8-9 (Hebrew); cf. G. Barkay, "Judah in Israel: The Northern Distribution of the LMLK Seal Impressions," unpublished essay).

37. Khirbet el-ʿAbhar: 1[60]
38. Horvat Dorban: 1[61]
39. Horvat Maon (Khirbet Maʿin): 1[62]
40. Khirbet Qumran: 1[63]
41. Khirbet Rabûd: 1[64]
42. Khirbet es-Samrah: 2[65]
43. Horvat Shilhah: 1[66]
44. Tel Halif: 2[67]
45. Tel ʿIra: 1[68]
46. Tel Jezreel: 2[69]
47. Tell ash-Shuqf: 1[70]
48. Qh. el-Qom: 1[71]
49. ʿEin Yaʿel: 1[72]

---

[60]A. Mazar, "Iron Age Fortresses in the Judean Hills," *PEQ* 114 (1982) 107.

[61]Welten, *Die Königs-Stempel*, 187.

[62]Z. Ilan and D. Amit, "Maon (in Judea)," *NEAEHL* (ed. E. Stern; New York: Macmillan; Jerusalem: Israel Exploration Society, 1993) 942.

[63]Naʾaman, "Sennacherib's Campaign," 75, n. 37.

[64]Naʾaman, "Sennacherib's Campaign," 75, n. 37.

[65]1 impression from the gateway is reported in Cross, "El Buqeiʿa," 268; cf. Stager ("Ancient Agriculture," 140) for a detailed description of the archaeological context. A second inscription from a layer of occupational debris in a storage magazine was published by Stager ("Ancient Agriculture," 147, 149), but this impression did not appear in Garfinkel's corpus. The importance of these handles is discussed in Chapter 2 here.

[66]Z. Ilan, A. Mazar, and D. Amit, "Kh. Shilha," *ESI* 2 (1983) 94-95; A. Mazar, Amit, and Ilan, "Horvat Shilhah," 247.

[67]1 impression was found on April 5, 1924 by H. A. Kent, a member of Albright's survey team (Albright, "Researches," 6). The other impression was found during the renewed excavations (Borowski, personal communication).

[68]Aharoni, "Negeb of Judah," 36, pl. 16:D.

[69]1 impression was published by Yogev (O. Yogev, "Tel-Yizreʾel," *ESI* 7-8 [1988-9)] 192-193). Barkay ("Northern Distribution," no. 3) reports that about 1960 an additional impression was found by a group of children in an area just west of the tel. It is now kept in the I.A.A. stores (no. 91-6173).

[70]Naʾaman, "Sennacherib's Campaign," 75 n. 37.

[71]W. G. Dever, "Khirbet el-Qôm," *NEAEHL* (ed. E. Stern; New York: Macmillan; Jerusalem: Israel Exploration Society, 1993) 1233.

[72]G. Edelstein, "A Roman Villa at ʿEin Yaʿel" *Qad* 26 (1993) 116.

50. Nes Harim (west of Jer.): 1[73]
51. Hir. Jaresh: 1[74]
52. Adullam: 1[75]
53. Hir. Zawiyeh [(307)16-11/52/1]: 1[76]
54. Givat Haphurit South [(104)15-12/40/1]: 1[77]
55. Beit Ṣafâfâ: 1[78]
56. unnamed farming site (Dagan survey site no.62): 2[79]
57. unnamed farming site (Dagan survey site no.66): 1[80]
58. Khirbet Jannaba et Tahta (el Gharbiya): 1[81]
59. unnamed site with isolated building remains: 1[82]
60. unnamed agricultural settlement: 1[83]
61. Tel ʿEton: 1[84]

---

[73]G. Barkay, personal communication.

[74]The impressions was found by D. Amit in 1989 (G. Barkay, personal communication).

[75]The impression was found in D. Amit's survey (G. Barkay, personal communication).

[76]The impression was found in D. Amit's survey (G. Barkay, personal communication).

[77]The impression was found during Ofer's survey, by S. Ben-Shalom from Kefar Etzion (G. Barkay, personal communication).

[78]The two-winged impression was found in the as yet unpublished excavations of N. Feig. The site is in a modern Arab village which is a suburb south of Jerusalem. It was a an unfortified suburb of ancient Jerusalem (N. Feig, personal communication).

[79]2 two-winged impressions (MII? and ?II?) were found at this farming site located at grid point 15-12/13/12 (site no. 15105 12350)—approximately 8 km east Tel Azekah in the northeastern part of the Shephelah (Dagan, "Shephelah," 112).

[80]The impression was found at this farming site located at grid point 13-12/42/3 (site no. 13415 12260)—approximately 2 km southwest of Tell eṣ-Ṣâfi (Gath) on the northeastern edge of the Shephelah (Dagan, "Shephelah," 114).

[81]The two-winged impression was found at this site located in the north-central Shephelah about 3 km south of Tel Azekah and 4 km west of Tel Sokoh (Dagan, "Shephelah," 131-132).

[82]The impression was found at this site located just a few km north of Tel ʿEton. It was not fortified (Dagan, "Shephelah," 189).

[83]The impression was found at this farming settlement located at grid no. 14-10/43/7 (14442 10393)—a few km north of Tel ʿEton. (Dagan, "Shephelah," 196).

[84]The impression is now stored at the I.A.A. (no. 67-401; G. Barkay, personal communication).

62. Gedor: 1[85]
64. Betar: 1[86]

Unprovenanced *lmlk* seal impressions

a. Collection of Robert Deutsch: 53 (1 pithos).
b. Collection of Steve Adler, Jerusalem: 12
c. Collection of the Flagellation Museum, Jerusalem: 9
d. Private collection of William Stern and Steve Adler: 17
e. Private collection from Barakat: 3
f. Collection in the Brooklyn Museum: 7
g. Private collection of Arnold Spaer: 8
h. Collection of the Hecht Museum: 13
i. Collection of the Univ. of Southern California: 1
j. Collection of L. Alexander Wolfe: 98 (1 pithos)
k. Additional collection of L. Alexander Wolfe: about 50
l. Collection of D. Friedenberg: about 6
m. Collection of Shlomo Moussaieff: about 50[87]
n. Collection of Michael Welch: 16
o. Collection in Israel: 4 (1 pithos)
p. Collection of The Bible Lands Museum Jerusalem: 5
q. Collection of The Eretz Israel Museum: 2
r. Collection of James H. Charlesworth: 1

---

[85]Y. Dagan found this impression while conducting a survey (G. Barkay, personal communication).

[86]D. Ussishkin, "Archaeological Soundings at Betar, Bar Kochba's Last Stronghold," *Tel Aviv* 20 (1993) 91.

[87]Bruce Zuckerman, personal communication.

APPENDIX II
A New Corpus Of the Oficial Seal Impressions

The previous corpus of official seal impressions, by Garfinkel,[1] listed 105 "readable" official seal impressions even though this number also included partially readable impressions. In my collaboration with G. Barkay, this number has been increased to 236. If we include the remaining "unreadable" impressions and the pictographic impresssions, we can account for another 32 impressions, bringing the total as of February 1, 1996 to 267. Obviously, Since there are so many new impressions that are not in Garfinkel's list, these additional finds add important data to the phenomenon of the official seal impressions, and some sort of reference to them should be included. However, it is beyond the scope of this monograph to present a full description and photograph of each unpublished impression. In this Appendix, the various impressions are simply listed according to reading and a bibliographic reference is given, but the readings are not justified if the impression is unpublished. Barkay and I hope to publish a more complete corpus with photographs and detailed analysis in the near future.

The impressions are presented in alphabetical order. Each official is listed with a number in Roman numerals, and different seals belonging to the same official are identified with an alphabetic numeration added to the Roman numerals. For example, the official עזריהו (בן) צפן owned at least 4 seals, numbered as XXXa, XXXb, XXXc, XXXd. The reference listed is normally the *editio princeps* or the main excavation report, and additional references are cited only when necessary to provide essential data. The reader should also refer to the N. Avigad and B. Sass's important corpus of seals (*WSS*) which was published after the present monograph was already completed.

---

[1]Garfinkel, "Hierarchic Pattern."

Ia. תנחם / לאחא
Unknown provenance:
    1. Unpublished, in collection of S. Adler and W. Stern, Jerusalem
    2. Unpublished, in collection of Sh. Moussaieff, London

Ib. אחזיה/ו. תנחם
Beth Shemesh:
    3. Barkay and Vaughn, "New Readings," 44-46, no. 17, figs.
        20-21; I.A.A. no. P.422
Lachish:
    4. Barkay and Vaughn, "New Readings," 44-46, no. 16, fig. 19;
        Reg. No. 2057, Tel Aviv University
Tell en-Naṣbeh:
    5. McCown, *Tell En-Naṣbeh I*, 162, pl. 57:10. Badé Institute, no.
        2462
Unknown Provenance:
    6. BLMJ no. 911
    7. Unpublished, in collection of D. Friedenberg, New York
    8. Unpublished, in collection of Sh. Moussaieff, London

II. עזרם / לאחמלך
Unknown provenance:
    9. Deutsch and Heltzer, *Forty New Inscriptions*, 25; collection of
        Sh. Moussaieff, London

III. שלם / לבכי
Unknown provenance:
    10. Unpublished, in private collection in Israel

IV. יהוכל / לבנאי
Beth Shemesh:
    11. Grant and Wright, *Ain Shems V*, 80. I.A.A. I.8683
Ramat Raḥel:
    12. Aharoni, *Ramat Raḥel, Seasons 1961 and 1962*, 33, fig. 37:6, pl.
        40:4; I.A.A. 64-1771
Tell Beit Mirsim:
    13. Albright, "Seal of Eliakim," 77-106; F. No. 623; I.A.A. I.4936
    14. Albright, "Seal of Eliakim," 77-106; F. No. 860; Bible Lands
        Museum, Pittsburgh

V. לבכי / שלם

Beth Shemesh:

    15. Grant and Wright, *Ain Shems V*, 82. I.A.A. I.95

Ḥ. Shovav:

    16. Rahmani, "Notes," 82, pl. XX:1

VI. לבנאי / יהוכל

Mareshah:

    17. Bliss and Macalister, *Excavations in Palestine*, 119-121, pl.
        56:27; not located

Tell eṣ-Ṣâfi:[2]

    18. Bliss and Macalister, *Excavations in Palestine*, 119-121, pl.
        56:27; I.A.A. P.1501

    19. Bliss and Macalister, *Excavations in Palestine*, 119-121, pl.
        56:27; I.A.A. P.1502, Hebrew University, Jerusalem

VII. לגעי / אחא

Unknown provenance:

    20. Unpublished, in the collection of R. Führer, Jerusalem

VIII. הושעם / חגי

Jerusalem:

    21. Nadelman, "Hebrew Inscriptions," 130; Field No. 3558/20;
        Hecht Museum, Haifa

IXa. הושע / צפן

Gezer:

    22. Macalister, *Gezer II*, 211, fig. 360; published as [...] / תושב, not
        located

Kh. ʿAbbad:

    23. Unpublished, from Y. Aharoni's survey, 1966; Tel Aviv
        University

---

[2] 3 impressions with this name were found by Bliss and Macalister. At least one comes from Mareshah and at least one comes from Tell eṣ-Ṣâfi. Although it is possible that the third impression comes from Mareshah, it is listed as originating from Tell eṣ-Ṣâfi because no impressions from Mareshah were found during my examination of the Rockefeller collection.

Lachish:

24. Tufnell, *Lachish III*, 341; K.14/J.14 A.G.271.6; University of Leeds
25. Tufnell, *Lachish III*, 341; Pal. S.W.; BM 1980.1214.4152
26. Tufnell, *Lachish III*, 341, pl. 47A:3; L.15/46/6366; Cambridge University, no. 61.D.155.B(18)
27. Barkay and Vaughn, "*Lmlk* and Official Seal Impressions," 67, no. 5; K.14/J.14, no. 1548; I.A.A. 33.2114

Tell ej-Judeideh:

28. Bliss and Macalister, *Excavations in Palestine*, 119-122, pl. 56:20; I.A.A. P.537
29. Bliss and Macalister, *Excavations in Palestine*, 119-122, pl. 56:30; not located
30. Bliss and Macalister, *Excavations in Palestine*, 119-122, pl. 56:30; not located

Unknown Provenance:

31. Unpublished, in BLMJ, no. AC151
32. Unpublished, in collection of D. Friedenberg, New York
33. Unpublished, in Eretz Israel Museum, Tel Aviv, no. MHP 153463

IXb. הושע / צפן

Unknown Provenance:

34. Unpublished, in collection of L. A. Wolfe, Jerusalem

X. לחסדא / ירמיהו

Beth Shemesh:

35. Grant and Wright, *Ain Shems V*, 80. Ain Shems Exc. 1930 No. 1273, II T 32; I.A.A. I.8653

XI. חרי / חגי

Unknown Provenance:

36. Unpublished, in the collection of Sh. Moussaieff, London

XIIa. חשי / אלשמע
Jerusalem:
>37. Unpublished, from Y. Shiloh's excavations; Field no.
>D/12526; storage number R/5719

Unknown Provenance:
>38. Unpublished, in collection of Sh. Moussaieff, London

XIIb. לחשי / אלשמע
Ramat Raḥel:
>39. Aharoni, *Ramat Raḥel, Seasons 1959 and 1960*, 18-19; fig. 14:4,
>pl. 6:1 (published as אלשמע / [...]לל) I.A.A. 62-67

XIII. ידעיה / אלעזר
Unknown Provenance:
>40. Deutsch and Heltzer, *New Epigraphic Evidence*, 47-48, figs.
>53a, 53b; colliction of Sh. Moussaieff, London
>41. Deutsch and Heltzer, *New Epigraphic Evidence*, 49, fig. 53c;
>collection of Sh. Moussaieff, London

XIVa. יהוחל / שחר
Lachish:
>42. Ussishkin, "Lachish (1973-1977)," 81. F. No. 10612, Tel Aviv
>University

Ramat Raḥel
>43. Aharoni, *Ramat Raḥel, Seasons 1959 and 1960*, 44, fig. 31:2, pl.
>27:2; I.A.A. 62-61

XIVb. ליהוחיל / שחר
Jerusalem:
>44. Tushingham, *Excavations in Jerusalem*, pl. 69:13; Manchester
>Museum, Reg. no. 5649

Ramat Raḥel:
>45. Aharoni, *Ramat Raḥel, Seasons 1959 and 1960*, 44, fig. 31:3, pl.
>27:1; I.A.A. 62-63
>46. Aharoni, *Ramat Raḥel, Seasons 1961 and 1962*, 32-33, fig. 37:1,
>pl. 40:1; I.A.A. 62-417

Tell ʿAbbad:
    47. Unpublished, in the collection of Kefar Etzion
Unknown Provenance:
    48. Unpublished, in a private collection in Israel

XIVc. שחר / יהוחיל
Lachish:
    49. Ussishkin, "Royal Judean Storage Jars," 3; Barkay and
        Vaughn, "Impression Reconsidered," 94-97; I.A.A. 75-244
Unknown Provenance:
    50. Barkay 1992:117; S. Adler and W. Stern collection, Jerusalem

XV. זכא / לכסלא
Beth Shemesh:
    51. Grant and Wright, *Ain Shems V*, 84; Barkay and Vaughn,
        "New Readings," 33-34, no. 5, fig. 4; University of
        Pennsylvania, no. 61-14-1174
    52. Grant and Wright, *Ain Shems V*, 84, pls. 10a:10, 10b:10;
        Barkay and Vaughn, "New Readings," 33-34, no. 4, fig. 3
        University of Pennsylvania, no. 61-14-1176

XVI. יפיהו / כרמי
Lachish:
    53. Tufnell, *Lachish III*, 341, pl. 47B:7; BM 1980.12-14.4154
    54. Tufnell, *Lachish III*, 341, pl. 47B:7; D/X; Cambridge no.
        61.D.155.B(18)
Jerusalem:
    55. Unpublished,; reg. no. 267 from Kenyon's Jerusalem
        excavations, Area A; Manchester Museum

XVIIa. ויהבנה / מנחם
Beth Shemesh:
    56. Grant and Wright, *Ain Shems V*, 81-82; I.A.A. I.8652
Ramat Raḥel:
    57. Aharoni, "Ramat Raḥel, 1954," 145; I.A.A. 62-420
Unknown Provenance:
    58. Unpublished, in the collection of L. A. Wolfe
    59. Unpublished, in the collection L. A. Wolfe

XVIIb. למנחם / יובנה

Adullam:

>60: Found by the Rev. J. Voois (A. Mazar, personal
>communication)

Gibeon:

>61. Pritchard, *Stamps From Gibeon*, 28, fig. 10:7, pl. 11:7;
>University of Pennsylvania, no. 60-13-13

Kh. ʿAbbad:

>62. Unpublished, I.A.A. 92-101

Lachish:

>63. Tufnell, *Lachish III*, 341, pl. 47B:6; H.17; originally published
>as לפן בן / יחני Cambridge no. 61.D.155.B(18)

>64. Tufnell, *Lachish III*, 341; originally published as לתנחם / מגן;
>H.17/7070; Cambridge no. 61.D.155.B(19)

>65. Tufnell, *Lachish III*, 341; originally published as לתנחם / מגן;
>H.17/7070; BM no. 1980.12-14.4155

>66. Tufnell, *Lachish III*, 341; D/X; originally published as
>uncertain; not located[3]

Ramat Raḥel:

>67. Aharoni, *Ramat Raḥel, Seasons 1959 and 1960*, 17-18, fig. 14:3,
>pl. 6:4; I.A.A. 62-62

Unknown Provenance:

>68. BLMJ, *Guide to the Collection*, 31. BLMJ 863, seal 1824

XVIIc. מנחם / יבנה

Jerusalem:

>69. Avigad 1983, *Discovering Jerusalem*, 44; F. no. 3908/2; Wohl
>Museum, Jerusalem

Tell ej-Judeideh:

>70. Bliss and Macalister, *Excavations in Palestine*, 120. I.A.A.
>P.541

---

[3]This impression (registration no. D/X) was published in the final report
as "uncertain" (Tufnell, *Lachish III*, 341). Diringer (Diringer, "Ancient Hebrew
Inscriptions I," 52-53) reports a possible reading of כנבם in the upper register.
These letters are readily identifiable with impressions of למנחם / יובנה and parallels
were unknown to Diringer and Tufnell. The handle itself was not located, so this
reading must be tentative.

Unknown Provenance:

71. Unpublished, in BLMJ, no. 864
72. Unpublished, in the collection of L. A. Wolfe, Jerusalem
73. Deutsch and Heltzer, *Forty New Inscriptions*, :28, private collection in Israel
74. Barkay, "Stamped Handles," 118; collection of S. Adler and W. Stern, Jerusalem; published incorrectly as למנחם / יובנה
75. Barkay, "Stamped Handles," 118; collection of S. Adler and W. Stern, Jerusalem; published incorrectly as למנחם / יובנה

XVIII. משלם / אחמלך
Lachish:

76. Tufnell, *Lachish III*, 341, pl. 47A:4; Q.17; Cambridge 61.D.155.B(18)
77. Tufnell, *Lachish III*, 341; K.14/J.14; Pal. AG. 271.6; University of Leeds
78. Tufnell, *Lachish III*, 341; D/X/6115; Dublin, WM no. 354
79. Tufnell, *Lachish III*, 341, pl. 47A:5; F. No. 7167; I.A.A. 39.825
80. Tufnell, *Lachish III*, 341, pl. 47A:6; J.16; BM no. 1980.12-14.4153
81. Tufnell, *Lachish III*, 341; L.14; BM no. 1956.4-16.8
82. Tufnell, *Lachish III*, 341; L.15; not located
83. Hestrin and Dayagi-Mendels, *Inscribed Seals*, 29, no. 14; K14/J.14, F. No. 1547 (1933); I.A.A. 33-2113[4]
84. Ussishkin, "Royal Judean Storage Jars," 1-5, figs. 3-4
85. Ussishkin, "Royal Judean Storage Jars," 1-4, fig. 3
86. Ussishkin, "Royal Judean Storage Jars," 5-6
87. Ackerman and Braunstein, *Israel in Antiquity*, 71; K.15; Jewish Museum, New York, no. 12-73.278

Unknown Provenance:

88. Unpublished, in collection of L. A. Wolfe
89. Unpublished, in Studium Biblicum Franciscanum Museum, Jerusalem, no. SF 7096

---

[4]This handle was listed in Hestrin and Dayagi-Mendels's book on seals as being published in *Lachish III* (340-341). This attribution was in error, so the publication by Hestrin and Dayagi-Mendels is the *editio princeps*.

XIX. ‏למשל/ם אלנתן‎

Gibeon:

90. Pritchard, *Stamps From Gibeon*, 28, fig. 10:5, pl. 11:5;
University of Pennsylvania, no. 60-13-131

91. Pritchard, *Stamps From Gibeon*, 28, fig. 10:6, pl. 11:6;
University of Pennsylvania, no. 60-13-132

Lachish:

92. Tufnell, *Lachish III*, 341; published as ‏נחם‎?; D/X, Weingreen
Museum, no. WM355. correct reading ‏למשל/ם אלנתן‎

Unknown Provenance:

93. Barkay, "Stamped Handles," 116; collection of S. Adler and
W. Stern, Jerusalem

94. Unpublished, in collection of Sh. Moussaieff, London

XXa. ‏לנחם / הצליהו‎

Gibeon:

95. Pritchard, *Stamps From Gibeon*, 27, fig. 10:2, pl. 11:2

Jerusalem:

96. Nadelman, "Hebrew Inscriptions," 88, photo 141

Lachish:

97. Tufnell, *Lachish III*, 341, pl. 47B:3; Eretz Israel Museum, no.
MHA 55, D/X; F. No. 6113

Unknown Provenance:

98. Unpublished, in collection of collection, L. A. Wolfe,
Jerusalem

99. Unpublished, in collection of H. Kaufman, Tel Aviv

100. Unpublished, in collection of H. Kaufman, Tel Aviv

XXb. ‏לנחם / הצליהו‎

Unknown Provenance:

101. Barkay, "Stamped Handles," 117; collection of S. Adler and ·
W. Stern, Jerusalem

102. Barkay, "Stamped Handles," 118; collection of S. Adler and
W. Stern, Jerusalem

XXIa. לנחם / עבדי
Lachish:

103. Tufnell, *Lachish III*, 341, pl. 47A:10; H.17:1089, F. No. 7168; Weingreen Museum, Trinity College, Dublin, no. WM1210

104. Tufnell, *Lachish III*, 341, pl. 47A:11; D/X; Cambridge University, no. 61.D.155.B(18)

105. Tufnell, *Lachish III*, 341; K.14/J.14 Pal.AG.271.6; Cambridge University, no. 61.D.155.B(18)

106. Tufnell, *Lachish III*, 341; D/X; University of Leeds[5]

107. Tufnell, *Lachish III*, 341; BM no. 1980.12-14.4147, K.14/J.14 AG.271.6

108. Tufnell, *Lachish III*, 341; BM no. 1956.4-16.12, D/X

109. Tufnell, *Lachish III*, 341; BM no. 1980.12-14.4148, D 218 CO, 4771[6]

110. Barkay and Vaughn, "*Lmlk* and Official Seal Impressions," 69, no. 35; I.A.A. 33-2112, K.14/J.14 No. 1546

111. Barkay and Vaughn, "*Lmlk* and Official Seal Impressions," 69, no. 36; Metropolitan Museum, New York, no. 34.126.65

112. Barkay and Vaughn, "*Lmlk* and Official Seal Impressions," 69, no. 37; Jewish Museum, New York, no. 12-73.279, D/X

113. Barkay and Vaughn, "*Lmlk* and Official Seal Impressions," 69, no. 38; Jewish Museum, New York, no. 12-73.281, K/14/J.14 AG.271.6

114. Barkay and Vaughn, "*Lmlk* and Official Seal Impressions," 69, no. 39; Jewish Museum, New York, no. 12-73.283, K/14/J.14 AG.271.6

115. Barkay and Vaughn, "*Lmlk* and Official Seal Impressions," 69, no. 40; Jewish Museum, New York, no. 12-73.303, K/14/J.14 AG.271.6

Naḥal Arugot:

116. Hadas, "Naḥal ᶜArugot," 77

---

[5]This handle was listed as allocated to the University of Leeds in O. Tufnell's distribution list, but the handle was not located there.

[6]This findspot designation was written on the handle, but it appears to be in error. F. No. 4771 refers to an Iron Age jug from Tomb D 218. This handle is most probably to be identified with K.14/J.14 by the process of elimination. *Lachish III* (341) lists 7 impressions of לנחם / עבדי. 6 impressions were located in the various collections. Further, 3 impressions were listed as originating from K.14/J.14, but only 2 of them were located in the collections.

Tell ej-Judeideh:
> 117. Bliss and Macalister, *Excavations in Palestine*, 120. I.A.A.
> P.766

Unknown Provenance:
> 118. Unpublished, in BLMJ, no. 865
> 119. Overbeck and Meshorer, 11; collection of J. Sammel,
> Munich
> 120. Unpublished, in Eretz Israel Musuem, Tel Aviv, no. K-54501
> 121. Unpublished, in Eretz Israel Museum, Tel Aviv, no. K-350
> 122. Unpublished, I.A.A. 67-638
> 123. Barkay, "Stamped Handles," 116; collection of S. Adler and
> W. Stern, Jerusalem
> 124. Barkay, "Stamped Handles," 116; collection of S. Adler and
> W. Stern, Jerusalem
> 125. Barkay, "Stamped Handles," 116; collection of S. Adler and
> W. Stern, Jerusalem
> 126. Unpublished, in collection of R. Deutsch, Tel Aviv
> 127. Unpublished, in collection of R. Bakhar, Beth Shean

XXIb. לנחם / עבדי{י}
Unknown Provenance:
> 128. Barkay, "Stamped Handles," 116; collection of S. Adler and
> W. Stern, Jerusalem

XXIc. עבדי / ---
Unknown Provenance:
> 129. collection of L. Alexander Wolfe

XXIIa. לנרא / שבנא
Beth Shemesh (renewed excavations):
> 130. Unpublished, Tel Aviv University

Jerusalem:
> 131. Avigad, *Discovering Jerusalem*, 44-45; Wohl Museum,
> Jerusalem, F. No. 1388

Lachish:
> 132. Ussishkin, "Excavations 1985-1994," 57, no. 20, fig. 41; Tel
> Aviv University, F. No. 61358/1

Unknown Provenance:

133. Unpublished, in BLMJ, no. 866

134. Overbeck and Meshorer, 10; collection of J. Sammel, Munich

135. Deutsch and Heltzer, *Forty New Inscriptions*, 27; private collection in Israel

XXIIb. שבנא / לנרא
Ramat Raḥel:

136. Aharoni, *Ramat Raḥel, Seasons 1959 and 1960*, 16, fig. 14:2, pl. 6:2; I.A.A. 62-39

XXIIc. לנרא
En Gedi:

137. B. Mazar, Dothan, and Dunayevsky. *En-Gedi*, 34-35, pl. 26:1; Barkay, "King of Babylonia," 41-47; No. 208/4

XXIId. [...] / לנרא / שבנא
Unknown Provenance:

138. Overbeck and Mershorer, 12; collection of J. Sammel, Munich

XXIIe. לנרי ב/ן שבניו
Jerusalem:

139. Avigad, *Discovering Jerusalem*, 44-45; Wohl Museum, Jerusalem, F. No. 12311

XXIIIa. צפניהו / ן ב / לסמך
Jerusalem:

140. Unpublished, Shiloh's Jerusalem exacavations, I.A.A. 86-402
Lachish:

141. Tufnell, *Lachish III*, 341, pl. 47B:8; BM, no. 1980.12-14.4149, D/X

142. Tufnell, *Lachish III*, 341, pl. 47B:9; Cambridge University, no. 61.D.155.B(18), D/X

143. Tufnell, *Lachish III*, 341; Weingreen Museum, Dublin, no. WM 1209, D/X.6120

Tell ej-Judeideh:

144. Bliss and Macalister, *Excavations in Palestine*, 120, pl. 6:25

Unknown Provenance:
>   145. Overbeck and Meshorer, 10; collection of J. Sammel,
>   Munich
>   146. Unpublished, in the collection of R. Bakhar, Beth Shean

XXIIIb. לסמך / צפניהו
Unknown Provenance:
>   147. Deutsch and Heltzer, *New Epigraphic Evidence*, 45-46

XXIV. לעבד/י
Lachish:
>   148. Tufnell, *Lachish III*, 241, pl. 47A:8; Cambridge University,
>   no. 61.D.155.B(18), D/X

XXV. לעזר / חגי
Gezer:
>   149. Macalister, *Gezer I*, 211
Tel Azekah:
>   150. Bliss and Macalister, *Excavations in Palestine*, 121; not
>   located
Unknown Provenance:
>   151. Unpublished, in the collection of L. A. Wolfe, Jerusalem

XXVI. לעזר / שבנא
Unknown Provenance:
>   152. Overbeck and Meshorer, 10; collection of J. Sammel,
>   Munich
>   153. Unpublished, in the collection of L. Alexander Wolfe

XXVII. ערב / נבי
Unknown Provenance:
>   154. Avigad, "Titles and Symbols," 304-305, pl. 1:נז; collection of
>   A. Spaer, Jerusalem

XXVIII. לצדק / סמך
Beth Shemesh:
   155. Grant and Wright, *Ain Shems V*, 83; University of
      Pennsylvania, no. 61-14-1175

XXIX. לצפן. א/במעץ
Jerusalem:
   156. Avigad, *Discovering Jerusalem*, 44-45; Wohl Museum, F. No.
      6497
Tel Azekah:
   157. Bliss and Macalister, *Excavations in Palestine*, 121; PEF,
      London, collection no. 598183, F. No. 230
Tel Batash:
   158. Kelm and Mazar 1982:29
Tell eṣ-Ṣâfi:
   159. M. Israel, "Hebrew Stamp," 4; in museum at Kephar
      Menachem
   160. Unpublished, in museum at Kefar Menachem

XXXa. צפן ע/זריהו
Lachish:
   161. Tufnell, *Lachish III*, 341, pl. 47A:1; I.A.A. 39.824, H.17, F. No.
      7166
   162. Tufnell, *Lachish III*, 341, pl. 47A:2; Eretz Israel Museum, no.
      MH57, D/X, F. No. 6116
   163. Tufnell, *Lachish III*:341; Cambridge University, no.
      61.D.155.B(18), M.14, 268.01
   164. Hestrin and Dayagi-Mendels, *Inscribed Seals*, 38, no. 23;
      I.A.A. 36.2259; Room 1003, F. No. 5354[7]
   165. Barkay and Vaughn, *"Lmlk and Official Seal Impressions,"*
      70, no. 50; BM, no. 1980.12-14.8246, D/X, F. No. 6166
Unknown Provenance:
   166. Unpublished, in the collection of L. Alexander Wolfe
   167. Unpublished, in the collection of R. Deutsch

---

[7]Hestrin and Dayagi-Mendels list this impression as being published
in Diringer ("Ancient Hebrew Inscriptions I, 38-39). The handle was actually not
included in Diringer's list nor in *Lachish III*, so the publication by Hestrin and
Dayagi-Mendels is the *editio princeps*.

XXXb. ‏צפן. / עזר.‏
Beth Shemesh:
168. Grant and Wright, *Ain Shems V*, 80-1; I.A.A. I.5868

XXXc. ‏לצפן / עזר‏
Lachish:
169. Tufnell, *Lachish III*, 110; I.A.A. 38.715
170. Tufnell, *Lachish III*, 110; handle not located
171. Ussishkin, "Excavations 1985-1994," 58, no. 25; Barkay and Vaughn, "New Readings," 42-44, no. 14, fig. 17; Tel Aviv University, Reg. No. 638/1

XXXd. ‏לצפן / עזריהו‏
Ramat Raḥel:
172. Aharoni, *Ramat Raḥel, Seasons 1959 and 1960*, 44, published as unreadable; I.A.A. 64-1769
Gibeon:
173. Pritchard, *Stamps From Gibeon*, 28, fig. 10:4, pl. 11:4; originally published as ‏צפן ע/זריהו‏; University of Pennsylvania, F. No. 410 / S.146[8]
Unknown Provenance:
174. Unpublished, in collection of L. Alexander Wolfe

XXXI. ‏לשבניהו / בן המלך‏
Unknown Provenance:
175. Avigad, "Titles and Symbols," 304-305, pl. ‏נז‏:2. Hecht Museum, Haifa

XXXII. ‏לשבנ/א. שחר‏
Lachish:
176. Tufnell, *Lachish III*, 341, pl. 47B:1; BM, no. 1980.12-14.8245, K.14/J.14, Pal.A.G.271.6
177. Ackerman and Braunstein, *Israel in Antiquity*, 71; Jewish Museum, no. 12-73.286
178. Barkay and Vaughn, "*Lmlk* and Official Seal Impressions," 71, no. 56; I.A.A. 33.2115; K.14/J.14 No. 1549

---

[8]This handle is incorrectly listed in the publication as being stored in Amman, Jordan.

Ramat Raḥel:
>   179. Aharoni, *Ramat Raḥel, Seasons 1961 and 1962*, 60-61., fig. 37:3; pl. 40:3; I.A.A. no. 64-2286
>   180. Aharoni, *Ramat Raḥel, Seasons 1961 and 1962*, 61, fig. 37:2, pl. 40:2; I.A.A. no. 64-1768
>   181. Aharoni, *Ramat Raḥel, Seasons 1959 and 1960*, 19, fig. 14:5, pl. 6:3; I.A.A. no. 62-64

Tell En-Naṣbeh:
>   182. McCown, *Tell En-Naṣbeh I*, 160-162. I.A.A. 34.99
>   183. McCown, *Tell En-Naṣbeh I*, 160-162. I.A.A. 35.3085
>   184. McCown, *Tell En-Naṣbeh I*, 160-162. in Berkley, CA

XXXIIIa. שבניהו / עזריהו
Tell ej-Judeideh:
>   185. Bliss and Macalister, *Excavations in Palestine*, 119-120. I.A.A. P.892
>   186. Bliss and Macalister, *Excavations in Palestine*, 119-120. I.A.A. P.3638
>   187. Bliss and Macalister, *Excavations in Palestine*, 119-120. I.A.A. P.1500

XXXIIIb. שבניה / עזריה
Tell ej-Judeideh:
>   188. Bliss and Macalister, *Excavations in Palestine*, 120. I.A.A. P.1473

Lachish:
>   189. Tufnell, *Lachish III*, 341, pl. 47B:5; University of Leeds, D/X

Unknown Provenance:
>   190. Unpublished, in the collection of H. Kaufman, Tel Aviv

XXXIVa. לשוכ/י שבנ/א
Lachish:
>   191. Tufnell, *Lachish III*, 341, pl. 47B:2; Cambridge University, no. 61.D.155.B(18), D/X, J.15.6019
>   192. Tufnell, *Lachish III*, 341; Diringer 1941:90, fig. 1; I.A.A. 38.717, J.16.1028

Unknown Provenance:
>   193. Unpublished, in the collection of D. Friedenberg, New York

XXXIVb. לשכי / שבנא
Unknown Provenance:
   194. Unpublished, in the collection of H. Kaufman, Tel Aviv

XXXVa. אחא / לשלם
Arad:
   195. Unpublished, handle not located but reading identified by
        the collection card; I.A.A. 64-2563
Beth Shemesh (renewed excavations):
   196. Unpublished, Tel Aviv University
Jerusalem:
   197. Unpublished, Shiloh's Jerusalem excavations, Field no.
        11088.Locus 908, Area G, Season 1981
Kh. Rabûd:
   198. Kochavi "Khirbet Rabûd," 18, pl. 4:3; Field no. 188/1
   199. Kochavi "Khirbet Rabûd," 18, pl. 4:4; Field no. 188/2
Lachish:
   200. Ussishkin, "Excavations 1985-1994," 59, no. 26; Tel Aviv
        University, Field no. 210
Ramat Raḥel:
   201. Unpublished, I.A.A. 64-1772, Field no. 8123/1
Tell ej-Judeideh:
   202. Ben-Dor, "Two Stamped Jar-handles," 66-67; I.A.A. P.883
   203. Ben-Dor, "Two Stamped Jar-handles," 66-67; I.A.A. P.3639
Unknown Provenance:
   204. Unpublished, in BLMJ, no. 867
   205. Unpublished, in the collection of L. A. Wolfe, Jerusalem
   206. Unpublished, in Hecht Museum, Haifa
   207. Barkay, "Stamped Handles," 117; collection of S. Adler and
        W. Stern, Jerusalem
   208. Barkay, "Stamped Handles," 117; collection of S. Adler and
        W. Stern, Jerusalem
   209. Unpublished, in the collection of H. Kaufman, Tel Aviv
   210. Sternberg 1991:89, pl. XXXI:664g; present location unknown

XXXVb. אחאם / לשלם
Kh. Qeila:
   211. Hizmi and Shabbtai. "Khirbet Qeila," 170, fig. 188

Lachish:
    212. Tufnell, *Lachish III*, 341; pls. 47A:9; 78:1, 78:5; BM, F. No. 5400
    213. Tufnell, *Lachish III*, 341; K.17, not located
    214. Tufnell, *Lachish III*, 341, published as uncertain reading; University of Leeds, D/X
    215. Tufnell, *Lachish III*, 341; BM no. 1980.12-14.4156, G.17
Unknown Provenance:
    216. Unpublished, in the collection of L. A. Wolfe, Jerusalem

XXXVIa. לתנחם / מגן
Tell Erani:
    217. Unpublished, I.A.A. 61-506 (B. Brandl, personal communication)
Gibeon:
    218. Pritchard, *Stamps From Gibeon*, 28, fig. 10:8, pl. 11:8; The Archaeological Museum, Amman[9]
Lachish:
    219. Tufnell, *Lachish III*, 341; Cambridge University, no. 61.D.155.B(18), D/X.6118
    220. Tufnell, *Lachish III*, 341; BM, no. 1980.12-14.4151, D/X.6118
    221. Tufnell, *Lachish III*, 341, pl. 47A:7; Eretz Israel Museum, Tel Aviv, no. MH 56A, D/X.6118
    222. Tufnell, *Lachish III*, 341; BM, no. 1980.12-14.4150, K.15.6118[10]
    223. Tufnell, *Lachish III*, 341; University of Leeds, R16 Surface
    224. Ussishkin, "Excavations 1985-1994," 58, no. 23; Tel Aviv University, Field No. 330
    225. Ussishkin, "Lachish (1973-1977)," 81
Ramat Raḥel:
    226. Aharoni, *Ramat Raḥel, Seasons 1961 and 1962*, 32, fig. 37:5, pl. 40:5; I.A.A. 62-1770

---

[9]The publication incorrectly lists this handles as being stored in at the University of Pennsylvania.

[10]The Lachish final report (*Lachish III*:341) states that there are 4 handles with F. No. 6118. 3 of these handles are reported from surface finds (D/X), and the fourth is reported from square H.17. I located 4 handles with F. No. 6118. 3 of them contained the D/X designation, but the fourth contained the following designation on the reverse of the handle: "K.15; Pit E. of fill; x 4; 6118." It seems that the most logical explanation for the discrepancy is that the final report mistakenly lists H.17 instead of K.15; however, it is possible that there was a fifth handle with F. No. 6118 coming from square H.17 that was not located.

Tel Tekoa:
    227. Unpublished, from survey of D. Amit, 1989
Unknown Provenance:
    228. Overbeck and Meshorer, 11; collection of J. Sammel,
        Munich
    229. Barkay, "Stamped Handles," 117; collection of S. Adler and
        W. Stern, Jerusalem
    230. Barkay, "Stamped Handles," 118; collection of S. Adler and
        W. Stern, Jerusalem

XXXVII. לתנח/ם. נגב
Beth Shemesh:
    231. Grant and Wright, *Ain Shems V*, 83; University of
        Pennsylvania, no. 61-14-1173
    232. Barkay and Vaughn, "New Readings," 46-48, no. 24, fig. 19;
        I.A.A. P.423
Gibeon:
    233. Pritchard, *Stamps From Gibeon*, 28, fig. 10:3, pl. 11:3;
        University of Pennsylvania, no. 60-13-130
Jerusalem:
    234. Unpublished, Shiloh's Jerusalem excavations, Field. no.
        4733
Ramat Raḥel
    235. Aharoni, *Ramat Raḥel, Seasons 1961 and 1962*, 44, fig. 31:1, pl.
        27:3; I.A.A. 62-66
Unknown Provenance:
    236. Overbeck and Meshorer, 11

Partial Name:

XXXVIII. יהוקם / [...]
Unknown Provenance:
    237. Unpublished, in a private collection in Israel

Indecipherable Names:

ᶜEin Yaᶜel:
  238. Edelstein, "ᶜEin Yaᶜel," 116; listed as "personal impression," not located.[11]
Jerusalem:
  239. Unpublished, Broshi's Western City Wall excavations, Jerusalem; Field no. CW 1067
  240. Unpublished, Kenyon's Jerusalem excavations; Manchester Museum, Reg. no. 369
Kh. el-Burj:
  241. Unpublished
Lachish:
  242. Tufnell, *Lachish III*, 341; published as שבניה / ...לש, not located
  243. Tufnell, *Lachish III*, 341, pl. 47B:10; published as "Yrshlm"; Cambridge University, no. 61.D.155.B(18), K.14, Pal. B, 272.2
  244. Ussishkin, "Excavations 1985-1994," 58, no. 21; Tel Aviv University, Reg. No. 39502
  245. Ussishkin, "Excavations 1985-1994," 59, no. 27; Tel Aviv University, Reg. No. 127/1; square impression that possibly reads לאחא / תנחם
  246. Ussishkin, "Excavations 1985-1994," 58, no. 22; Tel Aviv University, Reg. No. 285
Naḥal Zimra:
  247. G. Barkay, personal communication
Ramat Raḥel:
  248. Aharoni, *Ramat Raḥel, Seasons 1961 and 1962*, 61, pl. 40:6; published as possibly לנחם / הצליהו; Tel Aviv University
Tel Batash:
  249. Z. Ilan, *Land of Butter*, 188
Tel Mareshah:
  250. Bliss and Macalister, *Excavations in Palestine*, 119; no reading given, not located
  251. Bliss and Macalister, *Excavations in Palestine*, 119; no reading given; not located

---

[11]It is uncertain if this impression is an official seal impression or not. Edelstein (1993:116) lists it in conjunction with a *lmlk* impression and defines this impression as a "personal impression" (טביעה של חותם אישית).

252. Bliss and Macalister, *Excavations in Palestine*, 119; no reading given; not located
253. Bliss and Macalister, *Excavations in Palestine*, 119; no reading given, not located
254. Bliss and Macalister, *Excavations in Palestine*, 119; no reading given, not located

Tell ej-Judeideh:

255. Bliss and Macalister, *Excavations in Palestine*, 1902:120, pl. 56:26; published as מכא / [...]; not located
256. Gibson, "Tell Ej-Judeideh, 203; listed as חנס...; not located
257. Gibson, "Tell Ej-Judeideh, 203; listed as בניהר / שריהן; not located
258. Gibson, "Tell Ej-Judeideh, 208; listed as ..ברע.. / ..לנש Reg. no. 1056, not located

Unknown Provenance:

259. Unpublished, in the collection of R. Deutsch, Tel Aviv
260. Unpublished, in a private collection in Israel
261. Unpublished, in the collection of L. A. Wolfe, Jerusalem

Pictographic Seal Impressions[12]

XXXIX. "Prancing Horse"
Jerusalem:
    262. Avigad, *Discovering Jerusalem*, 44
En Gedi (Tel Goren):
    263. B. Mazar and Dunayevsky, "En-Gedi: Fourth and Fifth
        Seasons," 123
Azekah:
    264. Bliss and Macalister, *Excavations in Palestine*, 122, pl. 56:33
Tell en-Naṣbeh:
    265. *Tell En-Naṣbeh* I:154, fig. 35:6
Tell ej-Judeideh:
    266. Barkay, "Stamped Handles," 126-127
Unknown Provenance:
    267. Barkay, "Stamped Handles," 127; Hecht Museum no. 86-79

XL. "Lion Hunting a Deer"
Ramat Raḥel:
    268. Aharoni, *Ramat Raḥel, Seasons 1961 and 1962*, pl. 40:7

---

[12]These are official seal impressions that do not contain PNN; however, Barkay ("Prancing Horse," 124-129) has presented evidence for viewing these pictographic seal impressions as related to the phenomenon of the official seal impressions that do contain PNN.

BIBLIOGRAPHY

Ackerman, Andrew S., and Susan L. Braunstein. *Israel in Antiquity: From David to Herod.* New York: The Jewish Museum, 1982.

Ackroyd, Peter R. "History and Theology in the Writings of the Chronicler." *CTM* 38 (1967):501-15.

Aharoni, Miriam. "Inscribed Weights and Royal Seals." In *Arad Inscriptions,* Ed. Yohanan Aharoni, Trans. Judith Ben-Or, Ed. and revised Anson F. Rainey, 126-27. Jerusalem: Isreal Exploration Society, 1981.

Aharoni, Miriam, and Yohanan Aharoni. "The Stratification of Judahite Sites in the 8th and 7th Centuries B.C.E." *BASOR* 224 (1976):73-90.

Aharoni, Yohanan, ed. *Beer-Sheba I: Excavations at Tel Beer-Sheba, 1969-1971 Seasons.* Publications of the Institute of Archaeology. Tel Aviv: Institute of Archaeology, Tel Aviv University, 1973.

———. *Arad Inscriptions.* Trans. J. Ben-Or. Ed. and revised A. F. Rainey. Jerusalem: Israel Exploration Society, 1981.

———. *The Archaeology of the Land of Israel: From the Prehistoric Beginnings to the End of the First Temple Period.* Philadelphia: Westminster Press, 1982.

———. "Beersheba—The Fortifications." In *Beersheba I: Excavations at Tel Beersheba 1969-1971 Excavations,* Ed. Y. Aharoni, 9-12. Tel Aviv: Institute of Archaeology, Tel Aviv University, 1973.

———. "Beersheba—The Stratification of the Site." In *Beersheba I: Excavations at Tel Beer-sheba 1969-1971 Seasons,* Ed. Y. Aharoni, 4-8. Tel Aviv: Institute of Archaeology, Tel Aviv University, 1973.

———. "Excavations at Ramat Raḥel, 1954: Preliminary Report—II." *IEJ* 6 (1956):137-57.

———. *Excavations At Ramat Raḥel, Seasons 1961 and 1962.* Rome: Centro Di Studi Semitico, 1964.

———. *Excavations at Ramat Raḥel, Seasons 1959 and 1960.* Rome: Centro Di Studi Semitico, 1962.

———. "The Horned Altar of Beer-Sheba," *BA* 37 (1974):2-6.

———. *Investigations at Lachish: The Sanctuary and The Residency (Lachish V).* Tel Aviv: Gateway Publishers, Inc., 1975.

———. *The Land of the Bible, A Historical Geography.* Trans. and ed. Rainey. Philadelphia: Westminster, 1967.

———. "The Negeb of Judah." *IEJ* 8 (1958):26-38.

———. "Ramat Raḥel." In *NEAEHL,* Ed. Ephraim Stern, 1261-67. New York: Macmillan; Jerusalem: Israel Exploration Society, 1993.

Aharoni, Yohanan, and Ruth Amiran. "A New Scheme for the Sub-Division of the Iron Age in Palestine." *IEJ* 8 (1958):171-84.

Aḥituv, Shmuel. *Handbook of Ancient Hebrew Inscriptions. From the Period of the First Commonwealth and the Beginning of the Second Commonwealth (Hebrew, Philistine, Edomite, Moabite, Ammonite, and the Bileam Inscription)*. Biblical Encyclopedia Library. Jerusalem: Bialik Institute, 1992 (Hebrew).

Albright, William F. "The Chronology of the Divided Monarchy of Israel." *BASOR* 100 (1945):16-22.

————. *The Excavation of Tell Beit Mirsim in Palestine, Vol. I: The Pottery of the First Three Campaigns*. AASOR, vol. 12. New Haven: Yale University Press, 1932.

————. *The Excavation of Tell Beit Mirsim, Vol. III: The Iron Age*. AASOR. New Haven: American Schools of Oriental Research, 1943.

————. "A New Campaign of Excavations at Gibeah of Saul." *BASOR* 52 (1933):6-12.

————. "Recent Progress in Palestinian Archaeology: Samaria-Sebaste III and Hazor I." *BASOR* 150 (1958):21-25.

————. "Researches of the School in Western Judaea." *BASOR* 15 (1924):2-11.

————. "The Seal of Eliakim and the Latest Pre-exilic History of Judah, with Some Observations on Ezekial." *JBL* 51 (1932):77-106.

————. "Some Recent Publications." *BASOR* 132 (1953):46-47.

Alt, Albrecht. "The Formation of the Israelite State in Palestine." In *Essays of Old Testament History and Religion*, Trans. R. A. Wilson, 223-309. New York: Doubleday, 1967.

————. "Das Taltor von Jerusalem." *PJb* 24 (1928):74-98.

Amiran, Ruth. *Ancient Pottery of Eretz Israel: From Its Beginnings in the Neolithic Period to the End of the First Temple*. Jerusalem: Bialik Foundation and The Israel Exploration Society, 1971 (Hebrew).

————. "Arad 1980." *Hadashot Arkhiologiot* 34 (1980):74-75 (Hebrew).

————. "The Water Supply of Israelite Jerusalem." In *Jerusalem Revealed: Archaeology in the Holy City 1968-1974*, Ed. Y. Yadin, 75-78. Jerusalem: Israel Exploration Society, 1976.

Avi-Yonah. Michael. "The Walls of Nehemiah—A Minimalist View." *IEJ* 4 (1954):239-48.

Avigad, Nahman. *Corpus of West Semitic Stamp Seals*, revised and completed by B. Sass. Jerusalem: The Israel Academy of Sciences and Humanities, Israel Exploration Society, and the Institute of Archaeology, The Hebrew University of Jerusalem, 1997.

————. *Discovering Jerusalem*. Nashville: T. Nelson, 1983.

————. "The Epitaph of a Royal Steward from Siloam Village." *IEJ* 3 (1953):137-52.

———. "Excavations in the Jewish Quarter of the Old City, Jerusalem, 1970 (Preliminary Report II)." *IEJ* 20 (1970):129-40.

———. "Excavations in the Jewish Quarter of the Old City of Jerusalem, 1971." *IEJ* 22 (1972):193-200.

———. *Hebrew Bullae From the Time of Jeremiah: Remnants of a Burnt Archive.* Trans. R. Grafman. Jerusalem: Israel Exploration Society, 1986.

———. "Jerusalem, the Jewish Quarter of the Old City, 1975." *IEJ* 25 (1975):260-61.

———. "New Light on the Na῾ar Seals." In *Magnalia Dei, The Mighty Acts of Gods: Essays on the Bible and Archaeology in Memory of G. Ernest Wright,* Eds. F. M. Cross, W. M. Lemke, and P. D. Miller, 294-300. Garden City, NY: Doubleday, 1976.

———. "New Names on Hebrew Seals." *EI* 12 (1975):66-71 (Hebrew).

———. "A Note on an Impression from a Woman's Seal." *IEJ* 37 (1987):18-19, pls. 1:A-B.

———. "Seals and Sealings." *IEJ* 14 (1964):190-94.

———. "Titles and Symbols on Hebrew Seals." *EI* 15 (1981):303-05, pl. נ (Hebrew).

Bagatti, R. P. B. "Bethléem." *RB* 62 (1965):270-72.

Bahat, Dan, and Magen Broshi. "Excavations in the Armenian Gardens." *Qad* 5 (1972):102-03.

Barkay, Gabriel. "A Bulla of Ishmael, the King's Son." *BASOR* 290-291 (1993):109-114.

———. "A Group of Stamped Handles From Judah." *EI* 23 (1992):113-28.

———. "Judah in Israel: The Northern Distribution of the LMLK Seal Impressions." forthcoming.

———. "The King of Babylonia or a Judean Official?" *IEJ* 45 (1995):41-47.

———. "Northern and Western Jerusalem in the End of the Iron Age." Ph.D. Dissertation, Tel Aviv University. 1985.

———. " 'The Prancing Horse'—An Official Seal Impression from Judah of the 8th Century B.C.E." *Tel Aviv* 19 (1992):124-29.

———. "Response to 'Revealing Biblical Jerusalem'" In *Biblical Archaeology Today: Proceedings of the International Congress on Biblical Archaeology. Jerusalem, April 1984,* Ed. Janet Amitai, 476-77. Jerusalem: Israel Exploration Society, 1985.

Barkay, Gabriel, and Andrew G. Vaughn. "An Official Seal Impressions from Lachish Reconsidered." *Tel Aviv* 22 (1995):94-97.

———. "LMLK and Official Seal Impressions From Tel Lachish." *Tel Aviv* 23 (1996) 61-74.

———. "New Readings of Hezekian Official Seal Impressions." *BASOR* 304 (1996) 29-54.

Bartlett, J. R. "Iron Age and Hellenistic Stamped Jar Handles from Tell Es-Sultan." In *Excavations at Jericho*, Eds. Kathleen M. Kenyon and T. M. Holland, 537-45. London: British School of Archaeology in Jerusalem, 1982.

Beit-Arieh, Itzhaq. "An Early Bronze Age III Settlement at Tel ʿIra in the Northern Negev." *IEJ* (1991):1-18.

———. "Ḥorvat ʿUza." In *NEAEHL*, 1495-97. New York: Macmillian; Jerusalem: Israel Exploration Society, 1993

———. "Ḥorvat Qitmit." In *NEAEHL*, Ed. Ephraim Stern, 1230-33. New York: Macmillan; Jerusalem: Israel Exploration Society, 1993.

———. "A Small Frontier Citadel at Ḥorvat Radum in the Judean Negeb." *Qad* 24 (1991):86-89 (Hebrew).

———. "Tel ʿIra." In *NEAEHL,* Ed. Ephraim Stern, 642-46. New York: Macmillian; Jerusalem: Israel Exploration Society, 1993

———. "Tel ʿIra—A Fortified City of the Kingdom of Judah." *Qad* 18 (1985):17-25 (Hebrew).

Beit-Arieh, Itzhaq, and Cohen Rudolph. "Aroer in the Negev." *EI* 15 (1981):250-73 (Hebrew).

Beit-Arieh, Itzhaq, and Bruce Cresson. "Horvat ʿUza, A Fortified Outpost on the Eastern Negev Border." *BA* 54 (1991):126-35.

Biran, Abraham. "Aroer (in Judea)." In *NEAEHL*, Ed. Ephraim Stern, 89-92. New York: Macmillian; Jerusalem: Israel Exploration Society, 1993.

———. "Tel ʿIra." *Qad* 18 (1985):25-27 (Hebrew).

Biran, Abraham, and Rudolf Cohen. "Aroer in the Negev." *EI* 15 (1981):250-73 (Hebrew).

Blake, F. R. "The Word *zdh* in the Siloam Inscription." *JAOS* 22 (1901):55-60.

Bliss, Frederick J. *Excavations at Jerusalem, 1894-1897*. London: Committee of the Palestine Exploration Fund, 1898.

———. "First Report of the Excavations at Tell Es-Sâfi." *PEFQS* 31 (1899):183-99.

———. "First Report on the Excavations at Tell Ej-Judeideh." *PEFQS* (1900):87-101.

———. "Fourth Report on the Excavations at Tell Zakarîya." *PEFQS* (1900):7-16.

———. "Report on the Excavations at Tell Es-Sandahannah." *PEFQS* (1900):319-41.

———. "Second Report on the Excavations at Tell Ej-Judeideh." *PEFQS* (1900):199-222.

———. "Second Report on the Excavations at Tell Zakarîya." *PEFQS* (1899):89-111.

———. "Third Report on the Excavations at Tell Zakarîya." *PEFQS* (1899):170-87.

Bliss, Frederick J., and Robert A. S. Macalister. *Excavations in Palestine During the Years 1898-1900*. London: Committee of the Palestine Exploration Fund, 1902.

Bordreuil, Pierre, and Felice Israel. "À Propos de la Carrière D'Elyaqim Du Page Au Majordome (?)." *Semitica* 41/42 (1991/2):81-87.

Bordreuil, Pierre, and André Lemaire. "Nouveaux Sceaux Hébreux, Araméens et Ammonites." *Semitica* 26 (1976):45-63, pls. IV-VI.

Borowski, Oded. "Hezekiah's Reform and the Revolt Against Assyria." *BA* 58 (1995):148-55.

Bright, John. *A History of Israel*. 3d ed. Westminster aids to the study of the Scriptures. Philadelphia: Westminster Press, 1981.

Brin, Gershon. "The Title (המלך בן) and Its Parallels." *AION* 29 (1969):433-65.

Broshi, Magen. "The Expansion of Jerusalem in the Reigns of Hezekiah and Manasseh." *IEJ* 24 (1974):21-26.

———. "Recent Excavations Along the Walls of Jerusalem." *Qad* 9 (1976):75-78 (Hebrew).

Broshi, Magen, and Israel Finkelstein. "The Population of Palestine in Iron Age II." *BASOR* 287 (1992):47-60.

Bunimovitz, Shlomo, and Zvi Lederman. "Beth Shemesh." In *NEAEHL*, Ed. Ephraim Stern, 249-53. New York: Macmillan; Jerusalem: Israel Exploration Society, 1993.

Bunimovitz, Shlomo, Zvi Lederman, and Raz Kletter. "Tel Bet Shemesh—1990." *ESI* 10 (1991):142-44.

Clark, Colin. *Population Growth and Land Use*. New York: Macmillan, 1967.

Clermont-Ganneau, C. "Inscribed Jar-Handles of Palestine." *PEFQS* (1900):251-53.

———. *Recueil D'archéologie Orientale I*. Paris, 1888.

Clifford, Richard J. *The Cosmic Mountain in Canaan and the Old Testament*. Cambridge, Mass.: Harvard University Press, 1972.

Cogan, Mordechai, and Hayim Tadmor. *II Kings: A New Translation*. Anchor Bible, vol. 11. Garden City, N.Y.: Doubleday, 1988.

Coogan, Michael D., J. Cheryl Exum, and Lawrence E. Stager, eds. *Scripture and Other Artifacts: Essays on the Bible and Archaeology in Honor of Philip J. King*. Louisville, KY: Westminster/John Knox Press, 1994.

Cross, Frank M., Jr. "Alphabets and Pots: Reflections on Typological Method in the Dating of Human Artifacts." *Maarav* 3 (1982):121-36.

———. "A Reconstruction of the Judean Restoration." *JBL* 94 (1975):4-18; also published in *Interpretation* 29 (1975):187-201.

———. "El Buqeiʿa." In *NEAEHL*, Ed. E. Stern, 267-69. New York: Macmillan; Jerusalem: Israel Exploration Society, 1993.

———. "Judean Stamps." *EI* 9 (1969):20-27.

————. "The Seal of *Miqnêyaw*, Servant of Yahweh." In *Ancient Seals and the Bible*, Eds. L. Gorelick and E. Williams-Forte, 55-63, pls. ix-xi. Occasional Papers on the Near East. Malibu, CA: Undena Publications, 1983.

Cross, Frank M., Jr., and David N. Freedman. *Early Hebrew Orthography, A Study of the Epigraphic Evidence.* AOS 36. New Haven: American Oriental Society, 1952.

————. "Josiah's Revolt Against Assyria." *JNES* 12 (1953):56-8.

Crowfoot, John W., and Gerald M. Fitzgerald. *Excavations in the Tyropoeon Valley, Jerusalem, 1927.* London: Palestine Exploration Fund, 1929.

Dagan, Yehudah. "The Shephelah During the Period of the Monarchy in Light of Archaeological Excavations and Surveys." M.A. Thesis, Tel Aviv University. 1992.

Dalman, G. *Jerusalem und Sein Gelände.* BFCT. Gütersloh: Bertelsmann, 1930.

Davis, David, and Amos Kloner. "A Burial Cave of the Late Israel Period on the Slopes of Mt. Zion." *Qad* 11 (1978) 16-19.

del Olmo Lete, G. "Notes on Ugaritic Semantics IV." *UF* 10 (1978):37-46.

Deutsch, Robert, and Michael Heltzer. *Forty New Ancient West Semitic Inscriptions.* Tel Aviv-Jaffa, Israel: Archaeological Center Publication, 1994.

————. *New Epigraphic Evidence from the Biblical Period.* Tel Aviv-Jaffa, Israel: Archaeological Center Publication, 1995.

Dever, William G., ed. *Gezer II: Report of the 1967-70 Seasons in Fields I and II.* Annual of the Nelson Glueck School of Biblical Archaeology, vol. 2. Jerusalem: Hebrew Union College, 1974.

————. "Khirbet El-Qôm." In *NEAEHL*, Ed. E. Stern, 1233-35. New York: Macmillan; Jerusalem: Israel Exploration Society, 1993.

Dever, William G., and Dan P. Cole. "Gezer: The 1968-70 Seasons, Field II." In *Gezer II: Report of the 1967-70 Seasons in Fields I and II*, Ed. W. G. Dever, 47-87. Jerusalem: Hebrew Union College, 1974.

Dever, William G., H. Darrell Lance, and G. Ernest Wright. *Gezer I: Preliminary Report of the 1964-66 Seasons.* Annual of the Hebrew Union College Biblical and Archaeological School, vol. 1. Jerusalem: Hebrew Union College, 1970.

De Vries, Simon J. *1 and 2 Chronicles.* The Forms of the Old Testament Literature, vol. XI. Grand Rapids, MI: William B. Eerdmans Publishing Company, 1989.

Diringer, David. "Early Hebrew Weights Found at Lachish." *PEQ* (1942):82-103, pls. XII-XIII.

————. *Le Iscrizioni Antico-ebraiche Palestinesi.* Firenze, F. Le Monnier, 1934.

————. "On Ancient Hebrew Inscriptions Discovered at Tell Ed-Duweir (Lachish)—I." *PEQ* (1941):38-56.

————. "On Ancient Hebrew Inscriptions Discovered at Tell Ed-Duweir (Lachish)—II." *PEQ* (1941):89-109.

————. "The Royal Jar-Handle Stamps of Ancient Judah." *BA* 12 (1949):70-86.

Donner, Herbert. "Der Feind Aus dem Norden: Topographische und Archäologische Erwägungen Zu Jes. 10:27b-34." *ZDPV* 84 (1968):46-54.

————. "Der 'Freund Des Königs'" *ZAW* 73 (1961):269-77.

————. *Israel und Den Völkern*. VT Supp., vol. 11. Leiden, 1964.

Donner, Herbert, and W. Röllig. *Kanaanäische und Aramäische Inschriften*. 3 Volumes. Wiesbaden: Harrassowitz, 1964.

Dothan, Moshe. "Ashdod." In *NEAEHL*, Ed. Ephraim Stern, 93-102. New York: Macmillan; Jerusalem: Israel Exploration Society, 1993.

Dothan, Trude, and Seymour Gitin. "Tel Miqne, 1986." *IEJ* 37 (1987):63-68.

Dumbrell, William J. "The Purpose of the Books of Chronicles." *JETS* 27 (1984):257-66.

Dumond, D. E. "Population Growth and Cultural Change." *SWJA* 21 (1965):302-24.

Duncan, J. Garrow. *Digging up Biblical History. Recent Archaeology in Palestine and Its Bearing on the Old Testament Historical Narratives. Vol II*. London: Macmillan, 1931.

Edelstein, Gershon. "A Roman Villa at ʿEin Yaʿel." *Qad* 26 (1993):114-19.

————. "The Terraced Farm at Er-Ras, Jerusalem." Unpublished Article.

Edelstein, Gershon, and E. Eisenberg. "Emeq Refraim." *ESI* 3 (1984):51-52.

Edelstein, Gershon, and Mordechai Kislev. "Mavasseret Yerushalayim: The Ancient Settlement and Its Agricultural Terraces." *BA* 44 (1981):53-56.

Eitam, D. "Tel Miqne (Ekron)—Survey of Oil Presses—1985." *ESI* 5 (1985):72-74.

Eshel, Hanan. "The Late Iron Age Cemetery of Gibeon." *IEJ* 37 (1987).

————. "A *lmlk* Stamp from Beth-El." *IEJ* 39 (1989):60-62.

Finkelstein, Israel. "The Archaeology of the Days of Manasseh." In *Scripture and Other Artifacts: Essays on the Bible and Archaeology in Honor of Philip J. King*, Eds. Michael D. Coogan, J. Cheryl Exum, and Lawrence E. Stager, 169-87. Louisville, KY: Westminster John Knox Press, 1994.

Finkelstein, Israel, and Y. Magen, eds. *Archaeological Survey in the Hill Country of Benjamin*. Publication of the Israel Antiquities Authority. Jerusalem: Israel Antiquities Authority, 1993 (Hebrew).

Freedman, David N. "The Chronicler's Purpose." *CBQ* 23 (1961) 436-442.

Friedman, Richard E. "The Tabernacle in the Temple." *BA* 43 (1980):241-48.

Fritz, Volkmar, and Aharon Kempinski. *Ergebnisse der Ausgrabungen auf der Hirbet El-Msas (Tel Masos) 1972-1975.* 3 vols. Abhandlungen des Deutschen Palastinavereins. Wiesbaden: Harrassowitz, 1983.

Funk, Robert W. "Beth-Zur." In *NEAEHL,* Ed. Ephraim Stern, 259-61. New York: Macmillan; Jerusalem: Israel Exploration Society, 1993.

————. "The History of Beth-Zur with Reference to Its Defences." In *The 1957 Excavation at Beth-Zur,* Eds. Ovid R. Seller, Robert W. Funk, John L. McKenzie, Paul Lapp, and Nancy Lapp, 4-17. AASOR, vol. 38. Cambridge, Mass.: American Schools of Oriental Research, 1968.

Garfinkel, Yosef. "2 Chr 11:5-10 Fortied Cities List and the *lmlk* Stamps—Reply to Nadav Naʾaman." *BASOR* 271 (1988):69-73.

————. "The Distribution of the 'Identical Seal Impressions' and the Settlement Pattern in Judah on the Eve of Sennacherib's Campaign." *Cathedra* 32 (1984):35-53 (Hebrew).

————. "A Hierarchic Pattern in the 'Private Seal Impressions' on the *lmlk* Jars." *EI* 18 (1985):108-15 (Hebrew).

Garr, W. Randall. *Dialect Geography of Syria-Palestine, 1000-586 B.C.E.* Philadelphia: University of Pennsylvania Press, 1985.

Gibson, John C. L. *Textbook of Syrian Semitic Inscriptions: Vol. 1, Hebrew and Moabite Inscriptions.* Oxford: Clarendeon, 1971.

Gibson, Shimon. "The Tell Ej-Judeideh (Tel Goded) Excavations: A Reappraisal Based on Archival Records in the Palestine Exploration Fund." *Tel Aviv* 21 (1994):194-234.

Gill, Dan. "How They Met: Geology Solves Mystery of Hezekiah's Tunnelers." *BAR* 20, no. 4 (1994):20-33, 64.

Gitin, Seymour. *Gezer III: A Ceramic Typology of the Late Iron II, Persian and Hellenistic Periods at Tell Gezer.* 2 vols. Annual of the Nelson Glueck School of Biblical Archaeology, vol. 3. Jerusalem: Hebrew Union College, 1990.

Govrin, Yehuda. *Archaeological Survey of Israel: Map of Naḥal Yattir (139).* Jerusalem: Israel Antiquities Authority, 1991.

Graham, M. Patrick. *The Utilization of 1 and 2 Chronicles in the Reconstruction of Israelite History in the Nineteenth Century.* SBLDS, vol. 116. Atlanta, GA: Scholars Press, 1990.

Grant, Elihu, and G. Ernest Wright. *Ain Shems Excavations (Palestine): Part V (Text).* Biblical and Kindred Studies, no. 8. Haverford, Pennsyvania: Haverford College, 1939.

Gray, George Buchanan. *Studies in Hebrew Proper Names.* London: Black, 1896.

Greenberg, Raphael. "New Light on the Early Iron Age at Tell Beit Mirsim." *BASOR* 265 (1987):55-80.

Guthe, H. "Die Siloahinschrift." *ZDMG* 36 (1882):725-50.

Hadas, G. "Naḥal ʿArugot, Seal Impression." *ESI* 2 (1983):77.

Halpern, Baruch. "Jerusalem and the Lineages in the Seventh Century BCE: Kingship and the Rise of Individual Moral Liability." In *Law and Ideology in Monarchic Israel*, Eds. Baruch Halpern and Deborah W. Hobson, 11-107. JSOTSup, vol. 124. Sheffield: JSOT Press, 1991.

———. "Sacred History and Ideology: Chronicles' Thematic Structure—Indications of an Earlier Source." In *The Creation of Sacred Literature: Composition and Redaction of the Biblical Text*, Ed. R. E. Friedman, 35-54. Berkeley: University of California Press, 1981.

Hendel, Ronald S. "The Date of the Siloam Inscription: A Rejoinder to Rogerson and Davies." *BA* 59 (1996):233-237.

Herr, Larry G. "Paleography and the Identification of Seal Owners." *BASOR* 239 (1980):67-70.

———. *The Scripts of Ancient Northwest Semitic Seals*. HSM, vol. 18. Missoula, MT: Scholars Press, 1978.

Herzog, Zeʾev. "The Beer-sheba Valley: From Nomadism to Monarchy." In *From Nomadism to Monarchy: Archaeological and Historical Aspects of Early Israel*, Eds. I. Finkelstein and N. Naʾaman, 122-49. Washington: Biblical Archaeology Society; Jerusalem: Israel Exploration Society, 1994.

———. "Settlement and Fortification Planning in the Iron Age." In *The Architecture of Ancient Israel from the Prehistoric to the Persian Periods*, Eds. A. Kempinski and R. Reich, 231-74. Jerusalem: Israel Exploration Society, 1992.

———. "The Storehouses." In *Beersheba I: Excavations at Tel Beersheba 1969-1971 Excavations*, 23-30. Tel Aviv: Institute of Archaeology, Tel Aviv University, 1973.

Herzog, Zeʾev, Miriam Aharoni, Anson F. Rainey, and Shmuel Moshkovitz. "The Israelite Fortress at Arad." *BASOR* 254 (1984):1-34.

Hestrin, Ruth. "Hebrew Seals of Officials." In *Ancient Hebrew Seals and the Bible*, Eds. L. Gorelick and E. Williams-Forte, 50-54. Malibu, CA: Undena Publications, 1983.

Hestrin, Ruth, and Michal Dayagi. *Seals from the First Temple Period*. Jerusalem: Israel Museum, 1978 (Hebrew).

Hizmi, Ḥananya, and Zion Shabbtai. "Khirbet Qeila, Seal Impression." *ESI* 10 (1991):170.

Hooker, Paul K. "The Kingdom of Hezekiah: Judah in the Geo-Political Context of the Late Eighth Century." Ph.D. Dissertation, Emory University, 1993. Ann Arbor, MI: University Microfilms International, 1993.

Hopkins, David C. *The Highlands of Canaan: Agricultural Life in the Early Iron Age*. Social World of Biblical Antiquity Series, 3. Sheffield, England and Decatur, GA: Almond, 1985.

Ilan, Zvi, and David Amit. "Maon (in Judea)." In *NEAEHL*, Ed. Ephraim Stern, 942. New York: Macmillan; Jerusalem: Israel Exploration Society, 1993.

Ilan, Zvi, Amihai Mazar, and David Amit. "Kh. Shilḥa." *ESI* 2 (1983):94-95.

Japhet, Sara. "The Historical Reliability of Chronicles: The History of the Problem and Its Place in Biblical Research." *JSOT* 33 (1985):83-107.

————. *The Ideology of the Book of Chronicles and Its Place in Biblical Thought*. Beiträge zur Erforschung des Alten Testaments und des Antiken Judentums. Frankfort: Verlag Peter Lang, 1989.

————. *I & II Chronicles: A Commentary*. Commentary. The Old Testament Library. Louisville, KY: Westminster/ John Knox Press, 1993.

Jones, C. N. "The Citadel, Jerusalem, (A Summary of Work Since 1934)." *QDAP* 14 (1950):121-90.

Josephus, Flavius. *The Works of Josephus*. Ed. W. Whiston. Peabody, Mass.: Hendrickson Publishers, 1987.

Kelm, George L., and Amihai Mazar. "Three Seasons of Excavations at Tel Batash—Biblical Timnah." *BASOR* 248 (1982):1-36.

————. *Timnah: A Biblical City in the Sorek Valley*. Winona Lake: Eisenbrauns, 1995.

Kempinski, Aharon. "Tel Masos." In *NEAEHL*, Ed. E. Stern, 986-89. New York: Macmillan; Jerusalem: Israel Exploration Society, 1993.

Kenyon, Kathleen M. "The Date of the Destruction of Iron Age Beer-sheba." *PEQ* 108 (1976):63-64.

Kenyon, Kathleen M., and Holland T. A. *Excavations at Jericho, Volume 3: The Architecture and Stratigraphy of the Tell*. London: British School of Archaeology at Jerusalem, 1981.

————. *Excavations at Jericho Volume 4: The Pottery Type Series and Other Finds*. London: British School of Archaeology at Jerusalem, 1982.

————. *Excavations at Jericho, Volume 5: The Pottery of Phases at the Tell and Other Finds*. London: British School of Archaeology at Jerusalem, 1983.

Kitchen, K. A. *Third Intermediate Period in Egypt (1100-650 B.C.)*. Warminster: Aris and Phillips, 1973.

Klein, Ralph W. "Abijah's Campaign Against the North (II Chr 13)—What Were the Chronicler's Sources?" *ZAW* 95 (1983):210-7.

Kloner, Amos. "Mareshah (Marisa): The Lower City." In *NEAEHL*, Ed. E. Stern, 951-57. New York: Macmillan; Jerusalem: Israel Exploration Society, 1993.

————. "Mareshah (Marisa)." In *NEAEHL*, Ed. E. Stern, 948-57. New York: Macmillian; Jerusalem: Israel Exploration Society, 1993

Knoppers, Gary N. " 'There was None Like Him': Incomparability in the Books of Kings." *CBQ* 54 (1992) 411-431.

————. "History and Historiography: The Royal Reforms." In *The Chronicler as Historian*, Eds. M. P. Graham and S. L. McKenzie. Sheffield: JSOT Press, 178-203.

Kochavi, Moshe. "Khirbet Rabûd = Debir." *Tel Aviv* 1 (1974):2-33.

Kurylowicz, Jerzy. *Studies in Semitic Grammar and Metrics*. Prace jezykoznawcze (Polska Akademia Nauk. Komitet Jezykoznawstwa) 67. Wroclaw: Zaklad Narodowy Imienia Ossolinskich, 1972.

Kuschke, A. "Kleine Beiträge Zur Siedlungsgeschichte der Stamme Asser und Juda." *HTR* 64 (1971):291-313.

Lance, H. Darrell. "The Royal Stamps and the Kingdom of Josiah." *HTR* 64 (1971):315-32.

Lang, Bernhard. "Review of *Die Königs-Stempel. Ein Beitrag Zur Militärpolitik Judas Unter Hiskia und Josia.*" By P. Welten. *RB* 79 (1972):441-44.

Lapp, Nancy L., ed. *The Third Campaign at Tell El-Ful: The Excavations of 1964*. AASOR, vol. 45. Cambridge, MA: American Schools of Oriental Research, 1981.

————. "Other Finds from the 1964 Campaign." In *The Third Campaign at Tel El-Ful: The Excavations of 1964*, 109-15. AASOR, vol. 45. Cambridge, MA: American Schools of Oriental Research, 1981.

————. "Tell El-Fûl." In *NEAEHL*, Ed. Ephraim Stern, 445-48. New York: Macmillan; Jerusalem: Israel Exploration Society, 1993.

Lapp, Paul W. "The Excavation of Field II." In *The 1957 Excavation at Beth-Zur*, Eds. Ovid R. Sellers, Robert W. Funk, John L. McKenzie, Paul W. Lapp, and Nancy L. Lapp, 26-34. AASOR, vol. 38. Cambridge, MA: American Schools of Oriental Research, 1968.

————. "Late Royal Seals From Judah." *BASOR* 158 (1960):11-22.

Lapp, Paul W., and Nancy L. Lapp. "Iron II - Hellenistic Pottery Groups." In *The 1957 Excavation at Beth-Zur*, Eds. Ovid R. Sellers, Robert W. Funk, John L. McKenzie, Paul W. Lapp, and Nancy L. Lapp, 54-79. AASOR, vol. 38. Cambridge, MA: American Schools of Oriental Research, 1968.

Lemke, Werner E. "The Synoptic Problem in the Chronicler's History." *HTR* 58 (1965):349-363.

Lemaire, André. "Classifcation Des Estampilles Royales Judéennes." *EI* 15 (1981):54-59* + pl. VIII.

————. "Note Sur le Titre *BN HMLK* Dans L'Ancien Israël." *Semitica* 29 (1979):59-65.

————. "Remarques sur la Datation Des Estampilles 'LMLK'" *VT* 25 (1975):678-82.

————. "Royal Signature—Name of Israel's Last King Surfaces in a Private Collection." *BAR* 21, no. 6 (1995):48-52.

Lenski, Gerhard E. *Power and Priviledge: A Theory of Social Stratification.* New York: McGraw-Hill Book Company, 1966.

Longacre, W. A., James M. Skibo, and Miriam T. Stark. "Ethnoarchaeology at the Top of the World: New Ceramic Studies Among the Kalinga of Luzon." *Expedition* 33 (1993):4-15.

Lux, Ute. "Vorläufiger Bericht Über die Ausgrabung Unter der Erlöserkirche Im Muriston in der Altstadt von Jerusalem in Den Jahren 1970 und 1971." *ZDPV* 88 (1972):185-201.

Macalister, Robert A. S. *The Excavation of Gezer 1902-1905 and 1907-1909. Volume II.* London: 1912.

Macdonald, John. "The Role and Status of the Ṣuḥāḫū in the Mari Correspondence." *JAOS* 96 (1976):57-68.

————. "The Status and Role of the Naᶜar in Israelite Society." *JNES* 35 (1976):147-70.

————. "The Supreme Warrior Caste in the Ancient Near East." In *Oriental Studies: Presented to Benedikt J. Isserlin by Friends and Colleagues on the Occasion of His Sixtieth Birthday 25 February 1976,* Eds. R. Y. Ebied and M. J. L. Yound, 39-71. Leeds University Oriental Society Near Eastern Researches, vol. 2. Leiden: Brill, 1980.

Mader, Evaristus. *Mambre; die Ergebnisse der Ausgrabungen Im Heiligen Bezirk Ramet El-Halil in Sudpalastina, 1926-1938.* 2 vols. Freiburg: E. Wewel, 1957.

Manor, Dale W., and Gary A. Herion. "Arad." In *The Anchor Bible Dictionary of the Bible,* Ed. D. N. Freedman, 331-336. New York: Doubleday, 1992.

Martin, M. F. "Six Palestinian Seals." *Rivista Degli Studi Orientali* 39 (1964):203-10.

Mazar, Amihai. *Archaeology of the Land of the Bible-- 10,000 - 586 B.C.E.* ABRL. New York: Doubleday, 1990.

————. "Iron Age Fortresses in the Judean Hills." *PEQ* 114 (1982):87-109.

————. "The Northern Shephelah in the Iron Age: Some Issues in Biblical History and Archaeology." In *Scripture and Other Artifacts: Essays on the Bible and Archaeology in Honor of Philip J. King,* Eds. M. D. Coogan, J. C. Exum, and L. E. Stager, 247-67. Louisville: Westminster/ John Knox Press, 1994.

Mazar, Amihai, David Amit, and Zvi Ilan. "The 'Border Road' Between Michmash and Jericho and the Excavations at Horvat Shilḥah." *EI* 17 (1984):236-50 (Hebrew).

Mazar, Amihai, and Ehud Netzer. "On the Israelite Fortress at Arad." *BASOR* 263 (1986):87-90.

Mazar, Benjamin. "The Campaign of Sennacherib in Judaea." In *The Military History of the Land of Israel in the Biblical Times*, Ed. J. Liver, 286-95. Tel Aviv, 1964 (Hebrew).

Mazar, Benjamin, Trude Dothan, and I. Dunayevsky. *En-Gedi: The First and Second Seasons of Excavations, 1961-1962*. ʿAtiqot (English Series), vol. 5. Jerusalem: Israel Exploration Society, 1966.

Mazar, Benjamin, and I. Dunayevsky. "En-Gedi: Fourth and Fifth Seasons of Excavations—Preliminary Report." *IEJ* 17 (1967):133-43.

Mazar, Eilat. "Edomite Pottery at the End of the Iron Age." *IEJ* 35 (1985):253-69.

Mazar, Eilat, and Benjamin Mazar. *Excavations in the South of the Temple Mount: The Ophel of Biblical Jerusalem*. Qedem, vol. 29. Jerusalem: Keterpress Enterprises, 1989.

McCown, Chester Charlton. *Tell En-Naṣbeh I: Archaeological and Historical Results*. Berkeley, California: The Palestine Institute of Pacific School of Religion and The American Schools of Oriental Research, 1947.

McKenzie, Steven L. *The Chronicler's Use of the Deuteronomistic History*. HSM 33. Atlanta: Scholars Press, 1985.

Meshel, Ze'ev. "Kuntilat ʿAjrûd—An Israelite Site on the Sinai Border." *Qadmoniot* 9 (1976):119-24.

Miller, Patrick D., Jr. "El, The Creator of Earth." *BASOR* 239 (1980):43-46.

Mommsen, H., I. Perlman, and J. Yellin. "The Provenience of the *lmlk* Jars." *IEJ* 34 (1984):89-113.

Moore, Michael S. "The Judean *lmlk* Stamps: Some Unresolved Issues." *Restoration Quarterly* 28 (1985/86):17-26.

Moriarty, Frederick L. "The Chronicler's Account of Hezekiah's Reform." *CBQ* 27 (1965):399-406.

Naʾaman, Nadav. "The Brook of Egypt and Assyrian Policy on the Border of Egypt." *Tel Aviv* 6 (1979):68-90.

———. "Hezekiah's Fortified Cities and the *LMLK* Stamps." *BASOR* 261 (1986):5-21.

———. "The Inheritance of the Sons of Simeon." *ZDPV* 96 (1980):136-52.

———. "Sennacherib's Campaign to Judah and the Date of the *lmlk* Stamps." *VT* 29 (1979):61-86.

———. "Sennacherib's 'Letter to God' on His Campaign to Judah." *BASOR* 214 (1974):25-39.

Nadelman, Yonatan. "Hebrew Inscriptions, Seal Impressions, and Markings of the Iron Age II." In *Excavations in the South of the Temple Mount: The Ophel of Biblical Jerusalem*, Eds. E. Mazar and B. Mazar, 128-37. Qedem, vol. 29. Jerusalem: The Institute of Archaeology, The Hebrew University of Jerusalem, 1989.

Naveh, Joseph. "A Hebrew Letter from the Seventh Century B.C." *IEJ* 10 (1960):129-39, pl. 17.

————. "Review of *The Scripts of Ancient Northwest Semitic Seals* by Larry G. Herr. *BASOR* 239 (1980):75-76.

NFA Classical Auctions, Inc. *Egyptian, Near Eastern Greek & Roman Antiquities: New York, December 11, 1991*. Auction Catalog. New York: NFA Classical Auctions, 1991.

North, Robert. "Does Archaeology Prove Chronicles Sources?" In *A Light Unto My Path: Old Testament Studies in Honor of Jacob M. Myers*, Eds. Howard M. Bream, Ralph D. Heim, and Carey A. Moore, 375-401. Gettysburg Theological Studies. Philadelphia: Temple University Press, 1974.

Noth, Martin. "Das Reich von Hamath als Grenznachbar des Reiches Israel." *PJb* 33 (1937):36-51.

————. *Die Israelitischen Personennamen Im Rahmen der Gemeinsemitischen Namengebung*. BWANT, vol. 46. Stuttgart: W. Kohlhammer, 1928.

————. *The Chronicler's History*. Sheffield: JSOT Press, 1987.

————. *The History of Israel*. New York: Harper and Row, 1958.

Nylander, C. "A Note on the Stonecutting and Masonry of Tel Arad." *IEJ* 17 (1967):56-59.

Ofer, Avi. "'All the Country of Judah': From a Settlment Fringe to a Prosperous Monarchy." In *From Nomadism to Monarchy: Archaeological and Historical Aspects of Early Israel*, Eds. I. Finkelstein and N. Naʾaman, 92-121. Washington and Jerusalem: Biblical Archaeology Society; Israel Exploration Society, 1994.

————. "Hebron." In *NEAEHL*, Ed. E. Stern, 606-09. New York: Macmillian; Jerusalem: Israel Exploration Society, 1993

————. "Tell Rumeideh—1984." *ESI* 3 (1984):94-95.

————. "Tell Rumeideh (Hebron)—1985." *ESI* 5 (1986):92-93.

————. "Tell Rumeideh (Hebron)—1986." *ESI* 6 (1987-8):92-93.

Ovadiah, A. "Kefar-Ata." *Ḥadashot Archaeologiot* 14 (1965):8-9 (Hebrew).

Overbeck, Bernhard, and Yaakov Meshorer. *Das Heilige Land: Antike Münzen und Siegel aus einem Jahrtausend jüdischer Geschichte*. Munich, 1992.

Pitard, Wayne T. "A New Edition of the 'Rāpiʾūma' Texts: KTU 1.20-22." *BASOR* 285 (1992):33-77.

Pritchard, James B. *Gibeon, Where the Sun Stood Still: The Discovery of the Biblical City.* Princeton: Princeton University Press, 1962.

———. *Hebrew Inscriptions and Stamps From Gibeon.* Museum Monographs. Philadelphia: The University Museum, University of Pennsylvania, 1959.

———. "Industry and Trade at Biblical Gibeon." *BA* 23 (1960):23-29.

———. *The Water System of Gibeon.* Museum Monographs, vol. 4. Philadelphia: The University Museum, University of Pennsylvania, 1961.

———. *Winery, Defenses, and Soundings at Gibeon.* Museum Monographs. Philadelphia: The University Museum, University of Pennsylvania, 1964.

Provan, Iian W. *Hezekiah and the Books of Kings: A Contribution to the Debate About the Composition of the Deuteronomistic History.* BZAW, vol. 172. Berlin: Walter de Gruyter, 1988.

Puech, Şmile. "L'inscription Du Tunnel de Siloé." *RB* 81 (1974):196-214.

Rahmani, Levi I. "Notes on Some Aquisitions." ᶜ*Atiqot* 5 (1969):81-83.

Rainey, Anson F. "The Chronicles of the Kings of Judah: A Source Used by the Chronicler." In *Untitled Volume*, M. P. Graham. Sheffield: Sheffield Academic Press, 30-72.

———. "Early Historical Geography of the Negeb." In *Beersheba II: The Early Iron Age Settlements,* 88-104. Herzog, Z. Tel Aviv: Institute of Archaeology, Tel Aviv University, 1984.

———. "The Fate of Lachish During the Campaigns of Sennacherib and Nebuchadrezzar." In *Lachish V: Investigations at Lachish-- The Sanctuary and the Residency,* Ed. Y. Aharoni, 47-60. Tel Aviv: Institute of Archaeology, Tel Aviv University, 1975.

———. "Hezekiah's Reform and the Altars at Beer-sheba and Arad." In *Scripture and Other Artifacts: Essays on the Bible and Archaeology in Honor of Philip J. King,* Eds. M. D. Coogan, J. C. Exum, and L. E. Stager, 333-54. Louisville: Westminster/John Knox Press, 1994.

———. "The Prince and the Pauper." *UF* 7 (1975):427-32.

———. "Taharqa and Syntax," *Tel Aviv* 3 (1976):38-41.

———. "Three Additional Texts." In *Arad Inscriptions,* Ed. Y. Aharoni, 122-23. Jerusalem: Israel Exploration Society, 1981.

———. "Wine From the Royal Vineyards." *BASOR* 245 (1982):57-62.

Reifenberg, A. *Ancient Hebrew Seals.* London, 1950.

Rogerson, John, and Philip R. Davies. "Was the Siloam Tunnel Built by Hezekiah?" *BA* 59 (1996):138-149.

Rosenbaum, Jonathan. "Hezekiah's Reform and the Deuteronomistic Tradition." *HTR* 72 (1979):24-43.

Sass, Benjamin. "The Pre-exilic Hebrew Seals: Iconism Vs. Aniconism." In *Studies in the Iconography of Northwest Semitic Inscribed Seals*, Eds. B. Sass and C. Uehlinger, 194-256. OBO, vol. 125. Fribourg and Göttingen: University Press; Vandenhoeck & Ruprecht, 1993.

Sass, Benjamin, and Christoph Uehlinger. *Studies in the Iconography of Northwest Semitic Inscribed Seals*. Proceedings of a Symposium Held in Fribourg on April 17-20, 1991. OBO 125. Fribourg and Göttingen: University Press; Vandenhoeck & Ruprecht, 1993.

Sasson, Victor. "The Siloam Tunnel Inscription." *PEQ* 114 (1982):111-17.

Sayce, A. H. "The Ancient Hebrew Inscription Discovered at the Pool of Siloam in Jerusalem." *PEFQS* (1881):141-53.

———. "The Topography of Pre-exilic Jerusalem." *PEGQSt* (1883):215-23.

Seger, Joe D. *Gezer V: The Field I Caves*. Eds. H. D. Lance and R. G. Bullard. Annual of the Nelson Glueck School of Biblical Archaeology, vol. 5. Jerusalem: Nelson Glueck School of Biblical Archaeology, 1988.

Sellers, Ovid R. *The Citadel of Beth-Zur: A Preliminary Report of the First Excavation Conducted by the Presbyterian Theological Seminary, Chicago and the American School of Oriental Research, Jerusalem, in 1931 at Khirbat et Tubeiqa*. Philadelphia: Westminster Press, 1933.

Sellers, Ovid R., and Albright William F. "The First Campaign of Excavation at Beth-Zur." *BASOR* 43 (1931):2-13.

Sellers, Ovid R., Robert W. Funk, John L. McKenzie, Paul Lapp, and Nancy Lapp, eds. *The 1957 Excavation at Beth-zur*. AASOR, vol. 38. Cambridge, MA: American Schools of Oriental Research, 1968.

Sellin, Ernst, and Carl Watzinger. *Jericho: Die Ergebnisse der Ausgrabungen*. WVDOG, vol. 22. Leipzig: Hinrichs, 1913.

Selman, Martin J. *1 Chronicles: An Introduction and Commentary*. The Tyndale Old Testament Commentaries. Leicester, England; Downers Grove, Illinois: Inter-varsity Press, 1994.

Shea, William H. "Commemorating the Final Breakthrough of the Siloam Tunnel." In *Fucus. A Semitic/ African Gathering in Remembrance of Albert Ehrman*, Y. L. Arbeitman, 431-42. Current Issues in Linguistic Theory. Amsterdam/ Philadelphia: John Benjamins, 1988.

———. "Sennacherib's Second Palestinian Campaign." *JBL* 104 (1985):410-18.

Shiloh, Yigal. *Excavations at the City of David I*. Qedem, vol. 19. Jerusalem: Institute of Archaeology, the Hebrew University of Jerusalem, 1992.

———. "A Group of Hebrew Bullae from the City of David." *IEJ* 36 (1986):16-36.

———. "Jerusalem: The City of David, 1978." *IEJ* 28 (1978):274-76.

──────. "Jerusalem: The Early Periods and the First Temple Period." In *NEAEHL*, Ed. Ephraim Stern, 701-12. New York: Macmillian; Jerusalem: Israel Exploration Society, 1993

──────. "Judah and Israel in the Eighth-Sixth Centuries B.C.E." In *Recent Excavations in Israel: Studies in Iron Age Archaeology*, Eds. S. Gitin and W. G. Dever, 97-105. AASOR, vol. 49. Winona Lake, Ind.: Eisenbrauns, 1989.

Shiloh, Yigal, and Mendel Kaplan. "Digging in the City of David." *BAR* 5, no. 4 (1979):36-49.

Shoham, Yair. "A Group of Hebrew Bullae from Yigal Shiloh's Excavations in the City of David." In *Ancient Jerusalem Revealed*, Ed. Hillel Geva, 55-61. Jerusalem: Israel Exploration Society, 1994.

Simons, J. *Jerusalem in the Old Testament: Researches and Theories.* Leiden: E. J. Brill, 1952.

Smith, G. A. *Jerusalem, The Topography, Economics and History from the Earliest Times to A.D. 70.* Vols. I-II. London: Hadler and Stoughton, 1907-8.

Stager, Lawrence E. "Ancient Agriculture in the Judaean Desert: A Case Study of the Buqêᶜah Valley in the Iron Age." Ph.D. Dissertation, Harvard University. 1975.

──────. "The Archaeology of the Family in Ancient Israel." *BASOR* 260 (1985):1-36.

──────. "Farming in the Judean Desert During the Iron Age." *BASOR* 221 (1976):145-58.

Starkey, J. L. "Excavations at Tell Ed Duweir." *PEQ* (1937):228-41.

──────. "Lachish as Illustrating Bible History." *PEQ* (1937):171-79.

Stähli, Hans-Peter. *Knabe, Jüngling, Knecht: Untersuchung Zum Begriff ŞÀÿ Im Alten Testament.* BBET, vol. 7. Frankfurt am Main and Bern: Peter Lang, 1978.

Stern, Ephraim, ed. *The New Encyclopedia of Archaeological Excavations in the Holy Land.* New York: Macmillan; Jerusalem: Israel Exploration Society, 1993.

──────. "The Kingdom of Judah in Its Last Days." In *Scripture and Other Artifacts: Essays on the Bible and Archaeology in Honor of Philip J. King*, M. D. Coogan, J. C. Exum, and L. E. Stager, 399-409. Louisville, KY: Westminster John Knox Press, 1994.

Tadmor, Hayim. "The Chronology of the First Temple Period—A Presentation and Evaluation of the Sources." In *A History of Ancient Israel from the Beginnings to the Bar Kochba Revolt, A.D. 135*, Ed. J. A. Soggin, 368-83. Philadelphia: Westminster Press, 1984.

——. *The Inscriptions of Tiglath-Pileser III King of Assyria: Critical Edition, with Introductions, Translations and Commentary.* Jerusalem: Israel Academy of Sciences and Humanities, 1994.

Teixidor, J. "An Archaic Inscription from Byblos." *BASOR* 225 (1977):70-71.

Thiele, Edwin R. *The Mysterious Numbers of the Hebrew Kings.* New Revised Edition. Grand Rapids, MI: Zondervan, 1983.

Thronveit, Mark A. *When Kings Speak: Royal Speech and Royal Prayer in Chronicles.* SBLDS, vol. 93. Atlanta: Scholars Press, 1987.

——. "Hezekiah in the Books of Chronicles." in *SBL Seminar Papers, 1988,* Ed. D. Lull, 302-311. Atlanta: Scholars Press, 1988.

Tufnell, Olga. "Excavations at Tell Ed-Duweir, Palestine, Directed by the Late J.L. Starkey, 1932-1938." *PEQ* (1950):65-80.

——. "Hazor, Samaria, and Lachich: A Synthesis." *PEQ* (1959):90-105.

——. *Lachish III: The Iron Age.* Wellcome-Marston Archaeological Research Expedition to the Near East. Publications. London: Oxford University Press, 1953.

Tushingham, A. D. *Excavations in Jerusalem, 1961-1967.* Toronto: Royal Ontario Museum, 1985.

——. "New Evidence Bearing on the Two-Winged LMLK Stamp." *BASOR* 287 (1992):61-65.

Ussishkin, David. *The Conquest of Lachish by Sennacherib.* Tel Aviv: Institute of Archaeology, Tel Aviv University, 1982.

——. "The Date of the Judaean Shrine at Arad." *IEJ* 38 (1988):142-57.

——. "The Destruction of Lachish by Sennacherib and the Dating of the Royal Judean Storage Jars." *Tel Aviv* 4 (1977):28-60.

——. "Excavations at Tel Lachish (1973-1977): Preliminary Report." *Tel Aviv* 5 (1978):1-97, pls. 1-32.

——. "Excavations at Tel Lachish 1978-1983: Second Preliminary Report." *Tel Aviv* 10 (1983):97-175, pls. 13-43.

——. "Excavations and Restoration Work at Lachish 1985-1994: Third Preliminary Report." *Tel Aviv* 23 (1996):3-60.

——. "Lachish." In *NEAEHL,* 897-911. New York: Macmillan; Jerusalem: Israel Exploration Society, 1993.

——. "Royal Judean Storage Jars and Private Seal Impressions." *BASOR* 223 (1976):1-14.

——. "The Water Systems of Jerusalem During Hezekiah's Reign." *Cathedra* 70 (1994):3-28 (Hebrew).

Vaughn, Andrew G. "*LMLK* and Official Seal Impressions From Tel Beth Shemesh." in forthcoming preliminary excavation report of the renewed Beth Shemesh excavations. Eds. Sh. Bunimovitz and Z. Lederman.

————. "Palaeographic Dating of Judaean Seals and Its Significance for Biblical Research." *BASOR* 313 (1999):43-64.

Vaux, Roland de. *Ancient Israel: Its Life and Institutions.* London: Darton, Longman & Todd, 1961.

Vincent, L. Hugues. *Jérusalem de L'ancien Testament: Rescherches D'archeologie.* Vol. I. Paris: J. Gabalda, 1954.

————. "Les Récentes Fouilles De'Ophel." *RB* 9 (1912):544-74.

Wampler, J. C, and C. C. McCown. *Tell En-Naṣbeh II: The Pottery.* Berkeley, CA: Pacific Institute of Religion, 1947.

Warren, Charles. "Phoenician Inscription on Jar Handles." *PEFQS* (1869):372.

————. *Underground Jerusalem: An Account of Some of the Principal Difficulties Encountered in Its Exploration and the Results Obtained.* London: Richard Bentley and Son, 1876.

Warren, Charles, and Claude R. Conder. *The Survey of Western Palestine. Jerusalem.* London: Palestine Exploration Fund, 1884.

Weill, Raymond. *La Cité de David: Compte Rendu Des Fouilles Exécutées, A Jérusalem, sur le Site de la Ville Primitive. Campagne de 1913-1914.* Paris: Librairie Paul Geuthner, 1920.

Welten, Peter. *Geschichte und Gesichdarstellung und der Chronikbüchern.* WMANT, vol. 42. Neukirchen, 1973.

————. *Die Konigs-Stempel. Ein Beitrag Zur Militarpolitik Judas Unter Hiskia und Josia.* Abhandlungen des Deutschen Palastinavereins. Wiesbaden: Harrassowitz, 1969.

Wette, W. M. L. de. *Kritscher Versuch über die Glaubwürdigkeit der Bücher der Chronik mit Hinsicht auf die Geschichte der Mosaischen Bücher und Gesetzgebung.* Halle, 1806.

Wildberger, Hans. *Isaiah 1-12: A Commentary.* Trans. Thomas H. Trapp. Continental Commentaries. Minneapolis: Fortress Press, 1991.

Williamson, H. G. M. *1 and 2 Chronicles.* New Century Bible Commentary. Grand Rapids: Wm. B. Eerdmans Publ. Co., 1982.

————. *Israel in the Books of Chronicles.* Cambridge: Cambridge University Press, 1977.

Wilson, Charles W., and Charles Warren. *The Recovery of Jerusalem: A Narrative of Exploration and Discovery in the City and the Holy Land.* New York: D. Appleton & Company, 1871.

Wright, G. Ernest. "Review of *Lachish III.*" *VT* 5 (1955):97-105.

Yadin, Yigael, "Beer-sheba: The High Place Destroyed by King Josiah." *BASOR* 222 (1976):5-17.

————. "A Note on the Stratigraphy of Arad." *IEJ* 15 (1965):180.

Yeivin, Shmuel. *The First Preliminary Report on the Excavations at Tel "Gath" 1956-1958.* Jerusalem: The Gat Expedition, 1961.

————. "Son of the King." In *Encyclopedia Biblica II*, 160. Jerusalem: Bialike Institute, 1954 (Hebrew).

Yogev, Ora. "Tel-Yizreᶜel." *ESI* 7-8 (1988-9):191-95.

Younger, K. Lawson, Jr. "The Siloam Tunnel Inscription—an Integrated Reading." *UF* 26 (1994):in press.

Yurko, Frank J. "The Shabaka-Shebitku Coregency and the Supposed Second Campaign of Sennacherib Against Judah: A Critical Assessment." *JBL* 110 (1991):35-45.

Zadok, Ran. *The Pre-Hellenistic Israelite Anthroponymy and Prosopography.* Orientalia Lovaniensia analecta, vol. 28. Leuven: Peeters, 1988.

Zevit, Ziony. *Matres Lectionis in Ancient Hebrew Epigraphs.* American Schools of Oriental Research Monograph Series, vol. 2. Cambridge, MA: American Schools of Oriental Research, 1980.

Zimhoni, Orna. "The Iron Age Pottery of Tel ᶜEton and Its Relation to the Lachish, Tell Beit Mirsim and Arad Assemblages." *Tel Aviv* 12 (1985):63-90.

————. "Two Ceramic Assemblages from Lachish Levels III and II." *Tel Aviv* 17 (1990):3-52.

Zorn, Jeffrey R. *Tell En-Naṣbeh: A Re-evaluation of the Architecture and Stratigraphy of the Early Bronze Age, Iron Age, and Later Periods.* Ph.D. Dissertation, University of California, Berkeley. Ann Arbor, Mich.: UMI, 1993.

————. "Tell En-Naṣbeh." In *NEAEHL*, Ed. Ephraim Stern, 1098-102. New York: Macmillan; Jerusalem: Israel Exploration Society, 1993.

Printed in the United Kingdom
by Lightning Source UK Ltd.
124331UK00001B/95/A